Savage Theory

Savage Theory

CINEMA AS MODERN MAGIC

Rachel O. Moore

Duke University Press

Durham & London

2000

© 2000 Duke University Press

All rights reserved

Printed in the United States of America

on acid-free paper ∞

Designed by C. H. Westmoreland

Typeset in Carter & Cohn Galliard

with Frutiger Ultrabold display

by Keystone Typesetting, Inc.

Library of Congress Cataloging-in-Publication

Data appear on the last printed page of

this book.

To Santiago and Olivia

Contents

Acknowledgments

I would never have been in a position to write this book if someone hadn't looked after Santiago and Olivia during the years of my graduate study. During that time, Ximena Vargas kept them safe, warm, and full of fun. Ximena's enthusiasm and confidence were infectious; she maintained a patient and kind environment when, with the six of us all trying to get things done, and all of us, come to think of it, trying to read and write, it could easily have been otherwise. Her reader's comments since carry the weight of all that time, care, and fun.

In a truly fairy-tale fashion, Bruce Grant alighted one day and did everything that needed to be done so I could write that rainy summer week so long ago. By now he's read the entire document more than twice, and his reactions have been like fuel, their candor, brilliance, and wit vital to every stage in the transformation of some ashen-laden pages into a book.

Thanks to Dr. Laurie Jo Weeks for everything. For getting me a job, for turning me on to Thomas Bernhard (whom I also owe), for making me laugh outrageously again and again.

George Marcus and Lesley Stern gave me weighty, indeed quantifiable support. I also want to thank Anna Blume, Allen Weiss, Gertrud Koch, Mark Nash, and Mary Murrell for their assorted inspirations. I owe Swarthmore students too for their questions and responses over the years. As friend and mentor, Lesley Stern worked hard. She suggested crucial texts, and she attended to detail in a way we no longer expect. Roz Morris has been a true colleague; thanks to her and Yvette Christiansë for making the new neighborhood feel more like home.

Tom Gunning's work has long given me productive ways of interpreting my reactions to films, and it was an honor to have the benefit of his careful reading and rereading. Tom's suggestions and corrections permeate these pages, but the essential thing was the palpable, magical effect of his enthusiasm.

To my friends who were of particular help with everything from ideas to amusing the kids during crucial phases of putting this together — Barbara Kimball, Drew Walker, Lea Mansour, Paul Mendelson, Jenny Romaine,

Kyle de Camp, Sarah Wilson, Carolee Schneeman, Mark Sussman, Julie Taylor, Dick Hebdige, David Koester, Ranjani Mazumdar, and Anna Rubbo — thanks for all the wisdom and Scotch tape so freely dispensed.

Charles Silver facilitated invaluable access to films; Vincent Monnikendam generously provided background material about colonial imagery. The Revs. Robert and Viola Moore's vivacious optimism amazed if not inspired me. Tico encouraged me almost daily, and helped me to contextualize and to enjoy material foreign, starting with his childhood excitement over Radin's *The Trickster* and continuing through his astute comments as an adult reader. Olivia and Santiago did their best to give me time and space, and Santiago even lent me his computer so I could write.

Gifts, by their nature, exceed reciprocity. Such is the case for all gifts, but the problem has never been made so clear to me as at the present moment. Revealing the nature of the advice, tolerance, and love he gave daily risks revealing that Mick's gift far exceeds my offering. This too is part of the danger and pleasure of giving, receiving, and giving again.

Introduction

"All voodoo is at night." So concludes Pepe, Hunter's companion in his endeavor to save a missing aviator who has fallen victim to the Djukas, a tribe of savages living in the depths of Dutch Guiana's jungle. The Djukas are less famous for their successful slave rebellion than for the horrific ritual practices that were thus preserved from their African ancestry, which involve, among other things, human sacrifice. A newsreel journalist, Hunter is not without resources to save the dying flyer, as he watches through his camera's lens, perched amid the foliage of a distant tree. The victim is fussed over by men wearing large white feathers while others, wearing loincloths, dance on burning embers. "Wait a minute," says Hunter, "they go for magic don't they?" "Yes," replies Pepe, "everything in voodoo is magic." Hunter's strong jaw relaxes into a victorious smile, he beams triumphantly and says, "We're going to give them a little magic of our own!"

Come nightfall, the human sacrifice to fire is interrupted by the clang of a fire alarm, blaring sirens and giant fire trucks zooming across the night sky. The savage Djukas are held in trance. Locomotive horns blast their way toward the stunned and silent men; the threat posed by a close-up of the tracks' rock bed, that they too might be underneath the train's wheels, is relieved by a dynamite explosion of a glacier in slow motion. Bulls that bellow and pound the earth seem to stampede the awestruck spectators but pass them by, so that they look behind them to see where the bulls have gotten to. When a tank smashes just before careening out at them from the screen, they turn to their leader, who faces the screen boldly, only to see a diver reeling backward out of the water to the sound of a gentle waltz; the diver is suspended in air atop the diving board, and they all bend their heads and torsos way low, completing the anticipated action of falling back down with their own bodies. A cannon bends forward, its barrel as large as the screen, and points head on at them. They turn backward only to see their magical authority, who, more annoyed than scared, leads them to re-address the screen with gestures of protest. A man's voice in pidgin Spanish threatens to burn down their village if they don't behave, and a forest fire breaks out. Once they acquiesce, no less than the vast waterfalls of Niagara are called upon to quench the forest fire, and from the smoke and glare of a handy flare, Hunter emerges to pit "his magic" against Djuka voodoo.

Thus an MGM star vehicle delivers two minutes of "pure *photogenie*."[1] The danger of the scene forced Hunter (Clark Gable) to deploy every cinematic form of excess: the selection, magnification, reversal, and changes in speed of images as well as sounds. Normally, these appear in "fits and starts," wrote Jean Epstein in 1928, who then opined that he had "never seen an entire minute of pure *photogenie*." But in this scene from *Too Hot to Handle* (1938), as in the pivotal cream-separator sequence in Eisenstein's *The Old and the New* (1929), there is too much at stake to keep any cinematic tricks up the sleeve. And, like *The Old and the New* as well as countless lesser examples of cinema's awesomeness, such magic is at its most efficacious when shown to a primitive audience, that is, an audience that is markedly perceived to be naïve to the wonders of modern technology.[2]

The Hollywood banality that films are magic, or "our magic," as Hunter put it, stands here as a serious theoretical proposition. The repeated instances of primitive encounter with the cinema only make visual a similar, albeit more sober dependence on the primitive to account for the power of cinema in early film theoretical texts. Early theorists' dependence on primitive beliefs in animism, the sacred, ritual sacrifice, idol worship, and sympathetic and homeopathic magic to interpret the cinema's power for a modern audience suggest that technology did not lay the irrational to rest for good. On the contrary, the "metal brain"[3] prompted a fascination with the very primitive against which it is customarily shown in such sharp relief.

Contemporary film theory accounts for film's power by grafting the experience of cinema onto the rich terrain of the unconscious in psychoanalytic film theory, or limits its power by claiming that spectatorship takes place in a state of conscious cognition and is merely a process of reading meanings through cause and effect.[4] The difference between cognitive and cultural critical readings of films is merely one of refinement and taste, for cultural theoretical critiques too claim to *explain* films, but use instead social and historical contexts from within *and* without the film to show us what it really means.[5] The former approach ignores the public, social aspect of film spectatorship and the latter two neglect its intimacy. And none of these methods accounts for the magic of those two minutes of pure cinema. That is, no matter how much attention such film analyses pay to film form, they are interested in uncovering meaning — whether it is latent or manifest, psychological or intellectual, historical or social. The magic of cinema, its ability to touch you with no hands, elate you, shock you, though limited, as Epstein put it, to fits and starts, is nonetheless a defining feature of the medium. To address this magical feature of cinema, I suggest yet another look back at early film theory and its primitivist impulse in particular.

The Djukas' reaction to the white man's magic could easily be used to illustrate what Tom Gunning refers to as cinema's "primal scene," which has erroneously been constructed as a myth of origin for the cinema.[6] For the naïve audience characterized by "traditional accounts" of early cinema, "the absolute novelty of the moving image reduced them to a state usually attributed to savages in their primal encounter with the advanced technology of Western colonialists, howling and fleeing in impotent terror before the power of the machine." In reality, argues Gunning, early audiences did not take the image before them as real, but were "astonished," sensually entertained by the visual thrills of the cinema. As Gunning begins to suggest, this primitive construction belies the fears that plague the modern rather than the primitive creature. The waning of experience and the ascent of representation rendered the cinema a site for sore wounds: "The audience's reaction was the antipode to the primitive one: it was an encounter with modernity. From the start, the terror of that image uncovered a lack, and promised only a phantom embrace."[7] This too is enacted vicariously through Djuka eyes near the close of this episode in the film. "He's no God," one Djuka remarks to another, "he's only a white man."

Despite critical and anthropological efforts to dispel the myth of a primitive audience outdone by visual trickery, images of shocking first contact with the cinema that take the film image as real persist in film theory as well as in cinema itself. Reading Christian Metz on disavowal and fetishism suggests that whether or not spectators really were credulous at *Grand Café* in 1895 is *almost* irrelevant. The moment of credulity is continually "evoked by the incredulous spectators who have come *later*" precisely because, like all beliefs in a credulous "long ago," they "irrigate the unbelief of today."[8] Everything in the cinema happens as if someone would believe it, says Metz, yet any spectator will tell you that he or she "doesn't believe it." The primitive moment of credulity "irrigates by denegation" or "by delegation by attributing credulity to the child and to former times." It thus animates the "general refusal to admit that somewhere in oneself one believes they [the screen images] are genuinely true," on which cinema spectatorship at some hidden level nonetheless depends. For Metz, to enact these primal scenes on screen would then create a situation that allows spectators to "sustain their credulousness in all incredulousness." Further still, such persistent reenactments of naïve spectatorship, whether by viewers of cinema's first films or by people who have not yet been exposed to the movies because they are savages, serve, I argue, a distinctly modern cosmology. They reassure us of our superior position as spectators, while at the same time they enact our felt affinity to the primitive faced with our disappearing world.

The momentary delight and disappointment of cinema's "phantom embrace" creates, according to Gunning, a desire for more visual thrills. The image emerges as modern culture's most effective fetish, the fetish that stands in for experience now no longer available. This fetish power is animated by the mechanical nature of the camera, on the one side, whose image, on the other side, stands before an audience in a state of fatigue, distraction, or exhaustion. These two aspects of the cinema, working on each other, create a phantasmagoria of lively objects and muted subjects.

Magic, above all, must do something. As Marcel Mauss (1872–1950) wrote in his survey, *A General Theory of Magic* (1902–3), "[Magical] rites are eminently effective; they are creative; they *do* things."[9] Magic is used either to cure a variety of misfortunes or to ensorcell others to misfortune in a way that differs substantially from either religion or medicine, both in its form as well as the place it occupies in a culture: "Religious practices . . . are always predictable, prescribed and official," however solemn they may be, whereas magical rites, even though they "may occur regularly (as in the case of agricultural magic) and fulfill a need when they are performed for specific ends (such as a cure) are always considered unauthorized, abnormal and, at the very least, not highly estimable" (24). Magical rites are marked by their intimacy. However, they do not carry with them the kind of moral obligations that characterize religion, nor the apparently simple functionalism of medical healing. Mauss writes, "Isolation and secrecy are two almost perfect signs of the intimate character of a magical rite" (23). The "intimate character" of the magical rite also de-

4

fines the nature of the relationship achieved in the cinema, whose intimacy is the grounds for much of its theoretical attention.

Boris Eikhenbaum (1886–1959) remarked on the paradox that despite "all its 'mass' characteristics," we do not, apart from entering the theater, "feel ourselves to be members of a mass at all" and describes the situation instead as "intimate."[10] The anonymity of the cinema, I contend, along with its "mass characteristics," combine with its solitude in darkness to create a kind of public intimacy,[11] which may be more clearly apparent if understood in ritual terms.

To begin to align magical ritual with the cinema requires some familiarity with the practicalities of the former. We all know what it means to go to the cinema, how you choose a film, stand on line, that you're meant to be quiet, how we feel ourselves addressed by a film, and the particular relish with which one reads and talks about films. Although you know that the film has been seen by countless strangers in various places, you feel the viewing is yours alone. In this sense it is intimate and private. But cinema plays to the full range of "inner speech," which includes social understandings, myths, histories, nostalgias, as well as primal scenes.[12]

Ritual cures work in the same kind of public intimate way. Unlike, say, psychoanalytic healing, there is no mumbo-jumbo about one's innermost feelings, no bond with the healer. You show up, pay money or offer a gift of some kind, and partake in the ritual, often as part of a group of people you may or may not know. You hear about healers and rituals that work for various ailments, and you go and take what's offered. If you think it works, you stick around or return; if you don't, you search further. Like cinema, the mode of address from the healer is to everyone and to no one. There are specific maladies that can be cured by specific means, but your personal suffering plays no part in the cure from the curer's point of view. The audience in a magical ritual is made up of discrete people with varying concerns. As you lie there still in a hammock or sit on a stool, two worlds surface that seduce and distract by turns. Hallucinogenic visions of color and movement take you away from that dark room; the shaman's songs and stories and other people's shouts and laughter bring you back. Continually shifting between absorption and attraction, private mental meandering and public ritual, your vision will be yours alone, but the collection of inner speeches will intersect around the ritual's stories, songs, and images.[13]

Ritual was essential to Maya Deren as a model in her reflections on film form and also her in her filmmaking. Of *Ritual in Transfigured Time* Deren wrote, "I have called this new film *Ritual,* not only because of the importance of the quality of movement . . . but because a ritual is characterized by the de-personalization of the individual."[14] The depersonalized quality of ritual extends the individual into a larger sphere of significance: "Above all, the ritualist form treats the human being not as the source of the dramatic action, but as a somewhat depersonalized element in the dramatic whole. The intent of such depersonalization is not the destruction of the individual; on the contrary, it enlarges him beyond the personal dimension and frees him from the specializations and confines of personality."[15] The concept of art as ritual served Deren as a foil against the reigning "concept of the personality as a prime value," as well as in her critique of dramatic realism, romanticism, surrealism, and psychoanalysis.[16] But more than that, as Annette Michelson points out, she began to understand practices within her own culture, such as children's play at hopscotch, in ritual terms in which the stability and unity of the form transcended any particular performance of the ritual.[17]

This book puts forward a theory of film as magic in three ways. The first is to rearticulate the primitive beliefs already present in early film theory. The second, and admittedly most tentative, is to encourage the analogy between ritual and cinema. It is speculative because one is always "theorizing" when it comes to spectatorship in general, and because different kinds of films, or even portions of films, provoke different modes of perception. The third and perhaps boldest proposition is that the film image, drawing from Marx, Lukács, and Benjamin, is an eminently modern, magical fetish. As to the defining task of magic — that it *do* things — this book considers only one condition, modernity itself, in which cinema is both part of the cause as well as its cure.

The modern debt to the primitive took many forms in early film theory. Chapter 1 provides a summary of early theorists' use of the primitive and situates their primitivism within the context of modernism's many primitivisms. The concepts of the modern and the primitive are big, ubiquitous, and, at this point, hardly bound to time or space. On the one hand, they are real entities with dates, modes of production, and ritual gear; on the other hand, they are infinitely abstract and operate relatively instead of following a fixed chronology. To look to theorists who wrote amid the aftershocks from the vast changes of daily life that are attributed to the rise of technology, the reification of labor, or the Great War is to revisit a particular conjunction of the modern and the primitive. Inured to those changes that produced such profound effects, theoretical attention to a moment of radical encounter both in film theory and film spectatorship is melancholic work. It is impossible to work back and witness the moment of loss, a loss that is after all not really within our own historical experience, but a loss no less significant as it features so prominently in our intellectual heritage, at the very least. To continue this work is to hope that such attempts reawaken a time when the cinema was new, wondrous, and horrific—not for nostalgia's sake, but to disarm the process by which what is second nature appears as natural. Looking back at Eisenstein's, Lindsay's, Balázs's, Epstein's, Kracauer's, Benjamin's, and Bazin's encounters with the cinema produces, in short, an estrangement effect on our understanding of what cinema is today.

The most striking and most consistent concern of early film theory was the way modern language was seen as an impoverished expressive form whose arbitrariness and imprecision could be overcome by the moving picture. The space between the word and the thing is not arbitrary but magical. From Benjamin to Brakhage, this is the magical realm that cinema inhabits. Condensing much of Critical Theory, Brakhage wrote, "The original word was a trick, and so were all the rules of the game that followed in its wake."[18] This he says not so much to demean the word but to revere the trick and, by extension, suggest that it is magic that nourishes the artist's shadow garden. Those who confine themselves to thought and the word, he says, "know it [the world] without experiencing it, screw it lovelessly, find 'trick' or 'effect' derogatory terminology, too close for comfort, are utterly unable to comprehend 'magic.'"

Chapter 2 takes the problem of language as the first symptom of the modern condition. Using Eisenstein as my exemplar, I discuss the way in which a primitivistically rearticulated theory of language translated into not only his film theory but also his film practice. For Eisenstein, as well as for Benjamin, Epstein, and Balázs, the space between the word and its referent was a magical one. "Language is animistic," said Epstein, going so far as to say that it is the naming of a thing with a word that enlivens it. Benjamin took animism one step further, seeing language as a mechanism by which things talk to other things, and in so doing described all language, even that between us poor humans, as magical. Language communicates through a material community that is "immediate and infinite, and like every communication, it is magical"; its symbol, for human communication, "is sound."[19] For Balázs, language was impoverished by the loss of bodily gesture, which was once its full articulation. Finally, Eisenstein theorized a complex system of associations at work in language whose chain of association had been edited from its primitive richness so that it is now only a shortcut. Cinema, for Eisenstein, could reactivate the sensuous, primitive chains of meanings now lost. Chapter 2 gives an account of what was hidden by the language of words and how Eisenstein instead used the primitively charged language of cinema to reanimate that lost lucidity.

In chapter 3, I explore the analogous relationship of cinema spectatorship to the spectacle and the primitive's contact with technology. Both Vachel Lindsay and Béla Balázs theorize the cinema in terms of primitive encounter. This foregrounds the issue of modern-primitive encounter and begins to suggest that cinema, in its adolescence (1910–1925), provided a mirror of mankind in primitive form. Balázs's and Lindsay's encounters with cinema re-create first contact both in their examples of spectatorship as well as in the kind of prelinguistic, bodily form of expression they take cinema to be. In their unique occlusion of the camera's otherwise startling mimetic capacity, their theories perform first contact. Continuing the theme that film represents a form of contact otherwise unavailable, chapter 4 traces Balázs's understanding of spectatorship and his physiognomic divination of faces and things.

In one of Lindsay's enthusiastic reviews of cinema, he remarks, "Mankind in his childhood has always wanted his furniture to do such things [to move on their own accord]."[20] This "yearning for personality in furniture" (33) is a theme throughout early film theory. Balázs finds that in cinema things are as expressive as faces. Siegfried Kracauer sees the surface attraction of cinema's mass ornament as a thing, but a thing that resonates with people's thinglike experiences, and is therefore attractive; it draws the spectator toward it. It is a very lively thing. Walter Benjamin's preoccupation with the attractive pull of the commodity fetish, articulated in his work on Baudelaire, led him to try to use its power rather than try to defeat it.

Inspired by these theorists' often enthusiastic remarks about the liveliness of the object in the cinema, I pursue the reasons why we might be thought to have a "yearning for personality in furniture." This, it seems to me, is, or at least can be, the source of magic in modern life. Chapter 5 defines the status of the image as an object in itself. An analysis of Kenneth Anger's *Scorpio Rising* demonstrates the way a film image becomes a fetish. It then pursues the nature of the object whose meaning is not entirely contained by its function as a sign or a symbol, but whose function lies in its very objectness. Chapter 6 defines the status of the camera and the theoretical condition of its image. This involves looking again at André Bazin and Jean-Louis Comolli, not for their well-known differences but for the similar ways they define cinematic space. Chapter 7 defines the fatigued condition of the spectator. As things become more powerful, work more mechanical, and daily life more a series of disrupting noises than assimilable experiences, the person — so Epstein, Benjamin, and Kracauer believed — was fatigued, distracted, exhausted.

The fatigued, distracted, exhausted state of the modern subject affected his or her perception. He or she could not see things in perspective. At the same time, the assaults on the senses increased, as Simmel argued in "The Metropolis and Mental Life," such that one creates a dulled shield against them in daily life.[21] For Epstein cinema could take advantage of this fatigued state to bypass conscious cognition and provoke an unmediated effect on the spectator. For Kracauer, there was more of a sociological shape to the identity between the spectacle of cinema and the distracted spectator himself or herself. The identity between experience and representation was a step toward change if it led to the spectator's realization of this identity. Like Epstein, Benjamin was drawn by cinema's tactile apperception in a world in which in everyday life experience had "fallen in value."[22]

If representation has indeed consumed experience to an extent far beyond that which Benjamin saw in his lifetime, the pressure on the cinema to do the work of bodily felt and contingent experience is so much the greater. Perhaps no film better depicts the affectless fallen modern condition than Robert Bresson's *l'Argent* (1983). In this film, the fetish character of the cinematic object overpowers the fatigued subject, both within the story of the film and in the formal devices Bresson deploys to frame objects and people. Technology does not demystify the machinations of modernity but instead becomes a new form of magic. Ideally, the magic required of cinema would be to use the mysterious workings of its second nature to recycle images with transformative meaning and to reinvigorate the senses so as to perceive those meanings. Chapter 8 links together the theoretical construction of the phantasmagoria, made up of the image, camera, and spectator discussed in the previous three chapters, with an analysis of one film.

Chapter 9 reclaims part of cinema's archaic past by connecting its properties to the phenomenon of fire. Following Eisenstein's investigation of Disney's animation, this chapter aims to describe the attraction of attraction as a phenomenon, and even as a theoretical term. The intellectual meandering of watching the amorphous shapes twist and turn and the intimate nature of reverie before the fire are reignited in the cinema. Like fire, cinema brings us alone together, and although we watch the same embers and shoots of flame, its contemplation may take us in different directions. Like fire, cinema exceeds mere function. And like sacrifice, cinema is a form of ritual expenditure that restores the intimacy now lost to cultures organized around productive labor.

Benjamin stands between Epstein and Kracauer because, though mindful and generally enthusiastic about the new apperception cinema afforded, at the same time he had a creative project of his own. This project was to use the power of the commodity fetish (which he considered inexhaustible) to create immediate (the tactility of the cinema), archaic (the meanings that he wants to recover from the past), transformative (a reawakened, social presence) images, which he called dialectical images. These dialectical images, I argue, can be the curative magic of the cinema. Benjamin's theory was utopian and largely confined to creating these images in writing. The project of chapter 10 is to rearticulate this theory for the cinema by working through one film. The film, *nostalgia,* was made in 1971 by an American photographer and filmmaker who did not have the concerns of Critical Theory in mind. Hollis Frampton was interested in the relationship of the past to the present, and the film is about his own transformation from one person who was a photographer to another person who is a filmmaker. This involves a complex but nonetheless specific relationship to the past. I take advantage of this relationship to explicate Kracauer's and Benjamin's theoretical struggles with the topic of the relationship of the past to the present. In this sense, the film becomes a theoretical model not for prescription's sake but for the illumination of Kracauer's and Benjamin's ideas. In another sense, however, the film is a model of curing that is both psychological as well as ritualistic. Frampton is melancholic, nostalgic, homesick; to cure this condition, he burns images from the past and talks about them. The fact that he does this, and the **11** way he does this, constitute a model for cinema as a ritual cure.

Undergirding these early theorists' thoughts on primitive beliefs and customs is the suspicion that film signals a significant cultural change on the one hand, and a new, or renewed, mode of perception on the other. The primarily cultural importance of such changes, along with the primitive nature of the encounter with the form, prompted not only a look inward toward psychoanalytic theory, nor only outward toward theories of language, but also backward to primitive religion, language, and gesture. Nourished by the parallels found between film identification and primitive beliefs and customs, the cinema emerges in these theories both as an advanced form of modern communication and as a renewal of primitive faculties otherwise lost to postenlightenment culture.

An assumed teleology from magic to religion and finally to science would appear to place enlightened moderns at a disadvantage if compelled to accept magic as a serious category. E. E. Evans-Pritchard's *Theories of Primitive Religion,* along with Mauss's *A General Theory of Magic,* show that these are not rigid categories but rather that they borrow freely from and often depend on one another. Moreover, the idea that progress and development displace magic only belies those moderns' belief in their own magic. Evans-Pritchard argued against the evolutionist theory that animistic belief, for example, represents an early form of religion based on illusion, which progresses toward faith and rational science with the process of civilization. He even suggests that evidence would point to the contrary if one insists on these dubious, racist, and colonialist-inspired distinctions.[23] While we explore cyberspace, magical practices are rampant in traditional as well as invented and increasingly packaged forms. The fact that magic increases apace with technology begs us to consider the possibility that technology itself is magic.

The practices of attraction, distraction, tactility, shock, and repetition not only are film's stock-in-trade but also make for healing and sorcery. Directors who craft their films by deploying its specific devices, those who maintain the preeminence of the filmic, make magic.[24] Ironically, it is not just Hollywood narrative, but even more clearly a motion-sick, time-torn, *photogenie*-based cinema that shows film to be the ritual cure for modern misfortune.

CHAPTER 1 The Moderns

The prehistoric impulse to the past—this, too, at once a consequence and a
condition of technology—is no longer hidden.—Walter Benjamin,
" 'N' [Theoretics of Knowledge, Theory of Progress] "

Early film theory developed on the heels of modernity's most fulsome
transformations of everyday life. An ethnography of modernity would
include, for example, the shocks to the body and felt reconfigurations of
time and space produced by such modern icons as the train;[1] changes in
home living as produced by central gas and electricity that broke up its
internal communal spaces and destroyed the home as an independent
unit;[2] and, most important, changes in the nature of labor that tailored the
human body to fit a mechanical rhythm and speed.[3] Whether the reason
for these changes is then attributed to the politics and culture that gave
way to the machine, to the machine itself, or not found at all, would
depend on what kind of anthropologist you were.

Nonetheless, modernity's literature tells us that the senses had been
radically disturbed, if not reconfigured. Gone for good were the days-long
journeys of Gabriel Oak, whose feet felt the earth's contours in each step,
whose calendar was the stars and whose clock, the sun. Gone too was a
time when labor was couched in the succor of conversation, when relationships and stories, no less than grindstone and blade, shaped the wool
sheared from lambs—as it had in Thomas Hardy's (1840–1928) Wessex
of 1874.[4]

A different figure altogether is cut some twenty years later by Tess D'Urberville, plodding along to ever more distant and bleak villages in search of
work, only to find it in increasingly rough and monotonous forms. Her
final humiliation comes when she faces "the red tyrant . . . the threshing
machine."[5] The machine forces its pace upon the workers: "For Tess there
was no respite; for the drum never stopped, the man who fed it could not
stop and she, who had to supply the man with untied sheaves, could not
stop either" (416). Its beastlike noises make conversation impossible:

"The hum of the thresher, which prevented speech, increased to a raving whenever the supply of corn fell short of the regular quantity." Finally, at six o'clock, when they are still working, the sun's twilight casts the workers in a red glow not unlike the thresher's; the machine not only masters the working bodies but their senses as well:

A panting ache ran through the rick. The man who fed was weary, and Tess could see that the red nape of his neck was encrusted with dirt and husks. She still stood at her post, her flushed and perspiring face coated with the corn dust, and her white bonnet embrowned by it. She was the only woman whose place was upon the machine so as to be shaken bodily by its spinning, and the decrease of the stack now separated her from Marian and Izz, and prevented their changing duties with her as they had done. The incessant quivering, in which every fibre of her frame participated, had thrown her into a stupefied reverie in which her arms worked on independently of her consciousness. She hardly knew where she was, and did not hear Izz Huett tell her from below that her hair was tumbling down. (425)

The machine's brutalization of Tess's senses includes her hearing, her bodily sensation of her self and of her place in the physical world, as well as her contact with those with whom she labors. Vision alone guides her through the long evening's mechanical labor:

By degrees the freshest among them began to grow cadaverous and saucer-eyed. Whenever Tess lifted her head she beheld always the great upgrown straw-stack, with the men in shirt-sleeves upon it, against the grey north sky; in front of it the long red elevator like a Jacob's ladder, on which a perpetual stream of threshed straw ascended, a yellow river running up-hill, and spouting out on the top of the rick. (425)

The sensate assault on vision begins with the technological reproduction of reality in images. These images, both cause and consequence of the changing nature of seeing no less than the changed nature of modern labor and commodity production, are studied here as modernity's most prominent fetish. The newly ubiquitous image[6] ascends as a thing that draws a person toward it, not only in the form of billboard advertisements,[7] photographs, and films, but also in the form of mental images like those that Marcel Proust (1871–1922) followed to recollect his world. The task of a modern cosmology is to trace the power of its fetish, the image, and the effaced relations therein contained, or its "secret."[8] Modern magic, in turn, can use the power of these fetishes to reenliven the shabby modern condition with images that touch at the fragile, homesick, and exhausted human body.

Within the isolation and secrecy of the cinema, a new intimacy was established with a world that was, in many ways, its double and, in this and other ways as well, its negation. Although one can only speculate as to the reasons why early theorists consistently turned to the primitive when faced with such an awesome double — especially when compelled to name the source of film's power — the fact that this turn is fundamental to cinema's theoretical legacy demands attention. Modern artists and writers depended on the primitive as a source of affects that modernity itself denied, and surely this theoretical impulse partakes of some similar grasp at real referents in primitive culture that has left merely metaphoric residue in modern life. A general charge of yet another instance of modernist primitivism would only name, but not explain, this radical dependence. Moreover, it would beg the questions posed by the endurance, serviceability, and amorphousness of the primitive in modern artistic, literary, performative, and theoretical production.

Recent criticism has revealed modernism's significant debt to the primitive as regards painting and sculpture, literature, and performance, as well as in the violence of colonization itself. Primitivism is used today in three distinct senses. First, and apparently most simply, it means a lack of sophistication, a naïveté. This is the sense in which Noël Burch employs the term in his essay, "Primitivism and the Avant-Gardes," which deals with the relationship between primitive and avant-garde forms of cinema as regards spectatorship in particular.[9] Similarly, the commonly used "primitive gaze" is largely attributed to children, nonactors, and those new to the form who look at the filming camera. This term, while romantically privileged at times, according to Burch, is itself intended as neutral and is pejorative only in cases in which it is understood that one should have known more, the way in which Rousseau, for example, was considered a primitive artist, as Roger Shattuck notes with regret in *The Banquet Years*.[10] This use of the term simply means artlessness, but artlessness itself has effects when used by modern artists. Shattuck remarks, for example, that the construction of Satie's composition of "furniture music" for Rene Clair's *Entr' Acte* "could not be more primitive." It dampens, by its repeti-

MOTHER
DAO
THE TURTLELIKE

A Dutchman's photograph of a Javanese worker posed with his own movie camera is the publicity image for *Mother Dao the Turtlelike* (a kinematographic image of the Dutch Indies, 1912–c. 1933) (1995). Courtesy of the filmmaker Vincent Monnikendam.

tion, arbitrariness, and dull childish structure, "any strong tonal feeling."[11] This is similar to the result in avant-garde film which Burch remarks upon. Due to its lack of narrativity and nonsensical structure, avant-garde cinema shares some of the same feeling of "exteriority" that characterizes our conjuring in Burch's sense of primitive cinema spectatorship.[12]

Second, primitivism refers to the actual use of artifacts, dance, and musical forms borrowed — and stolen — from aboriginal people as models for painting and sculpture that feature prominently in the works of, for example, Picasso and Modigliani.[13] This rests on an "unqualified assumption of the inherent value of the historical, psychological or formal primitive."[14] Its motivation is characterized by John Goldwater in utopian terms: "By having its roots in fundamental and persuasive factors of experience, it will be both emotionally compelling to the individual and comprehensible to the many."[15] The "inherent" value of primitive forms, their simple and broad appeal, as understood in this sense, appears naïve to the colonial and race relations that served both their physical access to these artifacts and their exotic appeal, not to mention the disregard for the complex meaning of these artworks in their native contexts it betrays.[16]

It is the third term, as usual, whose sense is controversial and brackets the term's two former uses. Michael Taussig, for example, in *Shamanism, Colonialism and the Wild Man,* goes so far as to see the violence of colonialism, such atrocities as committed during the rubber boom in Colombia's frontier territory called the Putumayo (also the name of a thriving boutique since 1984 in New York's Soho, as well as a manufacturing label), as an instance of primitivism in this third sense.[17] White rubber barons and their employees feared Indians as the violent other to civilization and therefore reacted to their own mythology of savagery with horrifying violence that had been fueled by their own savage imagination. Primitivism in this sense is a projection of one's own fears onto unknown cultures. Primitivism as a form of projection is just as readily deployed, however, to express the pleasure and play so repressed by the authority of culture that emerges, for example, in the Dada movement.[18] The primitive also, in this sense, provided an affective richness to modern artists and writers that was no longer available to the modern sensibility. Primitivism in this third sense implies a lack.

Primitivism as a form of racist projection is a now a broad topic;[19] however, two significant contributions from the eighties laid the groundwork for current debates that continue to value the term. Hal Foster's "The 'Primitive' Unconscious of Modern Art" and James Clifford's "On Ethnographic Surrealism" share the conviction that modernism depends, to an important extent, on the primitive as its "other."[20] Certainly their elaborations on that dependence pursue various and different theoretical channels; however, they are not fundamentally at odds.

Foster stresses the necessity to contend with the ways in which Western society is constituted by its appropriation and colonization of the "other" (a term that includes the primitive, women, and people of color) and, further, that the most radical edge of postmodernism urges difference to the fore as the agent for dismantling Western hegemony. Though this may be the academic and artistic project of the day, this paradigm does not exhaust the impact of primitivism on the modern and postmodern world.

The idea of disrupting dominant discourses through the introduction of non-Western texts and artworks into the contemporary art and critical forum operates, to a large extent, in the very realm of representation and counterrepresentation rather than that of physical experience.

One might call Clifford's "On Ethnographic Surrealism," by contrast, a more primitive approach to the subject of primitivism because it deals with the way in which experiencing the primitive alters the senses themselves by expanding what they are able to perceive and thus reconfigures artistic and theoretical production. Focusing on primitivism as a moment of radical encounter with the other provided the surrealists of the twenties and thirties in France with an estranging "shock effect." The primary importance of this exposure was the real effect it had on sensate experience and the new ways of understanding the world these encounters produced.

Annette Michelson gives such an account for Maya Deren's experience of Haiti and Eisenstein's encounter with Mexico. Like Clifford, she calls on the College of Sociology's project of a "sacred sociology" to distinguish Deren's and Eisenstein's work in and on these cultures so foreign to them. "From these work projects," she writes, "both gained access to a dimension of experience which was undoubtedly decisive in every later enterprise: a glimpse, widely sought but denied to many of their generation, of the meaning of community in its most absorbing and fulfilling instance: of collective enterprise grounded in the mythic."[21] The care and rigor Deren brought to her task of making a film about vodoun was such that she abandoned the project and wrote *Divine Horsemen* instead. The theoretical refraction that emerged in her work was a serious consideration of children's play, dance, and social gatherings in her own society as ritual, enlarging their significance from the psychological to the social. Eisenstein, by contrast, appears overwhelmed by his sensual immersion in Mexico, its heat, blood, and its Indian mythic presence such that Mexico appears, by his account, in a general state of extasis. The nature of their engagement with a culture foreign to their own differed, but the fact that it radically altered their own work, both in theory and practice, remains.

Clifford situates his juxtaposition of ethnography and surrealism in interwar France; however, he intends it as a "utopian construct";[22] thus it can be transposed to different juxtapositions within the shattered framework of modernity. "Modern surrealism and ethnography began with a reality deeply in question," writes Clifford, in such a way that "Others appeared now as serious human alternatives," unlike the "exoticism of the nineteenth century" or the abstract empiricism that was to become one

18   sad recourse of British anthropology.[23] Sounds emanated from the forests of Africa and reverberated in the attics of Berlin; Aztec sacrifice regrounded our understanding of political economy so that its excess finally received the attention for which the subject had long begged.[24]

The primitive is a category projected by those who live upstream onto those who live downstream. On the one hand, it is always an imputed category, and hence often used with imprecision, as with the term "primitive gaze," for example.[25] On the other hand, the primitive is nonetheless a necessary referent replete with real practices and beliefs that serve to sustain modern practices of representation and modern belief, as with the phrase, "I was possessed."[26] Neither the seductive power of primitive contact's "shock effect," which characterizes Clifford's approach, nor its positive value as a medium for new vision that Foster espouses answers the implications, outlined above, of the charge that primitivism is an imputed power. The introduction to Barkan and Bush's *Prehistories of the Future,* a collection of essays that investigate the modernist debt to and invention of the primitive, puts it simply: "As for primitives, they never existed. Only Western 'primitivism' did, invented in heated arguments about human society, like the ones that swirled around Darwin's 1859 *On the Origin of Species* and Henry Maine's *Ancient Law.* We now consider 'primitive' a fighting word. Like 'savage,' it is a racist designation. In contrast, primitivism denotes an Occidental construction, a set of representations whose 'reality' is purely Western."[27] Far from containing primitivism as the use and abuse of the primitive other — far, in short, from calling names — my interest here is to acknowledge, define, and deepen modern primitivism for the theory of filmic representation in particular. The hope herein is that we understand not the primitive but rather something more about our relationship to the cinema, in the process.

Looking again at the film theoretical texts written when the cinema was still new enough to appear a strange phenomenon, we witness a scramble to explain not only the hold film has over the spectator but the many properties of the form as against those based in language like poetry and fiction, on the one hand, or those based on visual form as in the plastic arts, on the other. What surfaced most prominently in this scramble is the turn to "primitive" thought by the Russian, French, German, and American theorists who initially took to the task of theorizing film and who are canonized today as classical film theorists.

Ethnography and folk psychology, as well as borrowing from practices of distant and different contemporary societies such as Mexico and China, were crucial, for example, to the film theoretical work of Sergei Eisenstein (1898–1948). Eisenstein's "sensual thinking,"[28] derived in part from his own encounter with what he perceived as ancient Mexican society,[29] became one side of an abiding tension in his theoretical writing until his death. In his introduction to Eisenstein's monograph on Walt Disney, Naum Kleinman states that Eisenstein's insistence on a "dual unity" between sensuous and rational thought was for Eisenstein the fundamental problem of theory and art practice in general. Kleinman describes Eisenstein's thought as "The correlation of the rationally-logical and the sensuous in art: in a creative act, in the structure of a work, in the process of its perception."[30]

The foreign other weighs heavily on the "sensuous" side of this tension throughout Eisenstein's writing about cinema, beginning with his attention to Chinese ideograms as a model for montage structure.[31] His travel to Mexico, along with his making three films in midcareer that deal with peasant culture,[32] increased the tension between the sensuous and the rational. These tensions were made manifest in the essay "Film Form: New Problems" of 1935, and then finally barely fell short of breaking the balance in favor of sensuous thinking in *Nonindifferent Nature* and *Eisenstein on Disney*.[33] Eisenstein is unique in his consciousness of the implications of deploying the primitive in his theory and is mindful of the culturally charged nature of his sources, particularly Lévy-Bruhl. More than anyone, Eisenstein defines the effectiveness of magic in artistic production.

The encounter with cinema itself was often described in primitivist terms, most remarkably in the writings of Vachel Lindsay (1879–1931), for whom cinema partook of both the most primitive and the most developed forms of artistic expression: "The invention of the photoplay is as great a step as was the beginning of picture-writing in the stone age. And the cave-men and women of our slums seem to be the people most affected by this novelty, which is but an expression of the old in that spiral of life which is going higher while seeming to repeat the ancient phase."[34] The combination of the photoplay's blunt effectiveness and the fact that it calls upon pure, prelinguistic forms constitutes a shaky balancing act in

Lindsay's book on film, *The Art of the Moving Picture*. Lindsay's claim to theory rests on his chapter that uses Egyptian hieroglyphics to account for film's iconic (rather than mimetic) power. Lindsay's theory of film employs the primitive in two ways: first, in the stress he places on its function in society as a medium for contact between savage and civilized, and second, in the emphasis he places on its ability to call up primordial meanings in a modern world.

Like Lindsay, Béla Balázs (1884–1949) often stages film spectatorship in terms of a credulous spectator's encounter with an image, but his examples range from the Chinese belief that one actually enters the landscape painting one contemplates to his own experience of identification with the film image: "We walk amid crowds, ride, fly, or fall with the hero."[35] Unlike Lindsay, who was dealing with an earlier period in film history, Balázs's encounter with the cinema takes on the characteristics of a sacred rite. And here we move from the anthropological first contact meant to distinguish those raw moments when an "untouched" society is brought into purview, to what I term close contact, the intimacy that constitutes cinema's seduction for lost modernists. By regaining access to gesture, the cinema could reveal the secrets of things and souls inexpressible in the impoverished language of mere words. The cinema opened its subjects anew to physiognomic inspection, allowing the spectator to pursue the nonsensuous correspondences between image and meaning so as to convey, in Balázs's view, "non-rational emotions." Through its access to the nonrational, Balázs claimed a new expressivity for the cinema, one he believed existed, however erroneously, in primitive gestural language.[36]

Walter Benjamin (1892–1940) and Jean Epstein (1897–1953) provide striking examples of modernism's particular debt to the primitive regarding film. For both of them, cinema's central distinguishing feature was its mechanical nature. Whereas Epstein's "cinema machine" approaches the status of an independent will, and Benjamin's emphasis on "technological reproducibility" laid the ground for an immediate and bodily felt mode of perception that he called the "optical unconscious," it was the camera's perceived ability to circumvent human mediation that gave it such unnatural power. For Benjamin, "a different nature opens itself to the camera than opens to the naked eye — if only because an unconsciously penetrated space is substituted for a space consciously explored by man."[37]

The enigmatic and, I argue, "second nature"[38] of this "different nature" all but haunts early film theory. What was this thing, both object and image, that doubled the real world, its duality, in itself an enigma? Its power seemed to come from the mechanical, which, in the arena of commodity production and its labor, was busily at work endowing things with life such that they dominated people. The primary importance of the camera as a machine was, for both Benjamin and Epstein, inseparable from the connection it facilitated to primitive and archaic ways of perceiving and experiencing the world. Whereas today this connection has been deflected onto the unconscious, and thus psychoanalytic theory has achieved some dominance over the discipline of cinema studies as a whole, Critical Theory[39] conflates the unconscious and cultural anthropology so that the notion of the archaic is at one and the same time primal and primitive.[40] Freud himself combined the two in his early work. The very notion of the unconscious, for example, is derived from primitive animism. H.D.'s *Tribute to Freud,* which revolves around their discussion of Freud's primitive artifacts and their mythic delvings into the archaic past, shows how deeply Freud felt the relationship between the unconscious and the primitive.

Benjamin's distinction between the contemplative perception of auratic works of art and the tactile apperception of those that are reproduced through technology rests, in the "Work of Art" essay (1935–36), on pitting mystifying magic, the priest, and painting against science, the surgeon, and finally film. "The magician and surgeon," Benjamin wrote, "compare to painter and cameraman. The painter maintains in his work a natural distance from reality, the cameraman penetrates deeply into its web."[41] Benjamin has copious footnotes about medical surgery, but his reference to magic is a general one, deployed, along with the mystification of religion, as a rhetorical foil to the nearness and effectiveness of mechanically reproduced artworks. The distinction's prominence and didactic simplicity in "Work of Art" obscure the more complex and enigmatic relation modern technological forms had to primitive and archaic forms in Benjamin's theory of representation as a whole. In his essay, "On Language as Such and the Language of Man" (1916), for example, magic is the privileged mechanism by which words come to mean things.[42] Benjamin uses the primitive in a redemptive mode to locate the source of the mimicry and tactility that feature in his theory of modern representational forms. This theory poses the dialectical image and the redeemable wish image as methods by which new and redemptive meanings can be rescued from fetishism's mystification and history's authoritarian progress to produce transformative meanings in the present.

In contrast to Benjamin, Epstein, a former medical student and champion of the Bell and Howell, is clear and adamant about the camera's primitive power: "I would even go so far as to say that the cinema is polytheistic and theogonic. Those lives it creates, by summoning objects out of the shadows of indifference into the light of dramatic concern, have little in common with human life. These lives are like the life in charms and amulets, the ominous, tabooed objects of certain primitive religions. If we wish to understand how an animal, a plant or a stone can inspire respect, fear and horror, those three most sacred sentiments, I think we must watch them on the screen, living their mysterious silent lives, *alien to the human sensibility* [emphasis added]."[43] In this way, Epstein finds a parallel for film's particular prowess in primitive religion and at the same time accounts for its power by its alien, nonhuman, mechanical sensibility. The mechanism by which the film image takes on life has less to do with its "realism" than with the mysterious mechanical way in which that image is rendered real. For Epstein, the cinematic eye is an "eye independent of the eye" that allows us to escape "the tyrannical egocentrism of our personal vision" (19). The transfer of an object from reality to photographic image via the camera eye has added significance simply because it comes from a machine that leaves no traces of its handiwork. "Thus," wrote Benjamin, "for contemporary man the representation of reality by the film is incomparably more significant than that of the painter, since it offers, precisely because of the thoroughgoing permeation of reality with mechanical equipment, an aspect of reality which is free of all equipment."[44] The camera is a theoretical absent presence. On the one hand, it facilitates a direct, unmediated transfer of the real into an image, and therefore has no subjectivity; on the other hand, no matter how absent the presence of the camera may be, its alien and mechanical nature take on a subjectivity characterized by its subjective absence. The camera does not remain empty of character for long.

In 1926 Jean Epstein warned: "But the young black who used to kneel in worship before the headlights on explorers' cars is now driving a taxi in Paris and New York. We had best not lag behind this black."[45] Cinema appeared as a magical god, not to the primitive this time, but to the civilized. Cinema, whose power was evident but not understood, threatened or, alternatively, promised to recast the enlightened as archaic once again. Early theoretical writing on the cinema often enacts an encounter with the primitive wherein the audience is poised wonderstruck before the screen's bright lights. But this example goes further upstream. Here, "the black" shares an affinity with technology. The anxiety here is that the camera may well be that primitive, and it is the civilized who must hasten to avoid the headlights' blinding glare. Technology, an attribute of civilized society against which those upstream define those who live downstream (and in so doing, themselves), becomes, in the case of the image-producing machine, the very mark of their own primitiveness.

Siegfried Kracauer's (1889–1966) concepts of distraction and the mass ornament are crucial to an understanding of cinema's ritual function. In counterdistinction to Eikhenbaum, Kracauer found a very different experience in the cinema, one that had as much to do with the changed rhythms of mechanical labor as it did with the very architecture of Berlin's picture palaces. Kracauer's notion of a distracted subject, one unable to contemplate, unable to see things in perspective, parallels a society that is shattered into the oblivion of abstraction. Kracauer's distracted spectator sits alongside Epstein's fatigued viewer, their perception irretrievably altered by modern life's visual, physical, and mental noise. For Kracauer, one gains access to the truth of modern industrial experience in the cinema because the attention to the surface of things matches, for once, the thing-like nature of modern labor.

The result of Kracauer's distraction in his own film theory was to prove far less positive than Epstein's lyrical fatigue. In the exile of his later years he virtually vanished into the represented rather than the experienced world. Whereas reification merely laid the ground for its inverse fetish power in the active form of the mass ornament in Kracauer's early writing, his later work uses the reified image to redeem experience. Finally for Kracauer, the image simply becomes a thing that is easier to look at than reality. In his *Theory of Film,* he compares the film screen to Athena's polished shield given to Perseus.[46] By looking at the reflection of Medusa rather than Medusa herself, Perseus might safely see that which would otherwise destroy him, thus redeeming the horrors of experience from oblivion.[47] This model of redemption through reification, which defined his later theoretical writing,[48] places Kracauer finally in close proximity to André Bazin.

Bazin (1918–1958) saw in filming the same urge that once prompted

Egyptians to mummify their dead: an act of preservation that transcends time and space.[49] Just as important to Bazin's film theory as a whole, however, was the notion that cinema, like a clay mold, provided a direct transfer of the physical world that answers, once and for all, a "primitive desire" (11, 13–14). Bazin's reference to the primitive is both minimal and monumental. The primitive appeal of copying guides his theory as well as its critical consequences. His Aristotelian understanding of artistic representation begins with the premise that people have a desire to see copies. This he traces to the models, tracings, and reliefs made by primitive people. Their capacity to effect such a direct transfer from reality distinguishes cinema and photography from other art forms. Bazin is best known, and most often abused, for privileging the shot over the cut, mise-en-scène over montage. This forms the basis of his critical positions regarding German Expressionism and Soviet montage. The relationship of these criticisms to his basic aesthetic theory of a primitive desire for a direct, unmediated transfer of reality is clear. To make an impression, to cast a mold, to make a transfer of something real, the object, if only for a moment, must remain still. It is, I believe, this quality of stillness in a shot — the longer the take, the better the transfer — that executes such a profound influence over Bazin's critical assessments.

I have selected these theorists for discussion based not on the eventual outcome of the theory the thinker develops, nor by the quantity of references to the primitive. Rather, I have selected Epstein, Benjamin, Lindsay, Eisenstein, Balázs, Kracauer, and Bazin because of the crucial role, however fleetingly or systematically deployed, primitive thought plays in their theories of film within the context of their respective experiences of modernity. Although the writings discussed span fifty-odd years, they all write in the throes of awakening to cinema's impact on experience and representation. At the base of this primitive turn, I believe, one finds the reflections of a felt affinity to the primitive already so prevalent in modern artistic production.

"Only a thoughtless observer," wrote Benjamin, "would deny that there are correspondences between the world of modern technology and the archaic symbol-world of mythology."[50] Such correspondences, so bluntly displayed, for example, by Epstein's image of the young black bowing in worship of the car's headlights, appear in all of the theorists under discussion here. They appear strongest, however, in theorists who were also filmmakers. Their engagement with the cinema bears the marks of what Benjamin called "the next childhood memory," in which one understands technology not merely as new; instead, such childlike interest and curiosity as theirs inevitably links technology to the archaic: "Every childhood achieves something great, irreplaceable for mankind. Through its interest and curiosity about all kinds of discoveries and machinery, every childhood ties technological achievement to the old symbol-worlds. There is nothing in the realm of nature that would by definition be exempt from such a tie. But it takes form in the aura of habit, not in the aura of novelty" (6–7). Epstein and Eisenstein seem never to have lost the child's magical thinking. Their reverie with the form — its aura of novelty rather than of habit — does not share the spirit of melancholia that so pervades the work of Balázs, Benjamin, and Kracauer.[51] The reason for this, of course, is obvious: They were filmmakers. To put it in crude terms, modern affective scarcity created a market for their product.

And so we turn now to the story of language's poverty overcome by technology's bounty. In Eisenstein's *The Old and the New*, the cream separator announces a new product: the sensuous vision that is available now at the cinema.

CHAPTER 2 Savage Theory/Savage Practice

Our language is like dish washing: we have only dirty water and dirty dishrags, and yet we manage to get everything clean. — Niels Bohr[1]

Stephen. (looks behind.) So that gesture, not music, not odours, would be a universal language, the gift of tongues rendering visible not the lay sense but the first entelechy, the structural rhythm. — James Joyce[2]

The breaking of pure expression into a system of just so many dirty words has been variously marked by critical theorists as a move that can be characterized as one from primitive nature to rational culture. The impetus to see film, a medium distinguished by its technology, as a means of reestablishing relationships between the word and the thing it seeks to represent that have been lost through the rationalization of language, to make manifest the stages of thought between image and idea effaced by habits of association, nonetheless is very strong in early film theory. In his writing, Eisenstein addressed film's expressive potential only after having developed the cognitive line of intellectual cinema. When he did, like his contemporaries Vachel Lindsay and Béla Balázs, for example, Eisenstein turned to primitive theories of language and identification. In turning his attention to forms of expression such as gesture and the interior monologue that are less directly logic-bound than the cause-and-effect relations of montage theory, Eisenstein wished to establish an equal tension between the sensual and cognitive elements of film language.

The first section of this chapter deals with the dependence of enlightened thought on theories of the primitive to define the "shape" of sensual thinking in Eisenstein's theory of film. The second section introduces the relationships between Benjamin's and Eisenstein's theories of language and film. Benjamin's and Eisenstein's thoughts about children, language, and play are similar, and when taken together they illuminate the activities that occur within the very marked schism between word and thing, image and idea, which becomes the central arena of cinema and its theory for Eisenstein and his contemporaries. Thinking of cinema as such an arena, the final section of this chapter turns to the practical pressures to make a popular film that will create enthusiasm for excess rather than subsistence production that informed Eisenstein's project, *The Old and the New*. In the film's famous cream-separator sequence, Eisenstein greets a new magical god, which appears not by classical but by modern machinations.

The trajectories that map out a semiotic theory of language, based on arbitrary relations between the word and the thing on the one hand, and a sensuous or mystical connection between the word and the originary thing on the other, seem equally inadequate to describe Eisenstein's theory of how a word or image is produced and perceived in his formulation of "sensual thinking."[3]

In what follows, I draw from Critical Theory to map out a different trajectory more suited to sensual thinking, which takes the lack of the identity between the word and the thing not just as a priori but as *fons et origen*. Horkheimer and Adorno mark the split between word and thing in the *Dialectic of Enlightenment* as that which detonates the Enlightenment and clears the way for bourgeois formalism. What is more, it can be witnessed, for example, when Odysseus plays a word game, using linguistic cunning to save his neck in his encounter with Polyphemus. In the chapter, "Odysseus or Myth and Enlightenment," Horkheimer and Adorno chart Odysseus' worldly cunning. A physically weaker man than the forces of nature and myth that threaten him, Odysseus' power lies in his rationality. This enables him to distinguish the word from the sense of the word to his own advantage, which, in the two instances they select, saves Odysseus' life.

In response to the demand that he listen to the Sirens' song in order to pass through the choppy channel between Scylla and Charybdis, he binds himself to the mast, thus fulfilling the demand as uttered, but not the meaning of it, because he prevents his own seduction by the song. Odysseus places wax in the ears of the oarsmen so that they can't hear his orders to follow the sound of the Sirens' song. Thus, Horkheimer and Adorno assert, the point at which the "mythic destiny, *fatum*, was one with the spoken word" had been transgressed.[4]

In his encounter with Polyphemus, Odysseus "learns that the same word can mean different things." When Polyphemus asks Odysseus his name, he answers, "Nobody." "Because both the hero and Nobody are possible connotations of the name Udeis," Horkheimer and Adorno assert, "the former is able to break the anathema of the name. . . . The artifice of self-preservation depends on the process which decrees the relation [rather than unity] between word and thing. Odysseus' two contradictory actions in his encounter with Polyphemus, his answering to the name, and his disowning it, are nevertheless one. He acknowledges himself to himself by denying himself under the name Nobody; he saves his life by losing himself. This linguistic adaptation to death contains the schema of modern mathematics."[5] A play on words is not innocent but marks the beginning of language's rationalization into a system of tricks and shortcuts more concerned with self-preservation than expression.

Walter Benjamin situates the splitting of the word from its idea in the Garden of Eden. In the essay, "On Language as Such and the Language of Man," pure communication (what he calls the language-mind) falls into language itself: "the Fall marks the birth of the human word."[6] To consign language to either conventional semiotics or to maintain the myth of essential, unmediated meaning of the language-mind does not deal sufficiently with either reifying structures or expression, according to Benjamin: "Through the word man is bound to the language of things. The human word is the name of things. Hence it is no longer conceivable, as the bourgeois view of language maintains, that the word has an accidental relation to its object, that it is a sign for things (or knowledge of them) agreed on by some convention. Language never gives mere signs. However, the rejection of bourgeois by mystical linguistic theory equally rests on a misunderstanding" (116–17).

On the one hand, language never gives "mere signs"—there is something more to words than a simple, arbitrary signal; yet on the other hand, the "mystical theory" in which the word is simply the essence of the thing is incorrect because the "thing in itself has no word" (117). In "The Ground of Intentional Immediacy," Benjamin delineates the distance between the referent and the thing one intends to convey with the terms "pure name," "signifying word," and "mere sign." The pure name doesn't signify but refers us to the essence of the thing; the signifying word "contains the name within it but has an unclear relation to the object's essential nature"; and the mere sign merely refers to the signifier itself (it is not a word).[7] The second of these, which Benjamin labels "immediate and impure," situated between a thing's essence and its appearance, marks the material ambiguity that drove much of early film theoretical writing. Feeling their way around in the murky darkroom of language, cinema was to act as the developer's solution.

In a later essay, "On the Mimetic Faculty" (1933), Benjamin lays the foundation of a theory of language based on our ability to form nonsensuous correspondences between a word and the constellation of meanings that are stored within it, thus still connecting the word and the thing but placing human mimetic play rather than arbitrary signs as their mediation. While this will become important in relation to the discussion of sensual thinking below, here I only wish to highlight the gravity of the schism between words and their meaning that early film theory rushed in to fill.

Béla Balázs posits the gesture that precedes speech (which he locates in the primitive prelinguistic but not necessarily prevocal) as the unproblematic moment when the impetus to articulate coincides exactly with the (inarticulate) articulation of the orator's idea, a moment that the cinema, with its gestures and close-ups, could reintroduce:

Linguistic research has found that the origins of language lie in expressive movement, that is that man when he began to speak moved his tongue and lips to no greater extent than the other muscles of his face and body—just as an infant does to-day. Originally the purpose was not the making of sounds. The movement of tongue and lips was at first the same spontaneous gesturing as every other expressive movement of the body. That the former produced sounds was a secondary, adventitious phenomenon, which was only later used for practical purposes. The immediately visible message was thus turned into an immediately audible message. In the course of this process, as in every translation, a great deal was lost. It is the expressive movement, the gesture, that is the aboriginal mother-tongue of the human race.[8]

Balázs's theory is that cinema can recover the expressiveness since lost to spoken language because the ascent of the word effectively weakened the power of gesture as the body atrophied from neglect. Similarly, Epstein thought that a close-up could show not just the expressive gesture but the moments before the gesture, the curl of the lip that cracks the smile: "I know of nothing more moving than a face giving birth to an expression in slow motion. A whole preparation comes first, a slow fever, which is difficult to know whether or not to compare to the incubation of a disease, a gradual ripening, or more coarsely, a pregnancy. Finally, all this effort boils over, shattering the rigidity of a muscle. A contagion of movements animates the face."[9] Epstein aligns his pure cinema with primitive language: "Moreover cinema is a language, and like all languages it is animistic; it attributes, in other words, a semblance of life to the objects it defines. The more primitive a language, the more marked this animistic tendency. There is no need to stress the extent to which the language of cinema remains primitive in its terms and ideas" (22). Like language, cinema animates the object it represents. To name a thing with a word is to touch it with magic and thereby impart autonomous power to the word. The same is even more true for the representation of a thing on film because it is a more primitive form of language than words, and thus the visual naming it performs has none of the sophistications of convention that might mute this "animistic tendency."

Eisenstein as well sees primitive, prelogical speech as an important new element that he calls "inner speech" whose "syntax" is opposed to that of "uttered speech." "Inner speech," explains Eisenstein, "the flow and sequence of thinking unformulated into the logical constructions in which uttered, formulated thoughts are expressed, has a special structure of its own."[10] Although this primitive speech, unlike those to which Balázs and Epstein refer, has a syntax and a structure, it is still antithetical to uttered logical expression: "Inner speech is precisely at the stage of image-sensual structure, not yet having attained that logical formulation with which speech clothes itself before stepping out into the open" (130). Like Adam and Eve, inner speech is naked.

The apparent project of Eisenstein's speech/essay "Film Form: New Problems" was to provide a theoretical base for inner speech to become the new content of intellectual cinema (129).[11] His guiding principle of an organic whole induces him to relate the economic structure of the production of the work to its form and content (167). He first demonstrates this by showing how the form of the detective novel is an expression of private-property ideology, and again more elaborately later in the essay when he shows how Dickens's and Griffith's forms reflected the contradictions of capitalism. The argument of this essay then, in turn, should provide a theoretically dialectical, materialist context for the use of inner speech in Soviet film. But the essay/speech never connects the sense of the prelogical, the flow and sequence of unformulated thinking — with which, inspired by Joyce's inner monologues, he worked to create the shooting script for Dreiser's *An American Tragedy,* for example (103–7) — to, say, **31** the kind of egalitarian polyphony characteristic of the overtone that can be contextualized ideologically; thus, his quite broad and structural usage of the term "inner speech" never quite becomes to communism what the detective novel is to capitalism.

The concept of inner speech is still useful for opening theoretical ground today, as Paul Willemen demonstrates in his essay, "Cinematic Discourse: The Problem of Inner Speech." Willemen begins with the reminder that all these things — images, dreams, ideas, as well as the words — are language.[12] Willemen expands the concept of inner speech from the psychoanalytical discourse between the ego and the unconscious to include the social largely by taking up such thinkers as Eikhenbaum, Vygotsky, and Luria.[13] Eikhenbaum described the spectator's process of "internal speech" in the cinema as both complex and semi-automatic: "The film spectator must perform a complicated mental task in linking together the shots (the construction of cine-phrases and cine-periods), a task virtually absent in everyday usage where the word forms a covering and excludes other means of expression."[14] Here again, a distrust of the word emerges; the word forms a "covering" that "excludes other means of expression." In contrast to the enunciated word, the construction of meaning in film works backward "from the object, from the observed movement, to the comprehension of them to the construction of inner speech" (11).

Willemen constructively contrasts social speech (i.e., talking and writing) to inner speech to get at its richness, complexity, and instability. In social speech, "the meaning functions as the dominant element, while in inner speech — the frontier creature — words are saturated with sense."[15] The nature of this "frontier creature," chides Willemen, has continually been stripped of its social and historical characteristics. He proposes instead: "Inner speech is the discourse that binds the psychoanalytic subject and the subject in history, functioning as a locus of condensation, a site where the two overlap so that the 'mechanical' dialect must always be read as a function of the productivity of Ucs [unconscious] processes. This is not the same as subscribing to any notion of determination by the Ucs — quite the contrary" (51). Willemen goes so far as to accuse a strictly psychoanalytic understanding of inner speech as a form of repression: "Any discourse that essentialises and hypothesises notions of subject production/positions, autonomises the discursive and invokes the Ucs whenever the question of politics and the real is mentioned" (52). For Willemen, inner speech is the "site where the subjective and the social are articulated" (52). Inner speech appears as just such an articulation for Eisenstein's theory of sensual thinking. And, as we will see, film images are "closely related, although not for the reasons usually invoked, to dream images: both can be regarded as 'grounded in folklore, popular myths, legends, linguistic idiom, proverbial idioms and current jokes'" (52).[16] For it was precisely upon folklore and myth that Eisenstein called to further define sensual thinking in theory, as well as to activate expression in the cinema.

While in Paris, en route to the United States and then Mexico, Eisenstein picked up Lévy-Bruhl's *How Natives Think*. He could not find Frazer's *The Golden Bough*: "Never mind! Meanwhile, Lévy-Bruhl suffices, and through its pages I make the most dizzying excursions into the secrets of what already takes on the more precise definition of 'prelogic.'"[17] In the final section of his autobiography's chapter "Intellectual Cinema," Eisenstein leaps effortlessly from Paris and Lévy-Bruhl to Mexico and sensual thinking only to land finally at Joyce's door to hear him read "Anna Livia Plurabelle" on a gramophone. Like anthropologists and other travelers before him, Eisenstein uncovered the secrets of language through contact with the primitive on foreign turf, a contact unavailable at home in the magical and unproblematic way it had occurred:

that most unreal and most unpronounceable name:
Popocatepetl.

Ha, ha!

For I have only to raise my head from the page I am reading to see before my eyes the summit of that snow-white extinct volcano in the blindingly blue tropical sky.

I am in Mexico.

And I am sitting at the foot of this "verbal abstraction" that has borrowed, it would seem, the virginal accuracy of its slanting sides from those Japanese prints of Fujiyama's countenance, which has bored so many millions.

Popocatepetl is so real that once we nearly crashed in to its crater in the tiny plane. . . . Curiosity drove us to peer into the extinct crater of the mysterious Popo.

Not checking the contents of our fuel tank, we made an aerial detour up and around. . . .

I survived to sit at the foot of the volcano, surrounded by the representatives   **33**
of those very peoples whose system of thinking (for by that time I already knew that this kind of thing is also called sensuous) seemed so fantastic and unreal in the pages of Lévy-Bruhl or Frazer. (210–11)

Although he does not thoroughly immerse himself in the culture, as he claims Frank Cushing did with the Zunis (although he fails to mention that Cushing made himself an elder to do so), Eisenstein's contact with people in Mexico, and his seduction by the landscape, the colors, gave him the cultural experience of sensual thinking: "It is here in *tierra caliente* (burning earth) that I come to know the fantastic structure of prelogical, sensuous thinking — not only from the pages of anthropological investigations, but from daily communion with those descendants of the Aztecs and Toltecs, Mayas, or Huichole who have managed to carry unharmed through the ages that meandering thought" (211).[18] That "meandering thought" based in society becomes linked, for Eisenstein, with the "internal monologue," that is normally left unspoken: "The cramming of the Japanese language! Both this and the former language [Chinese] in its external speech have preserved that very same sensuous linguistic canon of prelogic, with which we ourselves speak when we talk to ourselves — our internal speech" (213). Eisenstein's inner speech has two origins: cultural, primitive "meandering thought," and the more personal, " 'asyntaxism' of Joyce's writing, overheard in the very origins of that internal speech which each of us speaks in his own way" (213).

These two origins[19] need to be kept in mind when Eisenstein begins his explication with the very general and great claim: "The laws of the construction of inner speech are precisely those laws which lie at the foundation of the whole variety of laws governing the construction of the form and composition of art-works."[20]

The essay clearly introduces new factors beyond a materialist-based theory of the cinema. In most of Eisenstein's previous writing, it was plain that one could account for any effect of a film through the content and most of all the arrangement of the images, and that the effects that Eisenstein was largely concerned with were those that produced ideas: "The specific quality of the intellectual cinema was proclaimed to be the content of the film. The trend of thoughts and the movement of thoughts were represented as the exhaustive basis of everything that transpired in the film" (129). The essay attempts to account for the production of feelings in the spectator as well, a "deepening" of his cinema/theory project. Although it is structured rhetorically so as to ground the concept of sensual thinking in yet another material base, in this case drawn from anthropology and folk psychology, the essay's prehistory (which includes his trip to Mexico, whose profound effects are documented in the book *Mexico According to Eisenstein*[21]) and the repeated use of the term "expression" suggest culture and the unconscious as factors in the creation of meaning.

This move to use and understand other forces that add to the creation of meaning that lie outside or beneath the material signs of the text is a shift very similar to that of another thinker who began with a material base, in this case the body, to explain effects on consciousness. Freud began with neurology, but finally abandoned the material body as the cause of effects on consciousness and introduced instead the unconscious. For both thinkers, human consciousness has always ceded the power to produce other meanings and effects to things and people outside it, beyond its control. Although in developed societies we no longer can abide a literal belief in, say, animism, we still account for the effects of those causes that remain unknown or outside our consciousness: for Freud, in his concept of the unconscious; for Eisenstein, in the sphere of artistic production and representation.

Eisenstein goes about his justification of the theory of sensual thinking as a reenactment of modes of primitive speech and thought in much the same way that Freud justifies the concept of the unconscious. The attribution of a consciousness to the unconscious, Freud believed, partakes of the long-standing logic by which we have formerly attributed consciousness to inanimate matter, to plants, and to other humans: "Consciousness makes each of us aware only of his own states of mind; that other people, too, possess a consciousness is an inference which we draw by analogy from their observable utterances and actions, in order to make this behaviour of theirs intelligible to us. . . . This inference (or this identification) was formerly extended by the ego to other human beings, to animals, plants, inanimate objects and to the world at large. . . . To-day, our critical judgment is already in doubt on the question of consciousness in animals; we refuse to admit it in plants and we regard the assumption of its existence in inanimate matter as mysticism."[22] Because we now regard the notion of consciousness in plants with some skepticism, "our critical judgment" renders unavailable the previous repository for meanings and feelings that impinge, yet cannot be consciously traced. The unconscious, in Freud's argument, effectively rushes in to fill the vacancy created by rationality's dispersion of an animated universe. This history of inferences of a consciousness to things and people outside ourselves lays the foundation for the concept of the unconscious.

Likewise, Eisenstein rests his case on inferences we at one point believed but that now resonate as artistic practice and poetic theory: "It is exceedingly curious that certain theories and points of view which in a given historical epoch represent an expression of scientific knowledge, in a succeeding epoch decline as science, but continue to exist as possible and admissible not in the line of science but in the line of art and imagery."[23] Sensual thinking is the prelogical structure by which we allow what have become, in our rational society, artistic associations. This has its basis in prelogical traditions and beliefs. Our poetic practices of metaphor and metonymy, for example, hark back to the magical forms that Frazer defined as the two kinds of sympathetic magic: homeopathic or imitative magic and contagious magic.[24] Eisenstein, as did Roman Jakobson, would surely have used the forms of sympathetic magic to make his connections more simply had he found Frazer in Paris and not Lévy-Bruhl.[25] In homeopathic magic, one works on the copy of the whole, like breaking the framed photo of an errant boyfriend or whipping the statue of an inattentive saint.[26] In contagious magic, one takes a piece of the original, like a piece of clothing or a pince-nez (132) and works on that piece. Both part for the whole and whole for the part rely on their believed identity, their sympathy, and in this essay Eisenstein sees them as variations of the same poetic theory.

Sensual, prelogical thinking, wrote Eisenstein, preserved in the "shape of inner speech among the peoples who have reached an adequate level of social and cultural development, at the same time also represents in mankind at the dawn of cultural development norms of conduct in general, i.e. the laws according to which flow the processes of sensual thought are equivalent for them to a 'habit logic' of the future" (131). The beliefs and practices that Eisenstein believes have become "habit logic" are varied and highly selected.

Eisenstein's most amusing example is the Bororo belief that a person has a simultaneous identity: He or she is both himself or herself and a red parakeet. Though this practice is unacceptable to the rational mind, nonetheless we are capable of maintaining, in fact when acting on the stage we must maintain such a dual conviction. His evidence concludes: "simultaneous actuality is present even in the most inveterate supporter of 'transsubstantiation.' There are, in fact, too few cases known in the history of the theater of an actor leaning on the 'fourth [nonexistent] wall!'" (137). This dual identification holds true as well for the spectator who refrains from rushing to the stage to save a character in peril. Though Eisenstein drew this example from Lévy-Bruhl, he could easily have found models, even among the Bororo, for other kinds of identification, such as identifying so much with a drawing that the mere sight of it would kill one.[27] The model of identification employed by Balázs, on the other hand, is that of actually going into Chinese paintings: The painter who fell in love with one of his painted women enters the painting, and a year later a picture of a newborn child appears.[28] Balázs is probably drawing from de Groot, but Lévy-Bruhl cites several similar examples of Chinese identification taken from de Groot's *The Religious System of China*[29] with which Eisenstein could have dealt.

Taking an example from Wundt's *Elements of Folk Psychology,* Eisenstein sees a Bushman's description of a colonial encounter as a series of "descriptive single images." The Bushman's "chain of concrete single images" functions, for Eisenstein, like a "shooting script," whereas the abstract language of the colonizer would have to be broken down to the Bushman's concrete formulation of the event in order to be translated into film.[30] For Wundt, gestural language is governed by the arrangement of words in their perceptual order: "The thinking itself may be called concrete."[31] Not only is it concrete, it is precise. Klamath language has not one word for walking but many, each specifying the particular gestures involved. Primitive language, which articulated concrete images and specified human gesture, was, Eisenstein maintained, precisely what the planning of a play or a film demanded.

The gesture, direct speech that can be expressed untranslated into filmed images, metaphor, metonymy, dual identification, the concept of the organic whole, are all rooted in primitive thought and language: "Art is nothing else but an artificial retrogression in the field of psychology toward the forms of earlier thought-processes, i.e., a phenomenon identical with any given form of drug, alcohol, shamanism, religion, etc.!"[32] This location of a model in the primitive is the same tactic Freud employed: "The psycho-analytic assumption of unconscious mental activity appears to us, on the one hand, as a further expansion of the primitive animism which caused us to see copies of our own consciousness all around us, and, on the other hand, as an extension of the corrections undertaken by Kant of our views on external perception."[33] Finally, Freud couples the proof of the unconscious with the logic of cognition. Just as Eisenstein's flight over and into Popocatepetl was fraught with danger, so too sensual thinking must not be left unchecked by the rational. Neither the unconscious nor the concept of inner speech can be left free to roam the interstices of volcanoes: "The dialectic of works of art is built upon a 'dual-unity.'" It is both "an impetuous progressive rise along the lines of the highest explicit steps of consciousness and a simultaneous penetration by means of the structure of the form into the layers of profoundest sensual thinking."[34] Finally, for Eisenstein, the primitive seems to be redeemed in the rational.

Mikhail Yampolsky pursues the difficulty of Eisenstein's dialectic between the primitive and the abstract in his essay, "The Essential Bone Structure, Mimesis in Eisenstein," a difficulty not unnoticed by Eisenstein himself. Yampolsky writes, "He admitted that he was 'disturbed' by a coincidence between the highest abstraction (the generalisation of the image) and the most primitive element, the line."[35] The line was at once for Eisenstein "purveyor of protoconcepts and the highest form of contemporary abstraction" (180). The line is both a literal trace, in the sense of a primitive transfer of a contour, and essence, in the sense that it partakes of "the essential bone structure" of the original. Yampolsky conjures Eisenstein's image of going to the museum in the dark (182). In darkness, knowing is both tactile and a mystical transmission of the conceptual world. In the dark, you know only by touching objects, yet at the same time an ethereal essence that is completely immaterial and unseen transfers itself directly, unmediated by the signs that vision would obscure. Like running your hand over a lover's finger, bold materiality and the deepest structural meaning constitute, in Yampolsky's view, Eisenstein's concern with mimesis. Thus the significance of the death masks of *Que Viva Mexico!* where the skull is repainted onto the mask: "Both the face like a skull and the skull like a face," as Yampolsky cites Eisenstein (187). The film director is he who masks the skull beneath the skin, deploying the pleasures of unmasking that the magician, the detective story, and physiognomy can all claim to hold. "The creation of meaning," Yampolsky concludes, "depends on the intuitively magic physiognomic disclosure of the line which lies concealed within the body of the object (or text) — of the 'bone-structure'" (187–88).

For Eisenstein, primitive language represents a stage in which language was less abstract, more descriptive of physical reality, of actions, where signifier and signified were closely bound together. The process by which a word signifies a meaning is given precise attention in the essay "Word and Image," written in 1938. The mental process by which a word signifies is based in part on convention, for example, the convention by which we read the time, but also on a set of consciously unacknowledged associations, the things that characterize the time of day denoted. "Psychological habit" tends to reduce this signifying chain so that we recognize only the resulting idea. This whole host of associations are precisely those that cinema can materialize so that not just the aggregate image, in this case the time of day, but its evocation in our consciousness and feelings is possible. Inner speech is not just the habitual shape of our thought but also, in terms of the relationship of signifier to signified, the chain of associations that transforms a word into an idea. What has been absorbed by Eisenstein's phrase "habit logic" (employed in both "Word and Image" and "Film Form") are not only the conventions that the semiotic theory of language uses to account for the way words mean but a sometimes primitive, sometimes unconscious constellation of possible associations whose nature is arbitrary only because the attendant chain of associations is ignored or forgotten.

Like Eisenstein's, Walter Benjamin's theory of language cannot be fit into either a semiotic or an essentialist mold. An identity between word and thing existed in what he calls the "language-mind" before man's fall into language in the Garden of Eden, but he holds no store in trying to reestablish that identity. Remnants of that pure identity exist in "the language of pure feeling," which Benjamin identifies with music, the lament of the mourning play,[36] and the "child's view of color." The child's sighting of color, writes Benjamin, "creates a pure mood." Because it is immediate, without adultlike "intellectual cross-references," a child's view of color is experience itself. Unlike the adult, whose "task is to provide a world order," who is not concerned with the "grasp of innermost reasons and essences" but their "development," the child is not interested in making things useful. "Instead," writes Benjamin, "the world is full of color in a state of identity, innocence, and harmony. Children are not ashamed, since they do not reflect but only see." The child viewing a rainbow sits alongside Eisenstein in the dark museum: "Because children see with pure eyes . . . it is something spiritual: the rainbow refers not to a chaste abstraction but to a life in art. The order of art is paradisiacal because there is no thought of the dissolution of boundaries—from excitement—in the object of experience."

Taking the child's experience of viewing color in a rainbow as an example of the limit ideal, semblance measures the degree to which something lives in the copy, and it is the quality of semblance that delivers pleasure.[37] It is in this space of imitation, between the thing and the copy, that the adult's playground lies. With his emphasis on the mimetic faculty, Benjamin is interested in galvanizing the constellations of meaning that a word suggests, using the human faculty to form what he calls nonsensuous correspondences to revitalize not only language but also perception. Nonsensuous correspondences are just that: Although their graphic appearance and sonic resonance bear no traces of the thing to which they correspond (unlike Chinese writing or hieroglyphics, for instance), they do nonetheless correspond through mental associations that are neither arbitrary nor conventional. Nonsensuous correspondences are imitative and associative. Benjamin's theory of the optical unconscious, which arises from a confrontation with the historical change in which artworks are produced and viewed, is part of our sensual retraining that is enhanced by technology. The optical unconscious represents, among many things, a way of restoring our special but languishing mimetic faculty. Like Eisenstein's concept of inner speech, Benjamin's concept of mimetic faculty finds its shape in archaic culture.

The mimetic faculty, the predisposition of human beings to form nonsensuous correspondences, finds its trace in mimicry, the play of animals, children, and primitives: "The highest capacity for producing similarities, however, is man's. His gift of seeing resemblances is nothing other that a rudiment of the powerful compulsion in former times to become and behave like something else."[38] In his monograph on Disney, Eisenstein was to call this compulsion the desire for "ability to become whatever you wish."[39] The freedom he finds in the animated cartoon, for example, is the elasticity with which forms move and change, the amorphous quality of cartoon animation. The attractiveness of what Eisenstein termed "plasmaticness" is characterized by a "rejection of once and forever allotted form, freedom from ossification, the ability to dynamically assume any form" (21). When Eisenstein refers plasmaticness to "a lost changeability," he conjures a sense of the archaic similar to Benjamin's "former times." Benjamin's "compulsion in former times," like Eisenstein's "lost changeability," suggests that this amorphous quality is a "faculty" as basic as deciphering the seasons, which is restimulated when it is needed.

Our powerful mimetic compulsion has weakened over time. Like Eisenstein, Benjamin recognizes cultural difference as a product of history and not evolutionist race theory: "It must be borne in mind that neither mimetic powers nor mimetic objects remain the same in the course of thousands of years. Rather, we must suppose that the gift of producing similarities — for example, in dances, whose oldest function this was — and therefore also the gift of recognizing them, have changed with historical development."[40] Marx produced the idea that the senses change with historical development in the very special context of predicting their change when we finally transcend the "life of private property." When in the life of private property, to see, for example, is to possess; after society changes in such a way that hidden ideology no longer so mediates the senses, they themselves will become theory.[41] The project of theorizing language through the mimetic faculty, and the tracing of aura through its transformation into the optical unconscious, should be understood within the context of Marx's historical sensitivity. Benjamin put great store in the gestures and play of children who, not yet marked by society's desensitization, by the life of private property, had not lost their mimetic faculty. As Susan Buck-Morss points out, Benjamin, embarking on a walk in Moscow, a society he at the time felt had undergone such a fundamental change as to affect the senses, wrote: "The instant one arrives, the childhood stage begins. On the thick sheets of ice of the streets walking has to be relearned."[42]

Like Eisenstein's use of primitive thought, Benjamin uses what were once real identities on which to base a concept of representation. Benjamin draws on astrology and graphology to explicate the concept. In astrology, for example, the "mimetic genius," "really a life-determining force for the ancients," produced a correspondence between the position of the stars and the newborn child. Although we can no longer speak of this kind of similarity, we do "possess a canon according to which the meaning of non-sensuous similarity can be at least partly clarified."[43] This canon is language. Rejecting the sensuous arena of similarity, onomatopoeia, to explain the meaning of words, he turns to the written rather than the spoken word, which by nature enacts a nonsensuous correspondence. Just as physiognomy reads the soul from the face, in graphology script reveals images that the writer's unconscious has hidden. It becomes, "like language, an archive of non-sensuous similarities, of non-sensuous correspondences" (162).

41

The semiotic element, the sign, like Eisenstein's ever serviceable timepiece, becomes the bearer of these correspondences whose perception is limited to a "flash." "It flits past," as Benjamin says (162). Eisenstein offers this example: "To recapitulate: between the representation of an hour on the dial of the clock and our perception of the image of that hour, there lies a long chain of linked representations of separate characteristic aspects of that hour. And we repeat: that psychological habit tends to reduce this intervening chain to a minimum, so that only the beginning and the end of the process are perceived."[44] Eisenstein reasoned that the reduction of the intervening chain, those nonsensuous correspondences, had to do with "psychological habit." Similarly, Benjamin thought that "the rapidity of writing and reading heightens the fusion of the semiotic and the mimetic in the sphere of language."[45]

One of cinema's early seductions was its potential to break the psychological habit of recognizing only signs. Cinema was able to produce the perception of such flashes of albeit highly condensed meanings as Benjamin described, as well as the fine nuances of the "intervening chain" Eisenstein theorized. Benjamin's optical unconscious, which springs forth at the technological crossroads of modernity and cinema, can be understood as a phenomenon capable of evoking and holding (on film at least) disparate, inarticulable associations around a meaning while reshaping, in a bodily mode, the habits of perception.

If Benjamin's essay "On the Mimetic Faculty" suggests not that faculty's loss but its transformation, one of the key elements of such a retooling would be the sort of perception cinema affords. Its "nearness,"[46] its tactile effect[47] displaces the meaning of the sign altogether. The close-up, the pan, slow, fast, and reverse motion provide us not with an object for contemplation, for an exercise in reading signs; cinema instead produces an immediate, tactile encounter with the modern world. In essence, as Gertrud Koch puts it, the eye touches what the hand cannot grasp.[48] The new perception cinema affords is revealing, analytical, and enchanting: "The film on the one hand extends our comprehension of the necessities which rule our lives; on the other hand, it manages to assure us of an immense and unexpected field of action."[49] The optical unconscious describes a mode of perception more suited to the modern world than auratic, distanced, perception. Before film, "our taverns and our metropolitan street, our office and furnished room, our railroad stations and our factories appeared to have us locked up hopelessly." Then "came the film and burst this prison-world asunder by the dynamite of the tenth of a second" (236). Benjamin opposes optical — and here the terminology is confusing because he uses the word optical to distinguish from tactile — contemplation, which he associates with auratic, nontechnological works of art, to tactile appropriation, which influences perception in an unconscious, habitual way, that is, without a conscious perspective. It is the mechanical aspect of the camera that allows these works of art to touch our senses so directly, because an "unconsciously penetrated space is substituted for a space consciously explored by man" (236). With its technological mimesis of a splintered and desensitized world, cinema provides the means to combat the perils of alienation.

Miriam Hansen has highlighted the political importance this held for Benjamin with her emphasis on his concept of "innervation."[50] In Benjamin's estimation, she writes, cinema could provide "a perceptual training ground for an industrially transformed physis: 'To make the vast technical apparatus of our time an object of human innervation — this is the historical task in whose service film has its true meaning.' "[51] It is in this sense of "social innervation" that we might understand Dziga Vertov's *The Man with a Movie Camera* (1929), for example, and even the "kino-eye" itself. "Collective innervation," writes Hansen, countered the "expropriation of the senses" by the "spiral of sensory alienation, phantasmagoria, and violence," which are the very handiwork of technology itself (38). These "can be countered only on the terrain of technology itself, by means of perceptual technologies that allow for a figurative, mimetic engage-

42

ment with technology at large, as productive force and social reality" (38). The new industrial world is a technological one, to be got at by technological means. This is similar to the effect of Vertov's film, as Annette 43 Michelson describes it in her introduction to *Kino-Eye*. "The editing structure culminates in the identification of film-making," writes Michelson, with "textile manufacture, itself seen as central in the economy's production."[52] The point, however, is to imbue this technology with the social relations and sensuousness that capitalism denies. With this Michelson suggests that Vertov achieves the "emancipation of the senses" that Marx proffered in the Paris manuscripts as part of revolutionary destiny, such that "The eye has indeed 'become a human eye,' and 'its object a human social object created by man and destined for him.' When the senses do thus become 'directly theoretical in practice,' the eye becomes, indeed, a kino-eye" (xl). This sensual emancipation through a technical penetration of spaces otherwise out of reach approximates in practice what Benjamin called "collective innervation."

Such a change toward spatial penetration is very apparent in Vertov's imagery in *Enthusiasm*,[53] for example, which at times pushes things so close to the surface that the things lose their identity as objects and become immediate sense impressions. A paean to the working men of the Donbass coal mines, the film stages the kind of renewal of perception that Benjamin had in mind. The coal, transported on a conveyor belt, is blasted out of contemplative time and space, imbued with rhythm and noise, reversed, slowed down, and enlarged. Rows of coal are no longer commodities on a production line but instead perform as a pulsating abstract pattern of black and white, assuring us indeed of the "immense and unexpected field of action" that lay stored in a coal conveyor belt. The space, previously closed to us, "hopelessly locked up," in this case the factory, is literally "burst asunder by the dynamite of a tenth [or less by half] of a second."[54] The question remains, however, whether Vertov, while making the mysterious world of technology and industry available to human perception so as to imbue the human senses with the very technology that would define human society, did not, at the same time, create another form of mystification.

Although it appears inconsistent with the modernization, proletarianization, and electrification that were the order of the day in Soviet society, Eisenstein's turn to primitive belief in order to theorize film is not only consistent with early impulses in film theory but bears directly on the problems faced by Eisenstein's film practice. Soviet society was in the throes of an encounter between technology and the primitive.

The extremely limited access to an understanding of precisely "how natives think," obvious in the assumption of superstition and ignorance that marks the beginning of Eisenstein's *The Old and the New* (1929) or in the cunning and treachery alluded to briefly in the encounter with the "Savage Division" in *October* (1927), where mutual suspicion uncoils into ecstatic spectacle, was an understanding that even Trotsky termed Tolstoyan at its best.[55] Leaders of the Revolution like Lenin and Trotsky grew up in landowner families on farms and had a lot of contact with peasants; nonetheless, Trotsky, for example, in *My Life,* rages against the peasants' stupidity when they failed to put his geometry lesson into practice to measure the land. Ironically, for Trotsky, what was wrong with primitive thinking — the "dull empiricism of the peasant"[56] — was peasants' inability to privilege theory over petty facts. Still, primitive speech and primitive customs became poetic theory for Eisenstein in 1935.

Eisenstein's "experiment intelligible to millions"[57] makes the encounter between technology and the primitive explicit, and also a comedy. The scene in *The Old and the New*[58] in which the land is broken up by turns into preposterously small proportions, for instance, is intended as a funny show of how the peasant can't see the forest for the trees. This not only misrepresents peasant production, it also belies a further clash of interests between the Soviet state and the peasantry whose results were humorless. Though it is common still today to couch debates about land tenure in terms of staving off the small and unworkable proportions that result from dividing land between the too many children peasants have begotten, this was clearly not the case in the Soviet countryside. By making fun of their land division Eisenstein is saying that peasants simply don't understand how to divide their land efficiently, whereas the Soviet, in this and many other things agricultural, knows better.

A. V. Chayanov's (1888–1939) study, *The Theory of Peasant Economy,* described the system of land division in Central Russia. This may well be where Eisenstein gets the image of land being divided into what seem like ridiculously small pieces, because the land was divided into very thin strips to ensure the allotment of similar quality of land first during the 1861 land reform and then far more extensively by further egalitarian repartitioning to individual family farms among the communes themselves. Indeed, the layout of the land, "the excessive intermingling of the peasant's household strips, their length, and the fragmentation of arable and meadow," as Chayanov described it in 1924, "frequently attain[ed] quite Homeric proportions."[59] Unwieldy as it had become, this organization of land had complex origins and solutions and by no means derived from the selfishness and stupidity that characterize the representation of land division in Eisenstein's film.

Chayanov's general thesis about peasant economy was that peasants produced according to what they needed and that they produced no more than what they required. Furthermore, he found, the household farm, which he contended was the basic unit from which to understand peasant economy, had an informal but nonetheless highly efficient system to see that they did just that. The basis of peasant farming, Chayanov emphasized, was minimizing "drudgery" rather than maximizing income. This basic fact, he contended, was not going to be changed by an infusion of enthusiasm for the new state but rather by carefully planned incentives for increased production.[60] Thus, the Soviet was up against not a stupid and inefficient peasantry, as shown in the film, but an extremely wily one. The poetic pressure for Eisenstein was to show the virtues, not merely of collectivization, for private cooperatives were not new, but more to the Soviet purpose, he had to demonstrate the joys of excess production to feed the growing proletariat of the cities.[61]

In meeting the task to hand, Eisenstein provides a clear demonstration of the transformation from auratic perception, one defined by its distance, however close the object may be, to the tactility of the optical unconscious along with a demonstration of the cream separator in *The Old and the New*. In *Nonindifferent Nature* (1945), Eisenstein laid out the contrasts he had intended to make with the sequence. He concedes that he gave priority to "'The pathos of the machine,' rather than to the social analysis of those profound processes, which our villages experienced in their transition to forms of collective farm economy."[62] Eisenstein thought that the issue of collectivization was addressed in the choice of a milk separator as the turning point for the film, because the separator collectivized, as it were, the milk into cream: "That drop of milk, undergoing a qualitative transformation into a drop of cream, as in a drop of . . . water, as it were, concretely mirrors the fate of a cluster of disunited individual peasant-owners. These peasants, impressed by the performance of the separator (which represents opportunities and resources of mechanized agriculture) just as suddenly undertake a gigantic qualitative leap in the area of social progress, from individual land ownership to collective agriculture, evolving from 'muzhiks' into collective farmers" (49). In a more poetic frame, the scene was designed to "clash and juxtapose . . . the different worlds of pathos and ecstasy" (51). To this end, Eisenstein deployed what he referred to as a "theatrical" style in the initial "prayer for rain," which I refer to as the auratic part of the sequence. He described the second part, the separator sequence, which I associate with tactility, the optical unconscious, and the mimetic associative play of inner speech, of nonsensuous correspondences, as "pure cinematography" (51). Through its extreme close-ups and vast waterfalls, everything, wrote Eisenstein, "either very close, or else very distant '(long-shots),' i.e., the same basic characteristic sign of ecstasy, in this case along the line of scale, everywhere is seeming to extend itself beyond the well-balanced norms, so that if there is a long-shot it becomes a 'super long-shot,' if it is a close-up, it becomes a super-close-up" (44).

The context of the sequence is that the village is suffering because of a severe drought. Led by their priest, the villagers perform a ritual procession and pray for rain. Their solemn, worried eyes fix on the priest, but in the next shot their eyes reveal a mean skepticism; the next shot shows not the priest but the spinning centrifuge of the cream separator. The eyes, we now can see, have graphically matched together two distinct scenes whose subjects are rivals for the observers' faith and skepticism.

The transformation from the ritual procession to the spectacle demonstrating technology can be characterized textually as one from images of drought to liquid plenitude; from looks of superstition and worry to skepticism and wonder; from bodies and icons to faces and the machine.[63] The stylistic change is even more pronounced. In the auratic sequence, the camera moves with the human figures such that our perception is apace with the movement of the procession, even to the degree that the camera bows with the supplicants.[64] By contrast, the movements that are recorded in the technological sequence with a static camera are beyond the median human scale of experience and range between extremes, from the slow first dribbles of cream to rushing torrents of water. The framing of the first part of the sequence takes the human figure as its base scale. The human figure is often severed by shots of legs walking or coasting, heads and shoulders looking and praying, but it is the representation of human action that determines the framing. The representation of perception itself **47** guides the framing of the second part of the sequence; the extreme close-up and the subjective shot become the scale of reference when technology renders the previously barren, dust-swept visual landscape plenteous, eyes in close-up fixed on the rapidly spinning centrifuge that fills the screen.

It is, to my mind, no accident that it is the eyes that provide the continuity match on which the "pivot"[65] from the failure of prayer to the success of the cream-separating machine turns. The film, which is about the transformation from manual to mechanical labor, from a "natural" to a market economy, from subsistence to excess production, from superstition to enlightenment, must address most of all the perception of such changes. The contradictions about how this in fact was felt in the countryside notwithstanding, the task was a mighty one: "For the tasks which face the human apparatus of perception at the turning points of history cannot be solved by optical means, that is by contemplation alone. They are mastered gradually by habit, under the guidance of tactile appropriation."[66] In *The Old and the New,* the eye itself is transformed. Aura becomes the optical unconscious; magic is not demystified but transformed. Primitive, sensuous thinking was well on its way to becoming a new "habit logic": "The point is that the forms of sensual, pre-logical thinking, which are preserved in the shape of inner speech among the peoples who have reached an adequate level of social and cultural development, at the same time also represent in mankind at the dawn of cultural development norms of conduct in general, i.e., the laws according to which flow the processes of sensual thought are equivalent for them to a 'habit logic' of the future."[67] Eisenstein described the associations he was counting on in terms of folklore and myth. These are the arenas of sensuous thinking, of mimetic correspondences: "A metaphor bursts into the action, 'fountains of milk,' echoing the folklore images of 'rivers of milk' and 'a land flowing with milk and honey' — symbols of material well-being."[68] This series of superscaled images of not just "well-being" but plenitude, excess, marks an accretion of the associations of inner speech that explodes into a state of extasis.

As to the magic of cinema: The camera, after all, does make it rain.

CHAPTER 3

First Contact

To see a thousand immobile heads whose gazes are aimed at, monopolized and haunted by a single enormous face on the screen towards which they all converge. Such a terrifying tête-à-tête. An idol and the crowd. Like the cults of India. But here the idol is living, and this idol is a man. — M. Jean Choux, cited in P. Adams Sitney, *The Avant Garde Film*

Early film theory often betrays a fascination with the audience's fascination with the cinema. The nature of this fascination is neither voyeuristic nor vicarious; rather, it is a complex refraction of theorists' felt contact with the image-producing machine. A model for this fascination on the part of early theorists can be seen in cinematic representations of first contact between the savage and the civilized, wherein primitives' reactions to the strangeness of civilized custom, ornamentation, and technology activate the spectator's nostalgia for the recent past in which technology was thought to be new and wondrous. It also confirms a sense of progress. But most striking is the way such representations of technology's magic enunciate the enlighteneds' own primitive wonder at the machine.

Contemporary popular cinematic reenactments of first contact produce the pleasures of voyeuristic irony when they simulate early viewers' responses to what was then new technology. Francis Ford Coppola's *Dracula* (1992), for example, represented the titillation and fear often projected onto first contact with the cinema and other related technology[1] when Count Dracula takes his blood bride through a gallery of the "cinema of attractions"[2] down turn-of-the-century London streets. Dracula chooses a motion picture gallery to reveal himself to Mina, whom he takes to be the incarnation of his long dead wife, Elizabeta. Fascinated and afraid — utterly seduced — she lies back and watches Dracula's eyes become those of his wolf/dog, then transform from cold blue to fiery blood red, then become once more Dracula's eyes, then match the cold blue shot of the moon. In the back of the frame a different sort of revelation altogether takes place. Trick films, such as that of a naked woman appearing by magic in a man's lap, form a gallery of taboos from perverse to cute, but the film that forms the backdrop for the scene's climax is a film made after **49** cinema's primal scene: Lumière's *Arrival of a Train* (1895, France). The image, in negative, is of the *Empire Express* from a 1901 Biograph film called *The Ghost Train*, a far more menacing version of the steel beast.³ The conflation of spectatorial and sexual seduction is not new; for example, in Max Ophuls's *Letter From an Unknown Woman* (1948, United States), the lovers take a simulated coach ride and travel scenes are run across the windows, creating a kind of protocinema. These examples not only highlight the idea that spectator seduction bolsters sexual seduction, they also demonstrate the way this new technology is and was often thought to leave one awestruck and vulnerable. It is in this vein that it is common to stage seduction scenes with new lovers watching old movies.

Quite a few popular period films whose represented era predates the moving picture extend this seductive interest in the fascination with visual technology to other devices such as the telescope. Protocontact, in this sense, has become part of the formula for historical films that deal in cultural conflict. In Kevin Costner's *Dances with Wolves* (1990), for example, the lone soldier Dunbar befriends a group of Sioux Indians. While they huddle together on a hill to observe a herd of buffalo, Dunbar uses his monocular to get a closer view. He passes it to Kicking Bird (Graham Greene), who jolts back, stunned by the close-up view from the white man's monocular. This scene is performed again in Kevin Reynolds's *Robin Hood: Prince of Thieves* (1991), when the sophisticated Moor (Morgan Freeman) unfolds a leather pouch that contains a telescope and hands it to Robin Hood (Kevin Costner), the primitive Englishman who sees in it a close-up of an advancing enemy. Milking the moment more than is customary, Costner's Robin Hood flails his arm pointlessly to fight off the aggressors who are still, of course, very much in the distance.

These moments of extreme voyeurism are generally intended as comic. They never announce themselves, they come and go quickly, but they recur over time and across genres. From the extended and prodding shot Robert Flaherty forces overlong when Nanook bites at a gramophone record at the fur trader's hut (*Nanook of the North*, 1921), to Lottie's (Butterfly McQueen) quizzical and easily missed gesture when she finds herself hearing a voice from a little black object, as if outdone by the

Nanook and the gramophone in *Nanook of the North* (1921). Courtesy of Museum of Modern Art Stills Archive.

mystery of phone communication, in *Mildred Pierce* (1945, directed by Michael Curtiz), this kind of encounter is standard stuff. These moments are not merely products of the well-worn dramatic device whose effect rests on the audience's superior knowledge to those on stage or screen. Rather, they partake of the double-edged bind to the primitive other that invigorates all representations of contact and early theoretical understandings of filmic representation itself. Through the contrivance of primitives' eyes we see the marvel of technology's recent past, and through the technology of the camera itself we enjoy the fine nuances of primitive gesture. Technology makes the primitive primitive and, at the same time, the primitive makes technology magical.

The position occupied by the film viewer in the examples above sustains portions of early theory as well. Béla Balázs and Vachel Lindsay often use examples in which the spectators are primitive or are made primitive by their lack of sophistication as regards the apparatus, or alternatively, by their primitive affinity with the machine. In effect, these theorists reproduce first contact outside the theater to master the audience's reactions to the viewing of cinema itself. Whether to serve spectator or theoretical pleasure, this position finds favorable ground in primitivism, that complex mangle of imputations to and fascinations with people whose very difference generally turns out to be marked by the stampede of progress over their bodies — their status in the realm of the real always circumvented by metaphor, myth, and misrecognition. Facets of theoretical first contact reach beyond mere moments of primitivist imputation. For not only is the primitive made primitive and technology made magical in this encounter, but modern man himself is thrown into primitive relief.

Béla Balázs's *Theory of the Film* and Vachel Lindsay's *The Art of the Moving Picture* are shot through with the metaphor of first contact. The people for whom the lack of distance was altogether new, for whom this nearness, whether an emotional absorption or a tactile hit, for whom contact with the work of art was a shock rather than a thrill, were those people who were acculturated to European aesthetics and art philosophy. Americans, women, children, and primitives, never so schooled, on the other hand, approach cinema with curiosity and readily accede to this immediate form.[4]

The distance that exists between spectator and work of art is, to Balázs's mind, culturally specific to Europeans. "The Chinese of Old," writes Balázs, "regarded their art with a different eye." He then recounts a tale in which the spectator is so taken by the beauty of a Chinese landscape painting that he enters the picture, follows the path to the mountains, and is never seen again. "Another story tells of a young man who saw a beautiful picture of lovely maidens disporting themselves in a meadow full of flowers. One of the maidens caught his eye and he fell in love with her. He entered the picture and took the maiden for his wife. A year later a little child appeared in the picture" (50). This literal absorption by the picture serves Balázs as a general model for film identification throughout his *Theory of Film*. He must conjure up a different model to explain the humor of old films, which becomes a form of alteric recognition.

The humor of old films, according to Balázs, stems from the fact that "we recognize ourselves in their clumsy primitiveness" (37). This is the kind of recognition on which Robert Flaherty counted when he built the gramophone scene into *Nanook of the North,* arguably the most critically successful and popular of ethnographic films. In this scene, Nanook listens to a gramophone at a fur trader's hut. He then reaches for the record, and places it in his mouth as if to bite it. The English version of *Theory of Film* includes a still from this scene, with Nanook smiling and bending over as if in conversation, pelts covering the wall of the trader's hut in the background and a gramophone playing off to the right. Absent from the German text, it was probably the editor, Herbert Marshall, who inserted it into the English translation with the curious caption " '*Nanook of the North*' The extra social-nature of the ice-pack as a social experience." This caption is taken from a section of the book subheaded "Instructional Films with a Hero." In this context, Balázs makes the point that we extract the most meaning from even the "realities of nature" if they are presented as a "social experience." Flaherty does something like this by presenting Nanook as a family man, sole breadwinner for the wife and children, a man alone against the elements, rather than a member of an Inuit community. The use of a "hero" in the film follows his simple model of technonarrative identification which tames the savage surroundings and different customs and beliefs so as to be understood as "social experience" by the audience in the theaters. But the still itself, often used to advertise the film, does not have a hint of anything that could be deemed nature, unless of course it is Nanook himself. Herbert Marshall's inclusion of this still as the book's first illustration is emblematic of the irresistible charm of contact.

This still is a very good illustration of the chapter entitled "Visual Culture," where Balázs tries to explain the humor of recently outdated technology in general, and old films in particular: "While a fifteenth-century Portuguese sailing-ship is a lovely sight, the early steam-engines and motor-cars are ridiculous because we see in them not something quite different, something no longer existent, but recognize a ridiculous, imperfect form of what is still in use to-day. We laugh at it as we laugh at the antics in the monkey-house—because the monkeys are like ourselves" (37). The "ridiculous, imperfect" form of technology is funny because it is similar but different, an imperfect copy of contemporary technology. To further explain, Balázs produces another analogy with a primitive species of man, this time emphasizing their similarity: "We laugh . . . because the monkeys are like ourselves." The humor in the felt similarity to ourselves in representational (or, in the case of the monkey house, performative) form is the humor of primitive mimicry. Though Balázs feels no need to explain its efficacy, the phenomenon of this humor is by no means minor to his theory of film: "For the culture of the film has developed so rapidly that we still recognize our own selves in its clumsy primitiveness. It is for this reason that this culture is of so great an importance for us, this art which is accessible to millions of ordinary people" (37).

The "millions of ordinary people" and the "cave dwellers in their slums" provided Balázs and Lindsay with the same staging of primitive encounter with the cinema screen that we witness from the point of view of the spectators they describe. The scene from *Nanook,* for example, or the felt contact between the recently out-of-date technology and our imagined (but offscreen) sense of superior technology is a contact analogous to that which the theorist witnesses as he speculates on the audience watching the film. The mimetic play between the primitive of the film and the primitive in the spectator is not just a laughing matter but the "culture of film's" very importance. Whether it is humorous or not, spectatorship relies on ordinary people's recognition and rejection of their own primitiveness. The humorous examples of primitive technology's appeal to the spectator are merely hypertrophied instances of a form of identification that "irrigates" cinema spectatorship at all times. Looking back at Balázs's treatment of Nanook, then, it is both Nanook and the gramophone together, both the primitive and technology, that produce the playful identification that interests Balázs.

Further examples of his use of the primitive to understand the effects of cinema include such disparate figures as the baffled "Colonial Englishman" who is uneducated in film language as compared to enthusiastic children (35). The cloistered Siberian Girl who understood shots of portions of bodies quite literally as bodily mayhem, and the famous instance of the panic caused in a Hollywood cinema at Griffith's severed head or big close-up all serve Balázs to teach us the value of learning "visual culture." These examples are simply too charming, too abundant to be mere didactic object lessons. Rather, the repeated use of contact throughout the work suggests that its appeal was a driving, if imperfectly understood, metaphor for Balázs's film theory.

Technology, as manifested in cinema at least, created a different mode of perception more equipped to work in the new dimensions and at the new speeds that characterize the advent of modernity. At the same time, the cinema forced a reencounter with that which progress was meant to have left behind. Film theory's primitivist reproductions of moments of contact between savage and civilized, the archaic and the enlightened, foreground

the perils and the promise of modernity itself.

Primitivism in film theory takes its most unselfconscious and even crude form in the work of the American poet Vachel Lindsay, who produced in 1915 one of the early attempts to theorize film in *The Art of the Moving Picture*. Though the work may appear today as naïve and eccentric, many of its observations and reflections can and will be seen again in more sophisticated, later formulations. It is also noteworthy because it addresses, as did Eisenstein and Epstein later on, the Americanness of the cinema. America, like cinema itself, was, to Lindsay's mind, both primitive and advanced. From its inception, cinema was an event that harkened back to primitive, gestural forms of expression on account of its silence, while at the same time it marked an advance in artistic form as well as technology because it no longer needed to trifle with the craft involved in representation. America, with no significant artistic tradition of its own, according to Lindsay, effectively skips developing its own art history and turns directly to cinema, thus putting it ahead, for once, of the Old World.

Lindsay begins his book with the study of the "Photoplay of Action," the "simplest" and "most often seen," which "dominates the slums."[5] The film he discusses is none other than Griffith's *Man's Genesis* (1912), which, as if a creation myth of cinema itself, produces all of the imagined pleasures of first contact as well as the rescue of culture by progress from the stronghold of the primitive. Lindsay remarks of the film, first, that the cavemen's "half-monkey gestures are wonderful to see" (9). The ingenuity of Weak-Hands prevails over the more primitive Brute Force, because he invents a weapon to win back his stolen bride, Lily-White. The technology of the photoplay provides primitive entertainment with his "half-monkey gestures," but, at the same time, technology's innovation rescues the weak from the brutish, the civilized from the primitive, in Lindsay's view. This film "provokes the ingenuity of the audience, not their sympathy" (10), confirming Tom Gunning's theory of the "Cinema of Attraction" but locating the fascination with cinema's ingenuity and innovation as a specifically American trait.[6] The audience consists, after all, of "mechanical Americans, fond of crawling on their stomachs to tinker with their automobiles," who are "eager over the evolution of the first weapon from stick to hammer."[7]

Man's Genesis was an important development in Griffith's progress away from the spectacle toward films with a message, and was billed as a comedy in order to sell it to the public. The film opens with the explanation that it is "A Psychological Comedy Founded upon the Darwinian Theory of the Evolution of Man." It begins with an elderly man and his two formally dressed grandchildren walking up a mountain cliff with all the regalia of a Sunday afternoon picnic. The two children are fighting, and when the little boy picks up a stick as if to hit the girl, the grandfather admonishes him and settles them down for a didactic lesson in the invention and use of weapons. They sit on a rock on the shrub- and stone-covered hillside, while fields of close-cut grass and young, symmetrically spaced trees of the town below form the eminently civilized background. Though the film within the film — the lesson about the successful invention of weaponry to outwit sheer brute force — does not really suit the grandfather's purpose, the boy does throw down his stick and kiss his sister in the end. The bodily gestures are not as impressive as Lindsay makes out; the cave peoples' hunched backs and extended arms move begrudgingly, while their faces subtly express fear and love rather than crude, comic reactions.

The climax of the picture's "comedy" comes when Weak Hands accidentally invents a weapon. All alone, he sits in his hut fumbling with his stick, which he accidentally inserts into a conveniently doughnut-shaped rock. He hits himself accidentally with the rock and feels the pain. The gesture of discovery is then extended as he tries to figure out what has just happened and, after much trial and error, re-creates the weapon, for it had fallen back into its two pieces. The comical extension of this moment is similar to Costner's antics in *Robin Hood* and Flaherty's construction of the scene in which Nanook bites the gramophone record. When Weak Hands finally connects the pain of accidentally hitting himself with the stone to the idea that he can make a weapon, he emerges from his cave victorious, holding it aloft to conquer Brute Force, first hitting him on each hand, then knocking him over the head, in the same order in which he had unwittingly experimented on himself. This extended scene of crude encounter and the creation of a weapon is surely what Lindsay refers to when he aligns the car mechanic with the primitive in his text.

Lindsay finds the audience's fascination with technology itself primitive in nature, although his own fascination with watching primitives' (Amer-

Weak Hands (Robert Harron) invents a weapon from a stick and a conveniently doughnut-shaped rock in *Man's Genesis* (1912). Courtesy of Museum of Modern Art Stills Archive.

icans', slum dwellers', children's) reactions to film is never interrogated. Instead, the entire work is propelled toward a return to what Lindsay takes to be the primitive.

Siegfried Kracauer was to suggest a far more compelling and complex relationship between the audience's experience with modern technology as laborers rather than primitives. The spectacle of moving things that the laborers on the assembly line saw in the cinema during their leisure time six years later in the essay "The Mass Ornament" was a reflection of such mechanical wage labor.[8] Lindsay, hardly a social theorist, does however make the important observation that audiences do not, at least in these action films, become absorbed by the films. Their primitive fascination is different from the possession by film about which Jean Epstein later writes so passionately. The viewer Lindsay describes is a decidedly distracted one: "But though the actors glower and wrestle and even if they are the most skillful lambasters in the profession, the audience gossips and chews gum."[9] In Lindsay's estimation, the audience goes to the cinema not to feel passions conveyed, but rather "simply because such spectacles gratify the incipient or rampant speed-mania in every American" (13). The assault on the senses and subjectivity that modernity represented to his European counterparts is simply American "speed-mania." American sensibilities are ready-made receptors for the antics produced by mechanical representation.

Lindsay contended that it was not a defect in photoplays that "human beings tend to become dolls and mechanisms, and dolls and mechanisms tend to become human" (32), but a quality to be used; for dolls, marionettes, and mechanisms pervaded American daily life. Repeatedly, Lindsay refers to the humanization of objects, or "this yearning for personality in furniture" (33). Although he does not identify it with reification, the erasure of meaning brought about by the object's exchangeability, and the object's rapid endowment with new lively meanings otherwise thought of as commodity fetishism, the appeal of animated objects to which he refers is similar to that which Karl Marx deployed to introduce the very topic of commodity fetishism itself. In the beginning of his chapter, "The Fetishism of Commodities (and the Secret Thereof)," Marx hit upon precisely the same example: "It is as clear as noon-day, that man, by his industry, changes the forms of the materials furnished by Nature, in a way as to make them useful to him. The form of wood, for instance, is altered, by making a table out of it. Yet, for all that, the table continues to be that common, every-day thing, wood. But so soon as it steps forth as a commodity, it is changed into something transcendent. It not only stands with its feet on the ground, but, in relation to all other commodities, it stands on its head, and evolves out of its wooden brain grotesque ideas, far more wonderful than 'table-turning' ever was."[10] The wood of the tree was once used to make an ordinary, serviceable table, but on the day that table became a commodity, it turned into a magically animated attraction. By introducing his chapter on commodity fetishism with such a magic act, Marx draws on the magical appeal of levitation and the animistic belief that a table can have ideas in its "wooden brain." Lindsay identifies the desire to bring things to life as a primitive one: "Mankind in his childhood has always wanted his furniture to do such things [to move on their own accord]."[11] The "mechanical or non-human object," says Lindsay, is "apt to be the hero in most any sort of photoplay while the producer remains utterly unconscious of the fact" (35). Lindsay then urges film producers to take up the object as the real hero of the photoplay. Drawing on a line from *Mother Goose,* he concludes, "Let [the stick] beat the dog most heroically" (35). The photoplay's animation of objects satisfies the noble caveman's delight in much the same way as did fairy tales, myths, and legends of old.

Lindsay's model operates with an extremely elastic notion of the primitive, flexible enough to include both the car mechanic and the cave painter. It fails, however, to name or explain "that thing in the cave-man attending the show that made him take note in other centuries of the rope that began to hang the butcher, the fire that began to burn the stick, and the stick that began to beat the dog" (128). In Lindsay's case, this fascination is above all a contemporary theoretical reaction to film as a mass phenomenon that is being deflected onto the primitive, but whose pleasures are archaic and noble by nature, whereas Marx simply counts on table-turning's appeal to show the fantastical nature of the commodity. The origin of the nature of spectator pleasure in magical acts, and the animation of objects in particular, is simply a given, for Lindsay as well as for Marx.

The significant cinematic properties Lindsay aligned with the primitive spectatorship were a distracted audience that was intrigued with technology and invention and an unabashed endorsement of cinema's ability to endow objects with life. Above all, Lindsay shares with other great primitivists a particularly modern notion that the primitive (in this case, the primitive art form he calls the photoplay) produces a step backward and a step forward at the same time. Cinema was "but an expression of the old in that spiral of life which is going higher while seeming to repeat the ancient phase" (171). Eisenstein's concept of a "dual unity," described in chapter 2, also expressed this desire: "The dialectic of works of art is both an impetuous progressive rise . . . and a simultaneous penetration . . . into the layers of profoundest sensual thinking."[12]

The cinema was also, and only apparently contradictorily, America's preeminent cultural project in Lindsay's view. He thought of the New World as a primarily literary rather than visual artistic culture and berated the low ratio of art museums to libraries. He says, for example, "The more characteristic America became, the less she had to do with the plastic arts."[13] The photoplay was the birth of visual art in America, its invention, "as great a step as the invention of picture writing" (171). He began his chapter on hieroglyphics, the only chapter in his book with theoretical aspirations, with the analogy between picture writing and the photoplay, and between cave dwellers and slum film audiences. As much as the photoplay is an invention, it also marks a return to pictorial literary communication, to which he finds a contemporary analogy in the modern billboard **59** advertisement.

The photoplay combined two artistic forms, the written and the plastic, to produce in turn a dual mode of signification. An image had its primary meaning, that is, it referred to its referent via conventions or iconic resemblance, and its secondary meaning: "From a proper balance of primary and secondary meaning photoplays with souls could come" (173). He proceeds to list select Egyptian hieroglyphics to illustrate these secondary meanings. For example, Lindsay proposes an exercise in which one cuts out the hieroglyphic figure from black cardboard that is white on the other side. First one gives the literal meaning, "then if he desires to rise above the commercial field, let him turn over each cardboard," and there on the white surface "write a more abstract meaning of the hieroglyphic, one that has a fairly close relation to his way of thinking about the primary form" (172). Here is one of his attempts: "Here is a duck: (picture of a duck). Roman equivalent, the letter Z. In the motion pictures this bird, a somewhat z-shaped animal, suggests the finality of Arcadian peace. It is the last and fittest ornament of the mill-pond. Nothing very terrible can happen with a duck in the foreground. There is no use turning it over. It would take Maeterlinck or Swedenborg to find the mystic meaning of a duck. A duck looks to me like a caricature of an alderman" (174).

The comparison between picture writing and Egyptian hieroglyph and the photoplay allows Lindsay to postulate a kind of dual signification wherein images have both literal and symbolic value. The symbolic value is the privileged value, the medium through which souls speak. Johann Caspar Lavater (1741–1801), the Swiss and very Catholic physiognomist, traced the best of physiognomy to the Egyptians and claimed that their capacity to read the soul through facial features was due to "the formation and constitution of their language, which consisted of hieroglyphic representations of figures and animals."[14] Hieroglyphics serve as an example of protofilmic communication not so much because they use pictures of a sort, but because these pictures correspond to primal, natural, and essential meanings that are otherwise obstructed by language. The facility to turn basic properties of a thing or animal that are invisible and languageless into a representation developed the Egyptians' ability to read the internal person from his or her external appearance. "This singular emicu-tion," Lavater continues, "according to Tacitus, obliged them to trace minutely the nature and properties of each before they could express their ideas by them; and this necessity undoubtedly brought on the habit of inquiring, which led them to their observations on human beings" (1:19). There is no direct connection from Lavater to Lindsay, but it is notewor-thy that Lindsay hits upon hieroglyphics as his code to the spirit just as Lavater had once traced physiognomy's roots to Egyptian hieroglyphics. Hieroglyphs combine a mythos of perfected ancient civilization and the fascination of coded secrets, still very much alive in the imaginations of today's schoolchildren.[15]

Lindsay is interested in hieroglyphics as a pared-down trace, one that is free of too many representational trappings. He unremittingly uses ever cruder forms that barely approximate a representation of a real person or thing as the model on which to base a theory of film. For example, he sug-gests that a Westernized Chinese play called *The Yellow Jacket,* which used two flags for a chariot, a red sack for a bloody head, and a dressed-up block of wood for a child, put "photographic realism splendidly to rout by pow-erful representation."[16] What he calls "primitive representative methods" are ripe with the potential to evoke abstract concepts. The primitive, in this case the originator of pictorial and symbolic forms of expression, provides the key to nonliteral and hence for Lindsay artistic expression. The rich meaning of the gesture, the animation of objects, and the sym-bolic nature of silent film combine to produce a form capable of retapping the primitive core of meaning. Because of its purity, cinema has the ability to manifest pure ideas, and as such, according to Lindsay, it can be a higher form of artistic expression than other art forms.

The symbolic form of representation that characterizes both hiero-glyphics and the photoplay is primitive because of its simplicity, its purity. The photoplay is nothing short of a platonic form of expression: "This invention, the kinetoscope, which affects or will affect as many people as the guns of Europe, is not yet understood in its powers, particularly those of bringing back the primitive in a big rich way. The primitive is always a new and higher beginning to the man who understands it" (262).

Lindsay uses the primitive to define what is most valuable both in film production and in film reception. First contact, that is, the primal reac-tions to a likewise primal but technological form, drives his study to a romanticization of the primitive rather than an inquiry into the effects of technology in daily life that occupied later German theorists such as Benjamin and Kracauer. The major reason for his staunch reliance on such notions of the primitive was that Lindsay was trying to redeem the photoplay in the tradition of art history, as is clear in his preface to the book, which is a lecture for the Art Institute of Chicago. As Arnheim was later to argue more rigorously, film could not proceed as an art form were it merely to copy things well. Lindsay, in fact, gives no attention to this aspect of the photoplay at all, unlike later theorists such as Bazin, Benjamin, and Epstein, for whom this aspect was crucial. The photoplay was a symbolic and expressive form and therefore the emotive, language-free powers of primitive representation were best emphasized for such an argument. To deploy the primitive as the bearer of expressive forms of representation helped to circumvent the idea of the photoplay as an otherwise crude technological advance and see in it merely a device that copies reality well.

Given the time in which Lindsay wrote, it goes without saying that his film theory refers to a cinema without synchronized sound. But one can go further to characterize it as antilanguage (intertitles) and also against the aural narrativization of piano accompaniment. He complains, "Almost every motion picture theater has its orchestra, pianist or mechanical piano. The perfect photoplay gathering-place would have no sound but the hum of the conversing audience" (189).

The silence of the cinema may also account for the consistency with which the primitive is called to serve early film theory, the great extent to which words are absent and gesture, in turn, is overpresent in early cinema. But people, of course, speak. It is the situation of contact and conquest that mutes language and incites gesture. And this, as the visceral and bodily conscious early film theory that developed bears out, is a two-way street. The silence of the cinema seemed to whisper the promise of a return to expression and communication that was not mediated by language nor debased by progress. For early film theory, it proffered the truth.

CHAPTER 4

Close Contact

The gestures of visual man are not intended to convey concepts which can be expressed in words, but such inner experiences, such non-rational emotions which would still remain unexpressed when everything that can be told has been told. — Béla Balázs, *Theory of the Film*

Béla Balázs, the Hungarian intellectual who wrote scripts, librettos, reviews, fairy tales, and novels, wrote three theoretical books about the cinema. *Der Sichtbare Mensch* (*The Visible Man,* 1924) and *Der Geist des Films* (*The Spirit of the Film,* 1930) were translated quickly into German, but only *Filmkultúra* (*Theory of the Film,* 1948), which borrows heavily from the former works, was translated into English in 1952. He was convinced that cinema made it possible to read the soul through the face and the gesture. Remembering that Lavater saw physiognomy as a route not just to truth, nor to the soul, but to the divine, Balázs's deployment of physiognomy secularizes a method in which reading God's traces gives access to the spiritual world. The meanings Balázs sought, on the other hand, were those that were inimical to language, those that with the ascent of the written word since "the golden age of the visual arts" had withered along with the neglect and atrophy of the body: "The expressive surface of our body was thus reduced to the face alone and this not merely because the rest of the body was hidden by clothes. For the poor remnants of bodily expression that remained to us the little surface of the face sufficed, sticking up like a clumsy semaphore of the soul and signaling as best it could. Sometimes a gesture of the hand was added, recalling the melancholy of a mutilated torso. In the epoch of word culture the soul learnt to speak but had grown almost invisible."[1] In cinema, the body communicates directly, without the mediation of language, says Balázs. Bodily communication itself, he goes on to argue, was a precursor to language. The sounds produced as the primitive or infant body contorted to communicate were a secondary, merely "adventitious" phenomenon only later to be organized into language. The origins of language lie in "expressive movement," and much has been lost in the process of these gestures' translation into language: "It is the expressive movement, the gesture, that is the aboriginal mother-tongue of the human race" (42).

Balázs's theory operates by opposing language to gesture; thus, the less linguistically complex a society, the more rich its gestures: The one displaces or disables the other. Yet gesture, he claims, expresses an entirely different order of meanings. Language is more rational than gestural communication and the rationalization that comes with language diminishes the body's ability to express. Balázs is quick to make clear, however, that within the opposition between rational language and expressive gesture there must be room for both modes of expression. He aligns "rational conceptual culture" with "human progress" and the "irrational" with fascism. Fascism, he claims, "has shown us where the tendency to reduce human culture to subconscious emotions in place of clear concepts would lead humanity" (43). Balázs thus places himself in a somewhat tenuous rhetorical position between rational language and irrational gesture. Language, which diminishes unconventional, individual expression also maintains a bulwark against fascism through its built-in rationality. Gesture encourages greater possibilities of expression, as well as "wider spirits" to express. Cinema, he lamented, will inevitably have the advantage of universal communication, but will sacrifice its direct expressivity as it too develops its own conventions. It would inevitably create a universal language of gesture, bringing linguistically and culturally distant folk together. Conventions will eventually congeal, spoiling its potential to evoke immediate, unique expression. Cinema's gestural form held within it both the dangers of irrationality and the inevitability of convention.

Post-Holocaust thought on rationalization, and that of Horkheimer and Adorno in particular, would question Balázs's assumption that irrationality is so much to blame for humanity's devastation. And postmodern thought would question the easy dichotomy between conventional and nonconventional gesture as well as their emotive capabilities. Balázs's attempts at social theory are often careless and illogical; however, his observations are useful when they address film in its medium specificity.

Balázs's sustained faith in the value of expressing what lies beneath the covers of language prompts one to ask, as does the work of Lindsay as well, what precisely are the kinds of meanings that are supplied by the physiognomic, expressive world of silent cinema. The film camera has revealed, wrote Balázs, "new worlds until then concealed from us: such as the soul of objects, the rhythm of crowds, the secret language of dumb things" (47). While these elements, along with an almost religious use of physiognomy, form the core of the book, he states here that cinema's uniqueness comes only secondarily from the new, "other things" shown; instead, he says here that the way they were shown was the key innovation.

At this point in his argument, Balázs cites the new lack of distance between the spectator and the work of art as the salient feature of cinema. Although barely attended to in the rest of the work, Balázs gives the concept of the "aura," now well-known via Benjamin's "Work of Art" essay, a slightly different connotation. Balázs repeats the idea from his 1930 *The Spirit of the Film:* "In the film the permanent distance from the work of art fades out of the consciousness of the spectator and with it the inner distance as well, which hitherto was the experience of art" (48). This loss of distance has all of the well-known effects of tactility: "We walk amid crowds, ride, fly, or fall with the hero" (48). Balázs compounds this tactility with "identification" to define the major element of film's novelty: "He [the film character] looks into our eyes from the screen, for our eyes are in the camera and become identical with the gaze of the characters. They see with our eyes. Herein lies the psychological act of 'identification.'" Moreover, "nothing like this 'identification' has ever occurred as the effect of any other system of art and it is here that the film manifests its absolute artistic novelty" (48). Later on, he explains that identification is controlled by the "angle and set-up," which are what style is to the narrator of a book (92). Though today we would argue that, just as in a novel, identification can be curtailed and even denied, his point is to register the degree of intensity with which one feels films. And there is a difference, not only of degree, between the immediacy of walking and flying along with the hero, which calls to mind watching something like *Man With a Movie Camera* (1928), and "psychological identification," which he accurately relates to realist continuity conventions. In the former, one feels on the order of physical touch; in the latter, one feels a mental emotion.

Gertrud Koch has pointed to Benjamin's obvious and unacknowledged debt to Balázs, whose *Der Geist des Films,* in which Balázs first formulated this idea, appeared some five years in advance of Benjamin's "Work of Art" essay.[2] The debt appears to be beyond question, but the directions in which they take this observation of film's immediacy seem to me quite different. Whereas both Benjamin and Balázs are primarily concerned with cinema's ability to present things to human sensibilities in such a way as to circumvent structured reasoning, Balázs is interested in the emotions cinema can convey that are otherwise inarticulate, while Benjamin is interested in its physical touch. This difference follows the same distinction Gunning marks out between a cinema of "attraction" and a cinema of "absorption." Attraction refers to the form of address to the spectator found in early cinema and later maintained in fragments of the musical and the avant-garde, which "aggressively subjected the spectator to sensual or psychological impact." Absorption, on the other hand, pulls the spectator into the diegesis of the film, into its "illusory imitativeness." Gunning borrows the term attraction from Eisenstein and emphasizes its context: "Then as now, the 'attraction' was a term of the fairground, and for Eisenstein and his friend Yuketvich it primarily represented their favorite fairground attraction, the roller coaster, or as it was known then in Russia, the American Mountains."[3]

Balázs's film theory just about dismisses the "cinema of attraction." He places the beginning of film as art, as opposed to the photographed stage, in America with D. W. Griffith's use of montage, variation of depth of field and camera angle, along with camera movement. The rest had all been what he calls "fairground sideshows."[4] Balázs's aversion to the tactile address to the spectator is borne out in his discussion of Vertov. Balázs finds Vertov's *Kino-Eye* so aggressive and overpresent that he associates the subjectivity of the kino-eye with Vertov himself. In Balázs's view, Vertov's subjectivity purloins the spectator's right to see for himself or herself and turns the objectivity Balázs finds inherent in the naturalistically rendered image into an extension of Vertov's imagination, no matter how documentary his footage originally might have been (164–65).

Although Balázs lauds Vertov as a filmic lyric poet, his interest in this sort of thing is clearly superficial. Balázs's interest is in carefully crafted, seamlessly sutured narrative cinema: "A good film director does not permit the spectator to look at a scene at random. He leads our eye inexorably from detail to detail along the line of his montage" (31).

Balázs does discuss film's ability to show crowds and landscapes, but it was the close-up that captivated his interest most of all. In the close-up he found not a copy of the real thing in image form but rather such close inspections revealed a hidden nature, which, as extended through to him in the cinema, he could intimately know. The cinema was like a sacred communion: it was private, intimate, and above all secret. Here the spectator could finally see "the very atoms of life and their innermost secrets revealed at close quarters . . . without any of the intimate secrecy being lost, as always happens in the exposure of a stage performance or of a painting" (31). If the aura created a distance, no matter how close the object might be, cinema, for Balázs at least, invited an intimacy, no matter how far, foreign, or new to the eye the object might be.

As Koch has pointed out, Balázs's focus on physiognomy follows the same path as Benjamin's discovery of the optical unconscious upon their mutual discovery that the perception of cinema is of a different order than that of other art forms. Following Koch on Balázs and Hansen on Benjamin, both Balázs and Benjamin are responding to a felt impoverishment of experience itself as a consequence of progress.[5] For Balázs, this partook of a kind of modernist romanticism, which led him to favor ambiguous expression over logical constructs and to criticize Eisenstein's montage constructions; Benjamin is as taken by the fine nuances of gesture as he is the rapid fire of montage.

Balázs and Benjamin's shared observation that the cinema lacked distance compared to other art forms took different shape not only as to the consequences for the kind of spectatorship they each conjured but also the status of the camera lens. The idea that the lens is impassive does not feature in Balázs's theory of film as it does in Benjamin's. After all, Balázs wrote scripts and directed "set-ups" for narrative cinema. Well-schooled in the manipulation of the impassive lens, and therefore perhaps inured to its charm, Balázs, unlike Benjamin, directs his attention instead to what he feels cannot be constructed. This is the physiognomic minutiae of faces, things, and landscapes: "The camera close-up aims at the uncontrolled small areas of the face; thus it is able to photograph the subconscious."[6] It is as if the closer he gets to the image, that is, the larger it becomes on the screen, the more he transcends the apparatus and so transcends the materiality of things as to float through the screen into the realm of pure expression.

Balázs's sustained reference to physiognomy reveals his modernist primitivism most clearly. Primitive thought in modern terms is thought that defies the logic of progress and the word, thought that Balázs imputes to prelinguistic societies. A point in time existed for Balázs in which language was unmediated and pure gestures were identical with the thought or, better, the feeling conveyed. Peter Sloterdijk in his *Critique of Cynical* **67** *Reason* confirms the idea that physiognomic perception preserves meanings of a different order to those conveyed by language: "A philosophical physiognomy follows the idea of a second, speechless language."[7] Its origins, for Sloterdijk, go further back than the primitive gestural speech to which Balázs was drawn, back to the senses of animals: "This notion of a speechless language is as old as human communication, indeed even older, its roots going back into the prehuman and the prerational, into the sphere of animal sensing and orientation" (139). Whereas Balázs saw the body's atrophy in the decline of gesture through the ascent of linguistic signs, Sloterdijk finds that the senses themselves have dulled, muting an entire field of expressions and perceptions: "The world is full of shapes, mimicry, faces; from all around us the hints of forms, colors, and atmospheres are received by our senses. In this physiognomic field, all the senses are tightly interwoven. Those who have been able to maintain their perceptual competence undamaged possess an effective antidote to the atrophy of the senses with which we pay for progress in civilization" (139). Though progress is to blame for the weakening of our physiognomic sense, the sense itself and the intimacy it nourishes with the world is the best antidote to modernity's "flood of signs." "Nonetheless," he writes, "there exists an undercurrent in our cultural life in which a mentally alert and self-evident capacity to enter into the language of shapes has reproduced itself—partly in the arts, partly in scattered traditions of knowledge about human nature in which, under various names (morals, the sorting of spirits, psychology, or the study of expressions) that other kind of perception of people and things is practiced." Surely Balázs would jump in to add the cinema to this list, for physiognomic perception as opposed to scientific objectification, like the close inspection provided by cinema, reveals our "proximity to the environment." Moreover, "its secret is intimacy, not distance; it dispenses not a matter-of-fact but a convivial knowledge of things" (139).

Physiognomy as a science of the nineteenth century allowed access to people's souls. In twentieth-century film theory, one reads the souls of things as well as the souls of people. The "entire kingdom on celluloid" has, according to Balázs, a corresponding spiritual world to which it refers, upon which the filmic world feeds. Physiognomy applies as much to the human face as it does to a footprint, a crumpled cloth, or a clock. As did Lindsay before him, Balázs observes that every image on film is leveled to the status of an object, be it an actor, his hand, his pipe, or the tree under which he sits. Every image has a physiognomy to which a corresponding spiritual double attends.

Like Lindsay, Balázs sees an equation of people with things on film: "In the silent film both a man and object were equally pictures, photographs, their homogeneous material was projected on to the same screen. . . . In significance, intensity and value men and things were thus brought on to the same plane."[8] This equation of man and thing as objects on film, their reification by technology, quickly incites their transformation. Just as soon as Balázs says that film drains the living of their human status, he reimputes that very life into the object: "The objects only reflect our own selves, and when we see the face of things, we do what the ancients did in creating gods in man's image and breathing a human soul in to them. The close-ups of the film are the creative instruments of this mighty visual anthropomorphism" (60). The close-up is a vessel from which a secret life emerges that can be different from the meaning of the entire picture. Koch embellishes Balázs's notion of the anthropomorphic expressiveness of things with her own example. In a shot for Hitchcock's *The Lodger* (1926) that Hitchcock later described to Truffaut, the oval-shaped rear windows of a news van frame the moving heads of the driver and his mate from the rear as they move from side to side in tandem. "As the van sways from side to side, you have the impression of a face with two eyes and the eyeballs moving," Koch writes. "A van with a face harbors a wide variety of connotations: thus, to the person who has just missed a ride, it may appear to be grinning."[9] The shot, Hitchcock says, "didn't work out," yet it does appear in the film's opening. Koch observes, "That kind of anthropomorphic visualization of objects, of inanimate things, permits transforming the whole world of dead matter into an animistic cosmos, rendering it as pure expression" (168). Koch's echo of Lucretius in titling the article "The Physiognomy of Things" is then in earnest; we picture such a cosmos as Lucretius described made of invisible atoms which, as they form and reform, configure the universe.[10] Things and people are made of the same atomic material, just as in the cinema they are made of the same celluloid material. In Koch's reading of Balázs, celluloid takes on the animistic character of the atom, the single element that fashions the universe.

Film images, including those of people, are things, and all things on celluloid are thereby reanimated and thus directly expressive.

Physiognomic readings of people, who are, after all, actors playing **69** emotions, rest nevertheless on the qualities of the face chosen to render requisite emotions. Balázs relies heavily on actresses such as Asta Nielsen and Lillian Gish, whose faces hold a complexity of sufferings, and also, I would contend, because they are women, and thus by nature hide secrets more deftly than men. Nielsen's facial deftness not only allows for great emotive power but also enables her to create many layers of emotions, artfully masked and unmasked. The interplay between acting and being on film, between masking and unmasking, is part of the appeal of physiognomic reading as a practice. Balázs performs this sort of analysis by uncovering veils of expressive features as if he were looking through a microscope. Physiognomy is based on the belief that one has all the evidence necessary to find the truth in the face itself, in its features and their gestural articulations of emotions. The job of an actor, however, is to manipulate those gestures and features in the service of a meaning for a film, to create a physiognomic map of, say, pain, love, or fear. The excitement of watching actors work is rooted in the fact that the "real" truth of the actor's character is bracketed. Balázs concentrates on examples in which masking emotions and subtly changing emotions are paramount. This suggests that the viewer's artful physiognomic reading is a compelling one in film spectatorship not because it offers a ready-made route to truth but because it involves the spectator in an intricate process of watching, suspecting, and unveiling the truth.

Physiognomy leads to an exploration of masking and unmasking in Balázs's text. He uses an example of Asta Nielsen attempting to create a face of youth in *Dirnentragödie* (*The Tragedy of a Whore,* 1927, Germany) before a cracked and dull mirror for what he calls "microphysiognomy."[11] In another example, Lillian Gish tries to force her face into a smile with the aid of her fingers, again in front of a mirror (*Broken Blossoms,* 1919, directed by D. W. Griffith). By virtue of "an intangible nuance," her "painful, even horrible mask" of a forced smile is turned into a "real" smiling expression. The mirror as the reflexive figure for scrutinizing the shifts between real and mask is taken over by a silent, vigilant observer within the frame in an example of what Balázs calls "the polyphonic play of features" (64).

Balázs, along with a generation of UFA film viewers, was fascinated by Asta Nielsen because of the virtuosity of her acting talent, the complexity of her face, and because of the childlike quality that kept her, no matter the circumstances, innocent.[12] With one scene, Balázs details the many layers of expression she can portray. Nielsen is being watched from behind a curtain by a man who has hired her to seduce a rich young man. She feigns love convincingly enough for the part, but "we are aware that it is only play-acting, that it is a sham, a mask." That is to say, the spectator is aware of the truth, whereas the other two men in the scene, who are, diegetically speaking at least, actually there, cannot see through her masks. The man behind the curtain is convinced that she is acting out her job successfully, but the man she seduces is convinced of something different altogether. The spectator, however, still has secrets to discover. As the scene continues, she actually does fall in love and her "expression changes only by a scarcely perceptible and yet immediately obvious nuance." Remembering suddenly that she is under observation, says Balázs, "she must further pretend that she is merely pretending to be in love." The actress must "pretend to be pretending," and now her face "shows a new, by this time threefold, change." "Now," writes Balázs, "she is lying that she is lying." The spectator has three layers of masks, three conflicting physiognomies to sort out: "And we can see all this clearly in her face, over which she has drawn two different masks. At such times an invisible face appears in front of the real one, just as spoken words can by association of ideas conjure up things unspoken and unseen, perceived only by those to whom they are addressed."[13] Balázs's analysis bears the traces of secrecy's seductions. He is watching, suspecting, unveiling, and he, the spectator, unlike the men in the room, is the only one who is so privileged as to discern the nuances of each small shift of feature.

The power of physiognomy as a theory of understanding silent film lies not so much in its certainty, as Lavater had claimed — that it is a readily catalogued route to spiritual truth — but in that it involves the spectator in a pleasure-filled game of knowing and not knowing, of belief and doubt in the face, of uncovering a secret to which only the spectator is privy.

I pointed out earlier that the impassive nature of the lens does not figure in Balázs's text as a salient feature of cinema. Interested in film's expressive potential, its ability to bring back the body and its attendant emotions, Balázs works with film as if it were an extension of nature. When he does refer to the camera's different perspective, it is as a process of unveiling: "When the film close-up strips the veil of our imperceptiveness and insensitivity from the hidden little things and shows us the face of objects, it still **71** shows us man, for what makes objects expressive are the human expressions projected on to them" (60). It is not the camera per se that gives us an image free of the trappings of representation, but the process of discovery it provokes. The mechanical nature of the camera's transfer of a real thing to the film image on screen is of little concern to Balázs because he is most concerned, it seems to me, not simply with the little detail that features so large in his text but with things that are even harder to see because they lack physical form altogether: "emotions, moods, intentions and thoughts" (61). Thus he emphasizes not the camera but the traces these emotions and thoughts leave on the face. In this sense, says Balázs, such representation approaches the status of objective documentary: "The most subjective and individual of human manifestations is rendered objective in the close-up" (60).

For Balázs and Lindsay, the significance of cinema came not through its power of technological reproduction, nor from the fact that the camera lens brought an image unmediated by human intervention (as it did for Benjamin, Epstein, and Bazin): Cinema's significance was due to the material path it beat to immaterial things. The traces of dormant and primal emotions, of thoughts, of the spirit and the soul were reactivated through physiognomic spectatorship, through close inspection of things that were secretive and small (for Balázs), and through cinema's iconic stimulation of quasiplatonic intimations (for Lindsay).

Lindsay and Balázs approach the cinema with a marked indifference to its representational aspect. As if captivated by a nautilus just found in the sand, they're not interested so much in its transformation from a living creature to a beautiful artifact, as they are in the secrets, upon inspection, its curves and chambers hold in store.

The nautilus has a secret beyond that marked out in its shape. Though it bears the traces of its former life, it keeps the secret of its transformation from being to thing. The image's secret, like the secret of the commodity, has to do with the effaced machinery of its production. And just as Marx came to associate this with the magical fetish, whose effectiveness was its secret nature, so too the film image takes on this fetish character. The transformation from live object to a dead thing to an image can be explained; its machinery is well understood. But the fact that it is none other than a machine that sends life back to us in such a sensate way is not so

easily gotten over. In contrast to Balázs and Lindsay, this paradox gave force to the thoughts about the cinema of Jean Epstein, Walter Benjamin, André Bazin, and Siegfried Kracauer.

The thinglike status of the image is tied to the mechanical nature of the camera's transfer of real objects to a screen image, as well as to the fatigued, distracted condition of the modern spectator. Taken together, they create the conditions for magic.

CHAPTER 5 The Secret Life of the Object

In Jean Epstein's essay, "On Certain Characteristics of *Photogenie*," he delivers a full account of cinema's phantasmagoric transformation of dead things to live objects, ripe with alien but nonetheless necessarily meaningful power, power that itself derives directly from the alien nature of the sensibility that delivers it to us: "I would even go so far as to say that the cinema is polytheuristic and theogonic. Those lives it creates, by summoning objects out of the shadows of indifference into the light of dramatic concern, have little in common with human life. These lives are like the life in charms and amulets, the ominous, tabooed objects of certain primitive religions. If we wish to understand how an animal, a plant or a stone can inspire respect, fear and horror, those three most sacred sentiments, I think we must watch them on the screen, living their mysterious silent lives, alien to the human sensibility."[1] That we may better understand real things through their image, through the eminently unreal realm of the cinema, stands as one of cinema's operative paradoxes. The genetic strands of the object's cinematic life as both a primitive magical object and a commodity fetish are immanent in this passage, and for Epstein cinema's animistic powers are directly linked to the absence of the human sensibility.

Epstein characterizes the object's transformation through cinema as "lives" that "have little in common with human life." This suggests that these objects are different from those daily-life objects from whence they came, but that nonetheless these objects are no less but rather even more alive than those objects. Objects burn bright as constellations of meaning and crackle with tactile effects; things take on life. One life is a spirit life, a magical world that is completely distinct from yet doubles our own. Primitive religion and folklore reveal this world of the spirit double to be ripe with magical sorcery and healing power. Zande witchcraft and divination and Cuna curing, but two examples, operate with a full set of copies of the physical world. Insofar as these doubles can move and change in ways that otherwise defeat earthly powers, they share the freedom and elasticity that the filmic world holds over the profilmic world. Like the film's frame, an object can be a vessel for those spirits and a vehicle for their power.

Eisenstein draws several analogies between images on film and the spirit world in his discussion of "sensual thinking."[2] Among the many examples that show how artistic practice operates on principles similar to magic and a primitive form of thinking that is by no means lost, are instances of the part substituting for the whole, or metaphor, where they function in the same way as homeopathic magic.[3] His illustration from *The Battleship Potemkin* (1925) shows how the surgeon's pince-nez substitutes for the surgeon himself in the surgeon's final appearance much more powerfully than his body could have done. He explains not how the well-known "artistic method" of the "so-called pars pro toto" works but rather, why it works. Belief in magic may be gone in practical life. We no longer think, for example, that the tooth of a bear can actually give its recipient the entire live bear's strength, as primitive belief might have done. But the very same magical belief that gave such power to things, Eisenstein argued, still obtains in the sphere of artistic representation: "It so happens that this method is the most typical example of a thinking form from the arsenal of early thought processes. At that stage we were still without the unity of the whole and the part as we now understand it. At that stage of non-differentiated thinking the part is at one and the same time also the whole."[4] The pince-nez fills the surgeon's "role and place" with a "huge sensual-emotional increase in intensity" so that we don't merely "register the fact that the surgeon has drowned, we emotionally react to the fact through a definite compositional presentation of this fact" (133). Eisenstein is claiming the power of homeopathic magic to make the pince-nez into a magic object that in turn adds intensity to the reaction to the surgeon's death. The difference between what it means to "register" and what it means to "react," the difference between conveying information and eliciting an emotional effect, is not one of degree. Rather, the first requirement of magic no less than artistic representation is that it must do something.[5]

The second kind of life an object can lead, while not unrelated to the theme of the magical double, bears a very different genealogy. This is the life with which objects are endowed that are mass produced and enter the market as objects of exchange. They are commodities: meaningless, empty ciphers that rapidly fill with new, fetishistic meaning. The camera turns nature into "second nature."[6] It lifts the image from the material thing and then creates a new thing, the image. This new thing is but one of many images, identical in size, interchangeable with other images. Taken from the embodied natural thing, this image/thing is freed from its context, that is, its own production. Set loose from its material context, second nature, the nature after nature, takes on a life of its own. The break from a thing's use value, once produced through "natural" social relations, turns a thing into a commodity. Once a thing becomes a commodity, an object of exchange, it is freed from its meaning as use value, or its natural meaning. It should therefore, by rights, have no meaning whatsoever, save that as an exchangeable commodity. Rather than being rendered meaningless, however, the commodity becomes the vessel in which "a definite social relation between [people] assumes, in their eyes, the fantastic form of a relationship between things."[7]

In its reified form, the commodity is a ready cipher for imputed meanings, for values that are grafted on in place of the value of labor and use lost to capitalist production. "The commodity" says Marx, "is therefore a mysterious thing, simply because in it the social character of men's labour appears to them as an objective character stamped upon the product of that labour: because the relation of the producers to the sum total of their own labour is presented to them as a social relation, existing, not between themselves, but between the products of their labour" (1:77). Substituting a relation between things for the lost relations between people, "the products of labor become commodities, social things whose qualities are at the same time perceptible and imperceptible by the senses" (1:72). This Marx called the "secret" or the "mystical character of the commodity" and finally "commodity fetishism" (1:77). The mechanical process by which a three-dimensional thing becomes a film image, crowded with technology so as to appear free of it, reducing all things to identically sized frames projected at a single speed, negates the nature of the three-dimensional object and its context and clears the way for new meanings and associations to take hold.

Walter Benjamin, when remarking on the autonomy of film space as opposed to the stage, emphasized the way the camera severs the image from its surroundings in the way that I here align with the commodity form. He concludes his thought with the now familiar paradox of an image that has been conjured from an environment choked with technology, an image that then appears, again via that very technology, to be free of all artifice: "The illusionary nature is that of the second degree, the result of cutting. That is to say, in the studio the mechanical equipment has penetrated so deeply into reality that its pure aspect freed from the foreign substance of equipment is the result of a special procedure, namely, the shooting by the specially adjusted camera and the mounting of the shot together with other similar ones. The equipment-free aspect of reality here has become the height of artifice; the sight of immediate reality has become an orchid in the land of technology."[8] If one understands cinema as the preeminent form of second nature, wrought by the alien machine, the question for a redemptive theory of film becomes what possible ways second nature can induce transformative meaning rather than merely perpetuate reification and further mystification. Epstein's wish, cited at the beginning of this chapter, the wish to "understand the lives of objects," registers both kinds of lives the object might lead in the cinema: as a commodity and as a religious fetish. These are the object's transformations through the cinema that the alien machine, the camera, was to release.

Kenneth Anger's *Scorpio Rising* (1962–64) is an extreme example of the transformative potential in the commodity wherein the commodity form itself almost narrates the film. Beyond mere reification, but still short of utopia, the objects in *Scorpio Rising* illustrate the object life of the commodity fetish, the ritual object, the religious fetish, and, most important, the transformative meaning that Benjamin believed should be wrought from such fetishes in modern representational practices.

In defining the commodity status of this particular film, we must bear in mind that all films are simulacra, copies of degraded icons. Though there is no original, the film, by definition, is nonetheless a copy, a reassemblage consisting of light, celluloid, a blank screen, speakers, and a (paying) audience. The authentic object never existed in cinema. "From a photographic negative, for example, one can make any number of prints; to ask for the 'authentic' print makes no sense," wrote Benjamin (224). But, as Baudrillard has pointed out, the simulacrum delivers an aura of reality far more effective than the original.[9] A Salem cigarette advertisement, for example, calls up an *ur*-image of freshness, mountains, and snow wintergreen free of telephone lines, sludge, runny noses, and smoker's cough. When Benjamin described the magical independence of the image from its apparatus and noted the artful absence of all the cameras and lights from the final product, he used the image of a carefully cultivated, rare flower, not a daylily, to describe the effect of the transformation from reality to film. As Miriam Hansen has pointed out, the German original uses the German Romantic Novalis's term *blaue Blume* instead of an orchid, enigmatically and perhaps ironically, she notes, suggesting that the unattainable telos of the romantic quest would be found in the cinema rather than in nature.[10]

Anger takes advantage of the cultivated rather than natural quality of cinema — that is, the image's acquisition of new vitality when completely divorced from its surroundings — by piecing the film together as a collage of dormant objects and found footage. His filming of objects also belies the irony and pathos Hansen suggests prompted Benjamin to deploy the romantic term. Instead of probing, revealing, provoking, or concealing, this camera is a roving spotlight shining on things that already appear to exist in their own right, independently of their screen time. We meet this film head-on as first of all a reified commodity, completely divorced from its means of production.

The commodity quality of the copy generates a familiar warmth. Instead of the authoritarian mystification that an art object commands, this commodity-rich montage democratizes the work of art and extends a casual invitation to enjoy its comforts. Anger is utterly at home in and can take full advantage of the referentless space provided by late capitalism; his is a work that revels in the art form of the simulacrum, as Fredric Jameson refers to it here: "The simulacrum (that is, the reproduction of 'copies' which have no original) characterizes the commodity production of consumer capitalism and marks our object world with an unreality and a free-floating absence of 'the referent' (e.g. the place hitherto taken by nature, by raw materials and primary production, or by the 'originals' of artisanal production or handicraft) utterly unlike anything experienced in any earlier social formation."[11] Recalling our commodity narrative, which moves from use value to exchange value when a thing is severed from its means of production and becomes reified, the commodity finally ends up just like any other thing and interchangeable with any other thing. The rough life story of the object reaching its maturity as reified commodity continues in its golden years among the great debates of aesthetics and politics in late capitalism. In Andy Warhol's *Shoes* or his prints of stars, Jameson tells us, he is referring to their repetition and interchangeability, and betrays an allegiance to surface rather than depth, the appearance of a thing (exchange value) rather than the function of a thing (use value), as Van

Gogh's well-worn boots had done (138–39). Well past Lukács's requisite saturation point, described in *History and Class Consciousness,* we are also beyond simple reification. In our late-night capitalism, the commodity seems to be emitting a radioactive glow, the shimmering attraction of the fetish's power.

Scorpio Rising's first sequence centers on a motorcycle, a song, and a man, alone together in a clean, sparse garage. The motorcycle shines to the peals of the simple and proud melody "Fools Rush in Where Angels Fear to Tread" that accompanies the camera, which spotlights the bike from above as if to track a star's walk up a stage ramp for an Academy Award. The guy is working on the bike, but more than that, he's watching it, kneeling by it, loving it. He doesn't love it as much as the camera does, however, following its every curve, licking it with light to polish the fenders for a brilliant showroom sheen. This is intercut with shots of windup plastic motorbikes, '50s paraphernalia of all sorts, pinups of Marlon Brando, James Dean, live shots of macho men flexing their smooth muscles, dressing, and grooming themselves. A series of '50s and early '60s rock-and-roll hits provide a disjointed narration to the film, with ballads of youth, death, and love religiously left to play out all their verses.

Like the commodities, the songs too have a formal narrative quality quite apart from the simple stories they tell. The songs have very strong melodies, often sung by multiple voices in unison. Melody is narrative itself in this instance, directing the flow of the film with an easy but forceful rhythm. A song's incongruous or ironic textual relation to the images on screen is overcome by the earnestness of the sound. Anger capitalizes on the pleasure of the melody (analogous to the comfort of narrative), the appeal of the stories within the songs (the fact that they progress from beginning to middle to end regardless of the particular content of the story), as well as the ambiguous textual relation of the words to the images on screen. Also, they are recognizable as cultural commodities; the film glows in the glitter of kitsch value that they now evoke. Viewing the film some thirty years after it was made, it is difficult to remove the new layer of nostalgia of these songs, that then were contemporary with the film, but he clearly intended to draw on their value as popular hits. Carel Rowe points to the problem that in later receptions, the film took on the vacuous qualities of nostalgia, which, Rowe maintains, "originally served as a critique against idolatry and romanticism," in

Anger's words "turned in on itself and beginning to rot."[12] To my mind, Anger can't have it both ways. He is, on the one hand, clearly deploying and enjoying their commodity value, with their reverent lyrics and clever juxtapositions, and on the other, they are what make the film go. Like his *Rabbit's Moon* (1971), the film could be seen as a form of opera.

Because of their repetitive value (a recorded song is also always a copy), the songs have a further ability to impart meaning to the film. As Jameson points out, "We never hear any of the [pop] singles 'for the first time.'" We are always aware of our aural belatedness. He argues that, instead, "we live in a constant exposure to them" in various contexts: car radio, market, boutique, restaurant, and lunch room. The pop single, then, "by means of repetition, insensibly becomes part of the existential fabric of our own lives, so that what we listen to is ourselves, our own previous auditions."[13] Each audition carries traces of other auditions, so that they accumulate a narrative of experiences associated with them that may come together in their full-fledged performances at a nightclub, in a dance hall, or in an instance such as their audition in this film.

The song "Torture" narrates the sequence in which the major scene is a rite of passage where hot mustard is smeared over a man's pelvis and a crowd of men hover over him to lick it off. A shot of his tense but smiling face is provided to show how the torture affects the initiate. This orgiastic scene is intercut with scenes from *The Road to Jerusalem* Anger claims to have found on the street, in which Jesus performs a miracle and walks with his followers, a crowd of men all dressed in Hollywood-style Arab gear, who are then spliced into the film to look as if they too are going inside to the orgy.

Many objects in *Scorpio Rising* appear to be important to gay culture in their commodity fetish form. Caught in the afterglow of exchange value, they have a brilliance that refers to them as part of a window display or a fashion show. The leather jackets, studded belts, chains, motorcycles, and biker's gear are filmed in adoring floods of light, again recalling Marx's fetishism of commodities, "in which a definite social relation between [people] assumes . . . the fantastic form of a relationship between things." Benjamin refers to the attractiveness of the fetish, the way commodities draw you near to them, in his discussion of crowds and arcades in *Charles Baudelaire: A Lyric Poet in the Era of High Capitalism*. "Baudelaire," he wrote, "was a connoisseur of narcotics, yet one of their most important social effects probably escaped him. It consists in the charm displayed by addicts under the influence of drugs. Commodities derive the same effect from the crowd that surges around and intoxicates them."[14] And of the proletariat's relationship to commodities he wrote: "If it wanted to achieve virtuosity in this kind of enjoyment, it could not spurn empathizing with commodities. It had to enjoy this identification with all the pleasure and the uneasiness which derived from a presentiment of its own destiny as a class. Finally, it had to approach this destiny with a sensitivity that perceives charm even in damaged and decaying goods" (59). In his "Arcades Project," Benjamin described the collections of recently out-of-date objects displayed in the glass cases of the Paris arcades as "dream-images of the collective," which were both, according to Susan Buck-Morss, "distorting illusion and redeemable wish-image," and so took on a political meaning.[15] Anger's parading of these commodities conflates sexual with consumer seduction in a way similar to that which developed with the department store in Paris of the 1850s. Of this development Buck-Morss writes, "If commodities had first promised to fulfill human desires, now they created them: dreams themselves became commodities."[16] No longer merely supplying goods for sale, "the use of display techniques and eye-catching design which developed rapidly over the next decades supplanted the commercial principle of supply with consumer seduction. As reification of desire, commodities generated dreams rather than satisfied them" (72). The display of objects and models in *Scorpio Rising* moves us farther, not only away from the utility of things (narrative or otherwise) but beyond commodity fetishism; Anger's displays become collective dream images.

The film proudly displays posters of male stars. Images of rebellious manhood become icons for the gay collective. They are not interested in the "aura of the person but the 'spell of the personality,' the phony spell of a commodity."[17] This spell of the commodity conjured up in *Scorpio Rising* is a magical way of being embraced by a hostile culture, one that, in its heterosexual hegemony of the early '60s, would not even have acknowledged gay culture. Warming themselves by the hearth-fire cinders of what was once use value, the answer to society's scorn is to steal the "aura" of its things, to make the dominant society's commodities the metanarrative of gay culture. Hence, the ritual of torture is interspersed with segments from a film version of one of Western culture's strongest narratives, *The*

Great Code, which, in its commodity form as film, knits together the shot sequence.[18] This, it seems to me, is a radical form of play.[19]

What I would call objecthood, or a filmic language that insists on an **81** extreme integrity of objects and valorizes them aesthetically, is the final kind of object life to consider in this chapter. Robert Bresson's *l'Argent* (1983, Switzerland/France) is a film of muted subjects and lively objects. Bresson's rationalizing shooting style, his direction of actors so as to appear as affectless automatons, and the visual richness of his film images serve to impart animistic significance to the film's visual tableaux. The central character, Yvon, who is at this point in the film a small-time thief, returns to his home demoralized and defeated from a court trial. Slowly, he opens the door just enough to reveal a generous cluster of brilliant orange carrots on the living room table. Raw food! Use value, as opposed to surface, exchange value if there ever was such a thing. But, as Bresson films the carrots not in the kitchen but where ornaments are usually displayed, they become a stunning if momentary still life, not edible nourishment. Though objects do have narrative functions, Bresson in this shot betrays an adoration of the object for its own sake. Not spirit, not symbol nor food, they are but pure matter. Bresson wrote, "Make the objects look as if they want to be there."[20] This still life of warm color insists on its presence.

This aspect of the object can be seen as the detail with an allegorical vocation, distinguished by its "oversignification" (Baudrillard), which Naomi Schor says "is not a matter of realism, but of surrealism, if not hyperrealism." It is a "disproportionately enlarged ornamental detail; bearing the seal of transcendence, it testifies to the loss of all transcendental signifieds in the modern period. In short, the modern allegorical detail is a parody of the traditional theological detail. It is the detail deserted by God."[21] The phantom detail, "the detail deserted by God" no longer transcendent, is distinguished by Schor for its excessive materiality. This detail deserted by God has characteristics similar to the pidgin *fetisso* or Portuguese *fetiço,* a term the Portuguese used to describe, in a colonial context, the adoration of certain objects in West Africa. The Portuguese believed that the Africans had endowed certain objects with godly power and then cut off recognition of those gods, that they'd forgotten those gods. Still, the Portuguese maintained, the West Africans believed that life was contained within those objects, but only the Portuguese, with their premise that the West Africans had forgotten those gods, knew why. Only they could see the West Africans' fetishization of the objects.

In "The Problem of the Fetish," William Pietz sees our current understanding of fetishism as a colonial construct, which erred when it followed this Portuguese interpretation. The fetish, he contends, in the African context is always, first of all, a material thing; it is not transcendent. It has an origin, a history that fixes together events that are otherwise incongruous. Its power and its identity come from its ability to repeat both the form of that historical unity and its effect in another situation. Its effect depends on a past set of social relations, now forgotten, but whose power has accrued in the material fetish. The fetish's control is external; it can't be manipulated by people because its power comes from the very effacement of its origins in historical social relations.[22]

Pietz's correction to the Western understanding of fetishism insists on the materiality of the fetish, as opposed to its being understood as a transcendental force. The fetish physically holds relationships and history that cannot be recovered. This insight provides a way of understanding the brilliant objectness of things often found in films whose characters have a dulled or muted subjectivity. Things have the vibrance that the characters do not possess. Douglas Sirk's objects in *Written on the Wind* (1956) stand out in this way. When Lauren Bacall opens her gifted closet, the outfits and their matching shoes neatly aligned below them shimmer such that she is almost frightened. The brilliant yellow sports car that begins the melodrama operates as an establishing shot for Robert Stack's poor rich boy's human vacancy. The most absurdly brilliant fetishes appear in Sirk's *Imitation of Life* (1959). The living room of the now successful actress (played by Lana Turner) is dominated by a three-foot-long multicolored clay fish that is shifted about the room by various characters each time a scene is enacted there.

Yvon's carrots, Lana's fish, and Lauren's shoes are visual props. They are details of material value. Yet it is almost impossible for a thing on film to be a thing in itself. For all of their visual brilliance, they seem to scream repressed emotions. Thomas Elsaesser reports on Sirk's remarks regarding the colors in *Written on the Wind*: "Almost throughout the picture I used deep-focus lenses which have the effect of giving a harshness to the objects and a kind of enameled, hard surface to the colours. I wanted this to bring out the inner violence, the energy of the characters which is all inside them and can't break through."[23] These objects—Sirk's fish, Bresson's carrots, and Anger's motorcycle—share the visual materiality of the fetish object. As deserted, enlarged details they have fallen from symbolic, narrative grace to serve an allegorical vocation. These objects are not transcendental: They persist as objects. The visceral materiality achieved by Sirk and Bresson through their lighting, color, and framing, and by Anger through his fashion-runway-style lighting and his spotlight roving camera movement, hold these objects to their substance. It is a substance, however, that looks as if it wants to be there.

The fetish character of the film image, if understood in magical terms, immediately lends itself as a cipher for roving, uncontained subjectivities. When characterizing the commodity fetish, Marx derived the fetish's power from the repressed, effaced, lost relationships and value produced by the market's reification of exchange value and labor. The commodity, in short, acquires the characteristics of the fetish because it is severed from its making. The film image is a modern, magical fetish in part because a similar kind of cut-off-ness characterizes its production. And so we turn now to the "scrupulous indifference" of the camera lens.

CHAPTER 6

The Metal Brain

The Bell and Howell is a metal brain, standardized, manufactured, marketed
in thousands of copies, which transforms the world outside it into art. The
Bell and Howell is an artist, and only behind it are there other artists: directors
and cameramen. A sensibility can at last be bought, available commercially
and subject to import duties like coffee or Oriental carpets. — Jean Epstein,
"*Bonjour cinéma* and Other Writings"

The belief that things take on life, meanings that are otherwise lost to
human experience via lapses of memory, the passage of time, the stampede
of progress, or the reifying structures of capitalism, plays a crucial role in
the early theorization and practices of cinema. This chapter discusses the
role of the camera as a representational apparatus and as a thing that is
itself a subject of fetishization in the creation of a magical, phantasmagoric cinema.

The most basic and of course most magical feat of cinema is to render
lifelike what is, after all, merely light and shadow, without volume, and,
early on, even lacked synchronized sound and often lacked color: "The
cinema names things, though in a visual way, and as a spectator, I do not
for a second doubt that they exist. All this drama, all this love are but light
and shadow. A square of white cloth, the only material element is all that's
needed to reflect all the photogenic substance with such intensity. I see
what is not and I see this unreal thing exactly."[1]

Cinema's capacity to let the viewer "see what is not . . . this unreal thing
exactly," of bringing that image of the absence of objects to life is fundamental to its enchantment. It is also, as Tom Gunning reveals in his discussion of spirit photography, "uncanny." Photography is a medium that
offers a "second glimpse . . . more sinister than the first" because of its
capacity to repeat, to double. Gunning argues, "While both Freud and
Rank demonstrate that the double has a long lineage (from archaic beliefs

in detachable souls to the romantic Doppelgänger), that predates photography, nonetheless photography furnished a technology which could summon up an uncanny visual experience of doubling as much as it was **85** capable of representing facts in all their positivity and uniqueness."[2] Spirits of the dead, for example, could use existing photographs of themselves as models to remind them of how they had looked, such that in some instances these images could occupy a place in photographs of those loved ones who were still very much alive. The indexical quality of photography, that it partakes in some way of the original, far from establishing "material certainty with apodictic clarity," released further phantasms whose "very fascination came from their apparent impossibility, their apparent severance from the laws of nature" (68).

A remnant of the enchantment by the uncanny double, which Epstein describes but to which through habit audiences are all but inured, can be recognized in films that animate objects within diegesis that otherwise obey basic physical laws. Norman Z. McLeod's *Topper* (1937), for example, is a screwball comedy in which two rich, carefree socialites die and become ghosts when they smash into a tree while driving home from a wild evening's escapades. While they are adjusting to their transformation, two drunkards are sitting on a distant log, sharing a bottle. The drunkards watch in amazement as the invisible ghosts move the wheel and jack to change their roadster's tire. The scene animates diegetically real things and tempts physical laws of causality. The two drunks, sufficiently primitivized by their consumption of firewater to believe that the laws of gravity are being violated in front of their eyes, are still attached enough to the laws of causality to know that everything is not as it should be. The scene initiates the drunken giddiness that ensues in increasingly uncontrolled doses during the film, until the ghosts' final ballroom bash where they invisibly hurl cocktails and make mayhem for a large, upscale audience and the scene becomes so over-the-top that the authorities are called in.

Outcasts from the film's plot, the drunken observers, who are the first observers of the ghosts' invisible movements of the props, mark the periphery of the film, the line between viewer and film, between reality and make-believe. They don't know it's only a movie; the viewer, on the other hand, knows better. The figure of the drunk is also a sort of wedge, easing open, albeit in a containable way, a porthole for the fantastical and the magical.[3] The drunks' amazement at seeing objects move of their own accord, of magic, weakens the sober viewer's reality resolve. We know the objects can't really move on their own, but we wish, ever so much, to see them do so. Like old demon rum, a kind of "no, not really, but wouldn't it be wonderful" spirit threatens the spectator's sobriety in exponential increments.[4] Such steadfast adult perception, with its sobriety, its sense of proportion, of "reality," faltered with the advent of modernist modes of representation in a variety of forms from literature to advertising. It was finally put to serious test on a massive scale by the cinema. Hence, *Variety*'s speculation about this otherwise innocuous 1937 comedy was that it might be "shocking to sensibilities" and would only be popular with "a small group who patronize the arty theaters and talk about pictures in terms of art expression."[5]

Epstein's plain and simple rendition — "I see this unreal thing exactly" — states film's fundamental paradox well. While real people and objects are more often the gums and varnishes of the form, a movie cannot be touched, smelled, or seen in the light of day. Even such disparate thinkers as Comolli and Bazin grounded their theories in cinema's uncannily mimetic nature, which further requires cinematic space to be discrete, completely distinct from real space in order that it be perceived as real. Cinematic representation depends on lack, on negation, on replacing the real entirely with a likeness to appear real. For Comolli, "Any representation is founded on a lack which governs."[6] The coexistence of the physically absent reality to which the image differs and defers and the presence of the film image fuel spectator desire. The spectator is "doubly racked by disillusion: from within itself as machine for simulation, mechanical and deathly reproduction of the living; from without as single image only" (760). Bazin, too, says that realism depends on a separate, neutral space outside of experience: "There can be no cinema without the setting up of an open space in place of the universe rather than as part of it."[7] Its difference from yet deference to physical reality is the source of its representational power: "First of all, the photographic reproduction, in projection, cannot pretend to be a substitute for the original or share its identity. If it could, then it would be better to destroy its aesthetic autonomy, since films or paintings start off precisely as the negation of that on which the aesthetic autonomy is based, the fact that the paintings are circumscribed in space and outside time" (142–43).

The "gap," as Philip Rosen refers to it, "between referent and signifier" without which "Bazin's ontology could not exist" is as much a part of cinema's appeal for Bazin, Rosen reminds us, as its indexicality.[8] With the example of Lamorisse's trick work necessary to create the mythic and real quality of Crin Blanc, Bazin states that "if it had been [instead] successfully created in front of the camera, the film would cease to exist, because it would cease, by the same token, to be a myth. It is that fringe of trick work, that margin of subterfuge demanded by the logic of the story that allows what is imaginary to include what is real and at the same time to substitute for it."[9] "It is precisely this gap," writes Rosen, "which is filled in by subjective projection as variable manifestations of human imagination."[10] The gap between the real and the made up is not only the porthole wedged open by the drunk but for the viewer's subjectivity in general. "All that matters," writes Bazin, "is that the spectator can say at one and the same time that the basic material of the film is authentic while the film is also truly cinema."[11] The pleasure for the spector resides not in the pure fantasy of illusion but in providing a screen upon which to exercise the "ebb and flow" between the real and the copy.

The film image can be seen as the spirit double of the real thing it shows, always independent of that thing, an exact copy that is thoroughly autonomous and exists as part of the spirit world that is cinema. The magical nature of the spirit double is very evident in films that play tricks with the frame and thereby highlight the delight got by its autonomy. When, in *Sherlock Junior* (1924, directed by Buster Keaton), and *Entr'acte* (1924, directed by René Clair), for example, characters step forward toward the audience, they momentarily break through the frame, tickling at the possibility that the film has in fact come to life. Georges Méliès, filmmaking's magician and trickster, gave the sanctity of the frame full measure by slipping around its edges. In *The Mermaid* (1904, France), the first frame shows a long shot of a room with a fish tank. Later, the framing places the viewer in close proximity to lazily swimming fish, as if to view an underwater paradise, disassociating it from the former diegesis. The camera moves backward so that we see the fish framed as if they are moving in a rather unlikely tableau vivant seeming to hang on a wall. Finally, the camera moves to reestablish the shot that reveals a room containing a small, rectangular fish tank. Sobriety. Such border violations thrill by breaking a taboo. Extending the conceit of film's reality one step further into the land of the living, these crossings momentarily activate a sensor between spirit and flesh, which sends out tantalizing jolts with each violation.

Cinema gains its magical quality from more than its paradoxical autonomy alone. The particular magic of making dimensionless things flush with the ability to activate the senses happens by virtue of two interdependent qualities. The first is the mechanical aspect of the camera, while on the audience's side brews what Jean Epstein termed a society in a state of "fatigue," or "distraction," as Kracauer and Benjamin put it. The unscrupulous, willful "camera-machine" takes advantage of the distracted, fatigued modern audience, catches them unawares, and makes things come alive.

The camera is, first of all, a machine. As such, it was a prime example of the alienating nature of modern production. At the same time, its images' mechanical movements at times mimicked the situation in the workplace and in that way addressed the audience's distracted perception. In Siegfried Kracauer's 1927 essay, "The Mass Ornament," the objectifying nature of assembly-line production is reproduced in popular spectacle.[12] The mass ornament removes the last vestiges of natural meaning and produces a spectacle ripe with surface splendor.[13] The legs of the Tiller Girls are no longer attached to bodies, but replicate the reifying structures of capitalist production: "The hands of the factories correspond to the legs of the Tiller Girls."[14] When Kracauer refers to the Tiller Girls he is referring to militarily trained dancing girls named after their choreographer, John Tiller, who were immensely popular throughout Europe.[15] Bertolt Brecht, too, while drinking a cup of coffee in New York City, was captivated by the "surface splendor" of cabaret dancing girls: "After enjoying black coffee I can look more tolerantly at concrete buildings. . . . I believe: surface has a great future. . . . I'm glad that in cabarets dancing girls are being manufactured to resemble each other more. It's pleasant that there are so many of them and that they're interchangeable."[16]

Kracauer does not directly refer to the film camera and the image it produces in the essay on the mass ornament, but the idea that the camera-machine is the vehicle for "the aesthetic reflex of the rationality to which the prevailing economic system aspires" is central to his argument.[17] Taken together with his essay, "Cult of Distraction," in which the "surface splendor" (323) is produced by the camera, cinema becomes the chosen art form that can produce a likeness in which society can examine itself.

Kracauer provides a firm footing for the aptness of the mechanical, thinglike nature of the film image to confront the perils of modernity. Insisting on radical attention to the surface meaning of things (attention, for example, to the legs of the Tiller Girls as an undulating abstract pattern rather than parts of real bodies), the route to truth "leads directly through the center of the mass ornament, not away from it" (86).

In turning toward the mass ornament, Kracauer is counting on its double-edged nature. Within its irrational, fragmentary continuity, built not upon meaning but its negation, lies the mass ornament's undoing, the revolutionary day for Marx when "all that is solid melts into air."[18] Kracauer writes, "In the streets of Berlin one is not seldom struck by the momentary insight that one day all this will suddenly burst apart. The entertainment to which the general public throngs ought to produce the same effect."[19] The fact that people flock to the movie theater only underscores the immanence of the mass ornament's undoing: "It could be done in Berlin, home of the masses who so easily allow themselves to be stupefied by the truth" (328). This would be possible if films first concentrated on what was really filmic and second displaced nature with reason: "[Movie theaters] should free their offerings of all trappings that deprived film of its rights and aim radically toward a kind of distraction that exposes disintegration instead of masking it" (328). Natural meanings and relationships between labor and its products have long since gone. Attempts to reestablish these meanings and relationships are doomed because they simply no longer obtain. Movies, in their form, their content, and their mode of exhibition, should perform instead the second nature of things.

Although Kracauer himself would be the first to object to such a comparison, the mass ornament is an apt illustrative figure for the concept of the "abstract totality" that Lukács defined in his widely influential essay, "Reification and the Consciousness of the Proletariat."[20] Once the commodity has become a universal category, Lukács says, "Time sheds its qualitative, variable, flowing nature; it freezes into an exactly delimited, quantifiable continuum filled with quantifiable 'things' (the reified, mechanically objectified 'performance' of the worker, wholly separated from his total human personality): in short, it [time] becomes space. . . . [In this] environment, at once the cause and the effect of the scientifically and mechanically fragmented and production of the object of labour, the subjects must likewise be rationally fragmented."[21] Lukács went on from describing a society reified by the commodity form to posit the proletariat as the class able to come to understand the identity of their own fragmented lives and bodies to that of the likewise fragmented world of commodities and their production. Through their consciousness of this identity, the proletariat could break the apparently infinite hold of the abstract totality and change the way things were done.[22] The same Lukácsian ring can be heard in Benjamin's discussion of the *flaneur* in his work on Charles Baudelaire: "To be sure, insofar as a person, as labour power, is a commodity, there is a need for him to identify himself as such. The more conscious he becomes of his mode of existence, the mode imposed upon him by the system of production, the more he proletarianizes himself, the more he will be gripped by the chill of the commodity economy and the less he will feel like empathizing with commodities."[23]

Kracauer's objection to Lukács rests, according to Miriam Hansen, on the spuriousness of this identity and the presumptuousness of the intellectual's theoretical position outside or above society. Kracauer's method instead, she argues, was that of immanent critique. Understandings of the meanings and functions of cultural products should be constructed from "within the material."[24] His manifest objection notwithstanding, Kracauer's call to arms that the route to truth runs through the mass ornament, not away from it, echoes the logic of Lukács's Hegelianization of Marx published four years earlier. As with Kracauer's insistence on radical attention to the surface, Lukács's conclusion to the problem of a state in which second nature is the nature of things is not to attempt to reverse the tide of reification. Like Kracauer, he finds the desire to reattach the legs of the Tiller Girls to real bodies a further mistake. His argument instead describes those whose life's work has been measured and meted out to fit the abstract pattern of the market, whose labor produces a commodity from which they are alienated, whose essence is that of a piece of this abstract totality, as the only people so equipped to see the identity between their fragmented limbs and those of the mass ornament. The same objection can be made to Kracauer's conclusion that he himself leveled against Lukács. Like Lukács's subject-object identity in the form of the proletariat, Kracauer's ultimate solution rings hollow: "[The process of change] can only move forward when thinking sets limits to nature and produces human beings in a way reason would produce them. Then society will change."[25] If the reason for society's lack of change in this regard is indeed due to the fact that "capitalism rationalizes not too much but too little," certainly Lukács could offer a similar rejoinder to the effect that the reification of society remains incomplete. "The Mass Ornament" and the reifica- tion essay share a profound sense of a society on the brink of consciousness of itself on the one hand, or absorption into reification's voracious machinery on the other. A condition that, if one is to gauge by today's writings on popular culture, has not changed all that much. The mass ornament still aptly describes a cinematic mode of address, an aspect of the apparatus, however unfulfilled Kracauer's utopian schema may now appear.

As much as the camera has been claimed to be an (ideological) apparatus,[26] and films are thought to be carefully manipulated by artists or socially constructed according to ideas of how things should look, for classical film theory, the camera's power was, time and again, accounted for by its alien, nonhuman, mechanical sensibility.

The alien quality of the camera does not lie in its status as a machine for the mass production of images alone. Along with mechanization, the camera brings with it the objectivity over which the human hand had cast such "doubt"[27] as well as a tool for seeing that is simply better than the human eye.

As a mechanism for making an impression of objective reality, the lens merely is itself. Its nature, or rather, the nature of the images it hands over, is still, however, enigmatic. André Bazin's "Ontology of the Photographic Image" (1945) confirms the subjective power of its objectivity, and also uncovers a further reason why cinema's mimetic power has such unequaled sway in relationship to other art forms.

Bazin credits the camera with a haunting objectivity but adds that this answers a specific need in human aesthetics: "the appetite for illusion." "No matter how skillful the painter," writes Bazin, "his work was always in fee to an inescapable subjectivity. The fact that a human hand intervened cast a shadow of doubt over the image. Again, the essential factor in the transition from the baroque to photography is not the perfecting of a physical process . . . rather does it lie in a psychological fact, to wit, in completely satisfying our appetite for illusion by a mechanical reproduction in the making of which man plays no part" (12). "The need for illusion" is a given element in the composition of the human mind. "It is purely a mental need, of itself nonaesthetic, the origins of which must be sought in the proclivity of the mind towards magic" (11). In the course of a few pages of the essay, an appetite becomes an obsession: "Photography and the cinema . . . are discoveries that satisfy, once and for all and in its very essence, our obsession with realism" (12). Each reference Bazin makes to this appetite, need, or obsession treats our fascination with the copy or "model" as something that is simply part of human nature.[28]

This belief in the power of duplicating is also fundamental to Aristotle's poetic theory. "Poetry in general," wrote Aristotle in the *Poetics,* "seems to have sprung from two causes, each of them lying deep in our nature. First the instinct of imitation is implanted in man from childhood, one difference between him and other animals being that he is the most imitative of living creatures, and through imitation he learns his earliest lessons; and no less universal is the pleasure felt in things imitated."[29] Given the primordial draw of the copy, Bazin's further claim is not for its superior imitative facility to other art forms, but rather the copy's unfettered origin. The appetite for illusion is satisfied completely by photographic reproduction because of the directness of the method of reproduction rather than because of the quality of the image.

As a result, the image "shares the being" of the original. Bazin writes: "Only a photographic lens can give us the kind of image of the object that is capable of satisfying the deep need man has to substitute for it something more that a mere approximation, a kind of decal or transfer. The photographic image is the object itself, the object freed from the conditions of time and space that govern it. No matter how fuzzy, distorted, or discolored, no matter how lacking in documentary value the image may be, it shares, by virtue of the very process of its becoming, the being of the model of which it is the reproduction: it is the model."[30] By claiming this identity between the model and the reproduction, Bazin, like Kracauer in *Theory of Film,* casts his faith in the image itself as superior, for the purposes of understanding an essence, to its model: "It is not for me to separate off . . . here a reflection on a damp sidewalk, there the gesture of a child. Only the impassive lens, stripping its object of all those ways of seeing it, those piled-up preconceptions, that spiritual dust and grime with which my eyes have covered it, is able to present it in all its virginal purity to my attention and consequently to my love" (15). Bazin's love, replete with "virginal purity," is the fulfillment of a long-standing human desire. The basis of his love is the mimetic pleasure that Aristotle defined as universal: the pleasure that offers the possibility of "inferring and learning."[31] Just as in the *Poetics,* which is nothing if not an attempt to erase artifice, so too we find in the lens itself, through its supposed omission of human intervention altogether, a chance "to learn." Film finally satisfies what Bazin called "the proclivity of the mind towards magic."[32]

Benjamin and Epstein, like Bazin, saw the camera's mechanical nature as film's central distinguishing feature. Apart from the obvious consequences for the scope of practical capabilities from these improvements on human faculties, the camera's alien superiority thrust it into an almost mythic realm. Maya Deren, criticizing the way photographers overplay their part in the success of an image, recounts Kodak's advertisement: "You push the button, IT does the rest!"[33] Yet it, the camera, she remarked, "creates, at times, the illusion of being almost itself a living intelligence which can inspire its manipulation on the explorative and creative level simultaneously" (47). The depersonalization of the camera—its itness—is for Deren, following Epstein, one of the magical features of cinema as a whole. She writes this passage upon the arrival of "L'Intelligence d'une Machine" by Epstein, which she had not yet read but nonetheless recommends "for those who share, with me, a profound respect for the magical complexities of the film instrument" (47). Epstein's "camera machine" approaches the status of an independent will, while Benjamin's emphasis on technological reproducibility laid the ground for an immediate and bodily felt mode of perception that he called the optical unconscious. For both of them, however, it was the camera's perceived ability to circumvent human mediation that gave it such unnatural power. "Evidently," remarked Benjamin innocently, "a different nature opens itself to the camera than opens to the naked eye—if only because an unconsciously penetrated space is substituted for a space consciously explored by man."[34]

The nature of this different nature operates like a phantom in Benjamin's writings about the reproduced image. He associates the different nature revealed in cinema with the properties of the camera itself: "The act of reaching for a lighter or a spoon is familiar routine, yet we hardly know what really goes on between hand and metal, not to mention how this fluctuates with our moods. Here the camera intervenes with the resources of its lowerings and liftings, its interruptions and isolations, its extensions and accelerations, its enlargements and reductions. The camera introduces us to unconscious optics as does psychoanalysis to unconscious impulses" (237). One thinks of John Cassavetes, working in the United States in the sixties and seventies, who put the gesture and the face in a new, intimate register, and of Stan Brakhage, who, beginning in the fifties, expanded what it meant to see. Such independent filmmaking gives full value to what Epstein termed "the independent eye" in his critique of the point-of-view shot: "But I do not mean to imply, as it was recently the fashion to state, that each image of the film should be conceived as seen by one of the characters in a preceding shot. Subjectivism like this is overdone. Why refuse to profit by one of the rarest qualities of the cinematic eye, that of *being an eye independent of the eye, of escaping the tyrannical egocentrism of our personal vision?* Why compel the sensitive emulsion simply to duplicate the functions of our own retina? Why not grasp eagerly at an almost unique opportunity to set a scene from a focus other than our own line of sight? *The lens is itself.*"[35]

The lens has a subjectivity of its own. However undefinable and unknowable the metal brain may be, "the lens is itself." The lens itself seems caught in the never-ending spiral twisting people into things and things into people. Terms that enliven the camera eye with human attributes are not even confined to the filming machine but extend to the filmstrip as well, which is too often tyrannically compelled to function as if it were a mere retina in mainstream film practice. In Benjamin's, Epstein's, and Bazin's manner of writing about the lens, with its gentle lowerings and liftings, its sensate emulsions, its virginal love, it is hardly artless. For Benjamin and Epstein it was even aggressive. Yet, at the same time they claim that it is its objective nature, its passivity, that gives it such artful power. The lens has the guile of an ingenue, the emotions of an executioner.

The camera is an image-producing machine, a thing. It is not exempt from the phantasmagoric transformations of capitalism Marx described, but rather, it too becomes animated by fetishism and by the theoretical process of naming. Naming, recalling Epstein, is animistic: "The cinema names things, although in a visual way."[36] This naming is the same kind of naming that defines language: "Moreover cinema is a language, and like all languages it is animistic; it attributes, in other words, a semblance of life to the objects it defines."[37] Just as cinema animates by naming things, naming, albeit in the hope of definition, animates the camera lens, the filmstrip, and the images they produce. Most generally, the camera becomes such a powerful thing because the fascination it attracts is animated by the primitive, archaic desire for a direct copy. By defining the camera as that which satisfies this primitive desire, the camera itself becomes a primitive whose nature is as beguiling as it is unknowable.

The images the camera produces partake of the same phantasmagoria; these things do not function to produce signs for our reading. What we are left with instead is the magical warm glow of the commodity fetish in which original meaning is forever effaced. In place of long lost meaning, the fetish produces new attractions. This is only half of the scene, however, for the spectator's fatigued and distracted condition, the subject of the following chapter, is another precondition for the dazzling life of the image.

CHAPTER 7

The Tired Lens

A road is a road but the ground which flees under the four beating hearts of an automobile's belly transports me. The Oberland and Semmering tunnels swallow me up, and my head, bursting through the roof, hits against their vaults. Seasickness is decidedly pleasant. — Jean Epstein, "Magnification and Other Writings"

The alien, mechanical nature of the camera highlights the object as discrete from human production and thus thrusts its image into a world of magical significance. At the same time, the mechanization of daily life, and of work in particular, changed the cognitive condition of the perception of the metamorphosing object. The different nature of these changes,[1] even their significance,[2] is now a subject for debate, but Epstein, Benjamin, and Kracauer granted them no small importance in the 1920s. The changes in the nature of experience brought on by what we loosely call modernity[3] were found not only in its forms of representation — the waning, for example, of the art of storytelling, and the ascent of the novel — but also, and most important, they were then understood to create a different, less broad kind of attention paid to those representations.

And indeed, in 1921, Jean Epstein declared his world in a state of fatigue, but that fatigue, he claimed, was an achievement: "We are all erudite and professional scholars of fatigue, neurasthenic esthetes."[4] According to Stuart Liebman, Epstein believed that modern society, via its whirring machines, and the changing nature of labor, produced an inability to contemplate and to focus on something for a long period of time. "Epstein's central premise," writes Liebman, "was that machines had drastically changed the nature of work. Manual labor was fast becoming the exception rather than the rule. Even where physical labor was still required, machines intervened to augment the power of workers."[5] Liebman cites Epstein's observation that, "In countless jobs, the arm, the hand, the shoulder, and the foot have been replaced by an electrical current, some

gears and pullies."[6] "Ever increasing numbers of jobs," Liebman summarizes, "were strictly 'white collar,' and even 'blue collar' occupations had
come to depend upon the mastery of the complex conceptual systems   **97**
required to operate the new mechanical tools. Work was becoming 'cere-
bral.'"[7] Modern labor made not just aural and visual but mental noise.

In the light of this dispersion of cognitive capabilities, Epstein saw his
opening. Liebman writes, "Machines, fatigue, and the subconscious cognition they brought to prominence were the principal features of a future
Epstein looked forward to optimistically" (140). Epstein's optimism lay
in his belief that fatigue afforded a new kind of perception, a sort of
haphazard apprehension that allowed the world to touch one unmediated
by structured reasoning. It is easy to recognize the wear of fatigue, but the
enthusiasm, as Liebman indicates, which became Epstein's impassioned
argument for film, requires a greater leap. Here is his translation of a
passage from Epstein's *La Poesie:*

I wonder whether man is not more intelligent when his overburdened intellect
is experiencing shocks, interruptions and failures; [I wonder] whether the
whole of civilization in which we live such complicated and active lives isn't
the product of accumulated fatigue, of incremental mental strain. . . . We
endure this fatigue almost continuously and are impaired by it. Certainly,
sometimes it is diminishing, but not always. In other respects, it is enhancing
and perhaps . . . that is why it interests me. Without it, one's intellect would
hardly ever experience moments of genius, of sudden flashes of understanding
of extraordinary scope, of incandescent lyricism, of victorious reason. Without
fatigue, man and civilization would be deprived of all this; civilization would
no longer be what it is. (181–83)

The effect of fatigue on people became, for Epstein, the cause of moments of genius and of victorious reason. In connecting the nature of
labor with the nature of creative activity, Epstein of course was not alone.
When Walter Benjamin wrote about the decline of the art of storytelling,
for example (and experience losing ground to representation), he noted
that one told stories while doing artisanal work: "This process of assimila-
tion [of a story] which takes place in depth, requires a state of relaxation
which is becoming rarer and rarer. If sleep is the apogee of physical relaxation, boredom is the apogee of mental relaxation. Boredom is the dream
bird that hatches the egg of experience. A rustling in the leaves drives him

away. His nesting place — the activities that are intimately associated with boredom — are already extinct in the cities and are declining in the country as well. . . . [Storytelling] is lost because there is no more weaving and spinning to go on while they are being listened to."[8] The nature of mechanical labor, the noise of its machines and the rapid repetitive tasks, had made not only storytelling but also the state of boredom, which had filled the idle mind, impossible. The tasks of the industrial laborer and office worker alike render boredom a thing of the past. Kracauer points to much the same thing in his essay "Boredom," in which he claimed that boredom had become close to impossible.[9]

To conjure a moment wherein "incandescent lyricism" is brought on by labor's fatigue, by "incremental mental strain," in contrast to the untormented quality of boredom which brings understandings that are readily assimilable to experience, requires acknowledging that fatigue is inevitably tied to repression, loss, or despair.[10] Benjamin's image of boredom as "the dream bird which hatches the egg of experience," and Epstein's theoretically quite different image of a fatigued laborer turning out epiphanies on the assembly line nonetheless both call cartoons to mind. An example to suit Epstein's lyrical fatigue can be found in a different form of visual comic animation. Charlie Chaplin's *Modern Times* (1936) portrays factory work in all its viscous effects on the soul. Chaplin's every move is timed, regulated, and determined by the conveyer belt as he tightens bolts on an assembly line with a quick turn of each wrist. Holding a wrench in each hand, this repetition finally stirs him into such a hypnotic frenzy that the motion of tightening bolts, two at a time, overtakes him and he throws himself into the factory's gargantuan machinery, only to be spit out again still tightening imaginary bolts as he traverses the shop room floor to the sidewalk outside, the wrenches still in hand. He performs an instant graphic match of imagined bolts to a woman's real dress buttons on her bustle and ends up paying for the incongruity by being taken away in a straitjacket. The animation of the object that is produced by shop room fatigue falls short of incandescent lyricism but approximates a moment of genius, however comic. Chaplin's screen performance served for Epstein as a clear demonstration of the creative effects of fatigue: "Chaplin has created the overwrought hero. His entire performance consists of reflexes of a nervous, tired person. A bell or an automobile horn makes him jump, forces him to stand anxiously, has hand on his chest, because of the nervous palpitations of his heart. This isn't so much an example, but rather a synopsis of his photogenic neurasthenia."[11] The basic form of Chaplin's representation of repetitive labor run amok through distraction from the task to the object is a familiar comic routine in films. But such comic heroes also bear out Lukács's observation that in capitalist production, one only has a soul when one makes a mistake.[12]

A more obvious fit to Epstein's description of fatigue is not the assembly line worker but, to the contrary, a writer, who, so exhausted by experience, and even more so by its memory, so sick as to spend his productive years literally lying down, always fatigued or in fear of absolute collapse, holds death at bay to witness a chance significant detail that then releases into a full meaning-laden image. The animation of the object that could bring forth meaning depended, for Proust, on chance on the one hand, and quieting the present on the other: "The past is hidden somewhere outside the realm, beyond the reach of intellect, in some material object (in the sensation which that material object will give us) which we do not suspect. And as for that object, it depends on chance whether we come upon it or not before we ourselves must die."[13] Proust, however, organized the conditions of his writing so that "chance" had every opportunity. Walter Benjamin describes the conditions of Proust's writing as "extremely unhealthy: an unusual malady, extraordinary wealth, and an abnormal disposition."[14] Benjamin's interpretation of Proust's method attempts to show that concentration is inimical to free recollection through images and sensation. Light and reason can undo a hard night's work: "the day unravels what the night has woven" (202). Finally, Proust confined himself to the evening's liminal state: "With our purposeful activity and, even more, our purposive remembering each day unravels the web and the ornaments of forgetting. That is why Proust finally turned his days into nights, devoting all his hours to undisturbed work in his darkened room with artificial illumination, so that none of those intricate arabesques might escape him" (202). Still, quiet, and dark. Such are the conditions for the chance perception of an important image. Tired but not sleeping, Proust recoiled from the light, "beyond the reach of intellect," so as to stumble upon a sensate recovery of the past through a material object. "Sudden flashes of understanding" or "incandescent lyricism" flood *Remembrance of Things Past* through gates impervious to reason, but rather wedged asunder by the material detritus time leaves in its wake. Images that animate the imagination beyond the reach of reason, like Proust's "fetiches"[15] and Chaplin's bolts to buttons, rescue the fatigued laborer

from modern times.

That modernity brought about a change in perception is by now a fairly familiar claim which perhaps gained most currency with the many readings of Benjamin's "Work of Art" essay as the "optical unconscious" and, to a lesser degree, Kracauer's concept of distraction.[16] From Vachel Lindsay's mechanically inclined Americans, so fond of crawling on their backs to tinker with their motor cars of a Saturday afternoon, to Kracauer's "Little Shopgirls,"[17] one's distractions in leisure time and the nature of one's daily experience, especially labor, are all of a piece. Although Epstein's observations were hardly novel, he went much further than Kracauer and Benjamin, for modern conditions not only changed perception, in his view; he claimed that the cinema, in particular, created the conditions for a modern creative practice.

The nature of one's daily experience and labor was so fragmented and confounding that the camera, which could function in a likewise fragmented fashion, was a good tool for its representation. But in order for the camera to so serve, "realist aesthetics" had to be abandoned. "Reality," writes Liebman, was for Epstein "too fast and volatile to be adequately conveyed by a realist aesthetic." Liebman then recalls Epstein's citation of Blaise Cendrars, the writer, actor, sailor, animal collector, who had a deep influence on Epstein. "Whirlpools of movements in space. Everything tumbles. The sun plummets and we after it. . . . Today everything opens, crumbles, melts, is hollowed out, constructed, expands. A new civilization. A new humanity. . . . And it's the machine that recreates and displaces our sense of orientation. Directions change. From this point of view then, the cinema, arbitrarily, has endowed man with an eye more marvelous than the faceted eye of a fly. One hundred worlds, a thousand movements, a million dramas enter the field of this eye simultaneously."[18] The camera matches the disorientation inherent in modern experience, illustrated here by the machine, shot for shot. And, like a fly whose multifaceted eye sees different angles simultaneously, a person, both while spectator in a film and living in the modern world, no longer has the time, nor the quiet, for contemplation's boredom.

Reminiscent of Epstein's fly, Benjamin describes the "jerky nearness" of the film image. The following passage from *One Way Street*, a series of short pieces Benjamin wrote in 1925–1926, illustrates the kind of change in perception of a work of art that he later referred to as its loss of "aura." Auratic works of art adhered to criticism, which was "a matter of correct distancing." In the piece entitled "This Space for Rent," Benjamin focused his attention instead on the modern billboard advertisement:

> Fools lament the decay of criticism. For its day is long past. Criticism is a matter of correct distancing. It was at home in a world where perspectives and prospects counted and where it was still possible to take a standpoint. Now things press too closely on human society. . . . Today the most real, the mercantile gaze into the heart of things is the advertisement. It abolishes the space where contemplation moved and all but hits us between the eyes with things as a car, growing to gigantic proportions, careens at us out of a film screen. And just as the film does not present furniture and façades in completed forms for critical inspections, their insistent, jerky nearness alone being sensational, the genuine advertisement hurtles things at us with the tempo of a good film.[19]

The raw vision that so captivated Benjamin and Epstein, which they express in these examples via the billboard advertisement, is now scattered across film genres from the action film to the avant-garde. The "unconscious optics" that are analogous to the psychoanalytic unconscious because they circumvent conscious cognition and are delivered as immediate sense impressions works, in this example, in the service of modern advertising. The camera's image is so "near," its effect so tactile that it "all but hits us between the eyes," and there is no longer any time for contemplation and no more room left for doubt. By doing away with the distance for contemplation that would have allowed one to think about it, the billboard advertisement works by visual assault to reign over the senses completely: "Thereby 'matter-of-factness' is finally dispatched, and in the face of the huge images across the walls of houses, where toothpaste and cosmetics lie handy for giants, sentimentality is restored to health and liberated in American style, just as people whom nothing moves or touches any longer are taught to cry again by films." Surely with this final line Benjamin is thinking of the more melodramatic forms of cinema. He could hardly have anticipated the split-second precision with which stones could be made to weep.[20] Nor could he have foreseen the mileage action films would get from those billboards where toothpaste lies handy for giants (and cars to smash through them). The mercantile gaze of the art collector who is interested in the price the artwork will bring is superior to the critic's gaze because the collector is attracted to the artwork's commodity value; he or she feels its warmth.

Perception of these bodily felt representations is no longer a matter of reading signs: "The warmth of the subject is communicated to him [the paid critic], stirs *sentient* springs. What, in the end, makes advertisements so superior to criticism? Not what the red neon sign says — but the fiery pool reflecting it in the asphalt."[21] Finally, Benjamin sees no sign at all on the billboard but instead turns his attention to its light's red reflection. The glow emitted by the fetish, like the commodity's warmth, draws the modern spectator near. In his or her distraction, the spectator is overwhelmed by this visual, tactile force.

Benjamin was not the only one to compare this new kind of physical apperception to the billboard advertisement. It is unlikely Kracauer had glanced at *One Way Street,* which Benjamin sent to him for publication in the *Frankfurter Zeitung,*[22] before he wrote "Boredom" in November 1924, but the similarity of the images suggests some cross-fertilization (332). The article discusses the decay of boredom, and how the visual and aural noise of the modern world prevents such pleasant empty-headedness. He suggests that even though one may desire the blankness of real boredom, "the world itself is much too *interested* for one to find the peace and quiet necessary" (332). Kracauer's language suggests the same sort of active pull of the person toward the physical world of mass reproduction that Benjamin saw in commodities: "Illuminated words glide by on the rooftops, and already one is banished from one's own emptiness into the alien *advertisement.* One's body takes root in the asphalt, and, together with the enlightening revelations of the illuminations, one's spirit — which is no longer one's own — roams ceaselessly out of the night and into the night. . . . Like Pegasus prancing on a carousel, this spirit must run in circles and may never tire of praising to high heaven the glory of a liqueur and the merits of the best five-cent cigarette. Some sort of magic spurs that spirit relentlessly amid the thousand electric bulbs, out of which it constitutes and reconstitutes itself into glittering sentences" (332). Though one's feet are firmly "root[ed] in the asphalt," the "spirit must run in circles" and, like Pegasus, takes up the overwhelmingly proportioned commodity. Like Benjamin, Kracauer's gaze finally rests on the glitter of the flashing sign. But here, unlike Benjamin, Kracauer appears to be an unwilling traveler. The spirit is "cranked away" to the cinema; "the posters swoop" and "drag it into the silver screen." Kracauer loses himself, but never finds the hearth fires of the commodity as did Benjamin, nor the moments of genius that emerge from Epstein's fatigue, which could, in the eyes of Benjamin and Epstein, have alleviated his condition: "One forgets oneself in the process of gawking, and the huge dark hole is animated with the illusion of a life that belongs to no one and exhausts everyone" (332).

Epstein, by contrast, evoked the billboard advertisement with predictable enthusiasm: "The motor-bike posters race uphill by means of symbols: hatching, hyphens, blank spaces. Right or wrong, they thereby endeavor to conceal their ankylosis. The painter and the sculptor maul life, but this bitch has beautiful, real legs and escapes from under the nose of the artist crippled by inertia. Sculpture and painting, paralyzed in marble or tied to canvas, are reduced to pretense in order to capture movement, the indispensable. The ruses of reading."[23]

"The ruses of reading," Benjamin's "not what the sign says," and earlier "language never gives mere signs" characterize the dissatisfaction Benjamin and Epstein share with privileging conscious cognition. These remarks chastise a rational approach to film, and could be productively deployed against cognitive or semiotic analyses of cinema. One kids oneself trying to read signs, and while paying attention to the letter of the word, one ignores but is still subject to the sensate assault of the image, even (as was the case in Benjamin's and Kracauer's examples) if the image is a word. Epstein's remarks about the billboard recalls Benjamin's "This Space for Rent," not only by dismissing auratic works of art and their criticism with the condemnation "the ruses of reading" but also in its concentration on the way these images overwhelm the spectator with their acceleration and size: "Acceleration. . . . Gearing up and gearing down." Like the "mercantile gaze," the effect of this new form is best compared to the market. Epstein concludes, "This new beauty is as sinuous as the curve of the stock market index. It is no longer the function of a variable but a variable itself" (10).

The differences between auratic and tactile perceptions have been addressed in the discussion of the cream-separator sequence in Eisenstein's *The Old and the New*. Implicit in that argument, which uses not just the same filmmaker but the same film to demonstrate both modes of perception, is the understanding that cinema partakes of both sorts of perception. Recall that Epstein wrote he'd "never seen an entire minute of pure photogenie," that it was "like a spark that appears in fits and starts" (9). When Epstein derides film conventions, such as point-of-view shot, or the "realist aesthetic," he underscores what is new, specific, and most responsive to the modern world about the camera. At the same time, however, this specifically modern form, under eminently modern conditions, was the archaic vehicle for magical power.

Epstein left Paris for Brittany in 1928 and began the third and last period of his career making films involving fishing village life and the sea. The films he made are perhaps closer to an ideal of ethnographic cinema than have ever been made, but that was not his concern. The last of these films made upon his return after the war is *Le Tempestaire* (1947–48). It was his first to use slow-motion sound and, consistent with his early attention to magnification, it also employed slow and reverse motion. Recapitulating his enthusiasm for the camera close-up where one can see the minute gestures that language leaves silent, Epstein wrote of his new use of sound: "In drawing out the detail, in separating the sounds, in creating a sort of close-up of the sound, slow-motion can allow all beings, all objects to speak. And so that misunderstanding of the latinists, which made Lucretius say that objects cry, becomes an audible reality."[24]

Le Tempestaire is the story of a fishing village during a storm, and the fears of a woman for her husband's life as the storm mounts. Finally, she gives in to her fears and goes to a shop in which the keeper pulls down from the shelf a crystal ball. They look into it together and see the sea. The entire frame is filled with the sea, which slows down, stops, calms, and rebels again.[25] Her husband, we infer from the momentary relaxation of the tempest, will be safe. The crystal ball sees as the camera does, but it is the camera-machine that stops the sea. With the worried eyes of the wife and confident eyes of the shopkeeper fixed on the crystal ball, the crystal ball hands its magic over to the camera.

In 1921, when describing the "drama of the microscope," which is movement in close-up, Epstein had described this scene with uncanny precision: "Young girls will consult them [dramatic microscopes] instead of the fortune teller."[26] The fortune-teller's signature tool for divination, the crystal ball becomes infused with the magical powers of the camera. As in the pivotal sequence where eyes were transfixed by the cream separator in *The Old and the New,* the magic of the spirits is replaced by the magic of mechanized perception.

Epstein's use of nonactors and slowed-down sound seems to hover over **105** real life, sapping the souls of people and things for a magical purpose. In 1928, after shooting his first film about the Sein and Ouessant islanders off Brittany, he wrote: "*Finis terrae* endeavours to be psychological '*documentary*,' the *reproduction* of a brief drama comprising events which really happened, of authentic men and things. Leaving the Ouessant archipelago, I felt I was taking with me not a film but a fact. And that once this fact had been transported to Paris, something of the material and spiritual reality of the island would henceforth be missing. An occult business."[27] Small wonder then that Eric Michaels tells us that "traditional peoples' first encounters with photography sometimes lead them to conclude that the camera is a dangerous, magical instrument capable of stealing some essential part of their being, causing illness or death."[28] For the modern artist, for the colonizer, for the man with the movie camera, it was a magical object, an object that could steal material and spiritual reality.

Reading Epstein, Benjamin, and Kracauer in tandem not only begins to build a consensus about the modern spectator's state of fatigue, distraction, and exhaustion, it also begins the process of cross-illumination. Because of his grounding in the theory of *photogenie,* Epstein makes distinctions between what we would divide into auratic and nonauratic works of art on film not only possible but even explicit. His writing about the moments of *photogenie* help to deflect Benjamin's almost too famous essay on the work of art in the age of reproducibility away from a functionalist interpretation. This interpretation errs by understanding him to mean that the machine's reproduction of images alone defines the difference between auratic and tactile works of art. Partaking of another sort of distance, the distance that defines its making, the invisible distance of the camera's machinations that leave no trace, the film also makes for a new and different intimacy. This intimacy, this closeness can touch the spectator in a way that a sculpture, "paralyzed in marble" (which one might actually physically touch), cannot. At the same time, Epstein used Rodin's efforts to create movement in the sculpture *St. John the Baptist* to explain the beginnings of the kind of sensate action that cinema was to develop.[29] Technological reproducibility on its own merely creates favorable conditions for tactile apperception, it does not guarantee such a facility. Epstein

wrote of the gramophone, another technological mechanism for reproduction, "The gramophone is a failure, or yet to be explored. One would
have to find out what it distorts, where it selects. Has anyone made re-
cordings of street noises, engines, railway concourses?"[30] By pointing out
where cinema distorts and selects, and by explicitly connecting this to
perception, Epstein eases the way for a finer interpretation of Benjamin's
essay than the functionalism with which it is often credited.

Epstein's, Kracauer's, and Benjamin's discussions of the perceptual
changes they saw around them present us with the empirical evidence that
they at least were fatigued by their experience of modern life. In their
encounters with the machine's image, we can see its felt superior vitality to
the straining, weakened, and ever tiring observer. Taken together with the
image as a fetish object and the camera as a machine, this is the final
element that sets the conditions for the modern phantasmagoria of magical cinema. A "new way of feeling," Bresson called it.

CHAPTER 8 Bresson's Phantasmagoria

Idle horror is always accompanied by the words, "I told you so!"

—Max Horkheimer and Theodor Adorno, *The Dialectic of Enlightenment*

Raul Ruiz defines shamanic cinema as one that records "a week that has never been experienced but still proves perfectly real."[1] Bresson's *L'Argent* depicts such a week, although the time frame is on the order of a year. The film simply follows the events that occur when two pubescent boys pass a forged banknote, "conjoining," as Steve Shaviro puts it, "absolute necessity to sheer contingency."[2] The two boys pass the forged bill at a photography shop.[3] Yvon, a man who supports his wife and daughter by delivering fuel oil, is given the note as payment and wrongly accused and convicted of passing counterfeit money after he in turn uses it to buy lunch. He then tries his hand at real crime, driving a getaway car for a bank robbery, fails miserably and gets caught and put into prison. Upon release from prison, he takes to murder. First, he knifes to death the keeper of a guest house in which he boards, then he kills an entire family and finally their housekeeper, who had befriended him.

The magical power of money, unleashed in the photography shop, initiates the metamorphoses of Yvon from an unremarkable working man to an ineffectual criminal and finally an affectless killer. At the same time, another form of sorcery takes hold in which the movie camera levels, indeed overturns, the distinction between people and things. The neutralized subjectivity of the film's characters is due to Bresson's particular use of actors, which strives to make them appear as natural automatons on the one hand, and his relish—both aural and visual—of textures and patterns, the details that maintain the preeminence of the surface value of things, on the other. His subjects, "drained of all affect," and his objects, brilliant, shimmering fetishes, produce a cinematography in which, indeed, "a definite social relation between [people] assumes, in their eyes, the fantastic form of a relationship between things."[4] The "fantastic form," the phantasmagoria, is opened up to us in such a way that it reveals not only its horrific potential but also its potential as, in Benjamin's terms, "redeemable wish image."[5] Bresson's repetitive form and the way he drains his actors of life's blood creates an aesthetic of fatigue that Epstein would surely recognize. And though Bresson rescinds subjectivity, one might say, once and for all, he offers back to us the object world — and it is brilliant, horrific, and alive.

With a mind to understanding bespoken subjects and animated objects, this analysis begins with a discussion of Bresson's repetitive style. To deal more specifically with the phantasmagoric effect of Bresson's style, it makes a temporary distinction between his objects and his subjects. Bresson's particular notions about acting replicate reifying structures to destroy subjectivity, yet his rich, balanced frames render the world of objects bounteous. Money, the title and subject of the film, in its estrangement as a Bressonian object enacts the unnatural liveness of capital: "i.e., past, materialised, and dead labour [is turned] into capital, into value big with value, a live monster that is fruitful and multiplies."[6] Tolstoy's story "The Forged Coupon," upon which the film is based, is set in late feudal rather than capitalist society, where the act of counterfeiting presages capital. Capital's unnatural life is finally absorbed by storytelling in Tolstoy's story. Bresson's version, by contrast, keeps the money alive.

Bresson's cinematography in *l'Argent* is so even, so measured that he can render the slap of a face through the consequent spilling of hot coffee with a violence that is on a par with if not greater than the massacre of a family. Though such immanent rationality displays a kind of reification of violence, Bresson's careful doses of reality create a form of repetition with its own poetic force: a resounding redundancy that makes things appear both inevitable and, at the same time, recuperable.

Bresson shoots his scenes as animated tableaux, each lasting approximately the same amount of time, often shot at medium range, usually with a 50mm lens straight on, simply cutting from one tableau to the next as if the film were a documentary slide show. Camera movement is confined; tracking shots sparsely follow significant movement; pans define the field, they don't reveal in any conventional fashion. Like the epic scene in Brecht, the shot in Eisenstein, these scenes are "so many tableaux," as Barthes developed the term in "Brecht, Diderot, Eisenstein."[7] Barthes writes that such scenes are *"laid out* (in the sense in which one says *the table is laid*)"; they "answer perfectly to that dramatic unity theorized by Diderot: firmly cut out (remember the tolerance shown by Brecht with regard to the Italian curtain-stage, his contempt for indefinite theatres — open air, theatre in the round), erecting a meaning but manifesting the production of that meaning, they accomplish the coincidence of the visual and the ideal *découpages*" (71). Such decoupage or "cutting out,"[8] wherein the viewing eye (or the mind) becomes the apex of a visual triangle, creates "sovereign" images with "clearly defined edges" in which "everything that it admits with its field is promoted into essence, into light, into view."[9] And like the "perfect instant," which Diderot conceived as the ideal moment chosen by the painter, these scenes are "hieroglyphs" that portray an instant that is "totally concrete and totally abstract" (73).[10]

Sound, almost always diegetic, is magnified just a notch, selected out as a contrapuntal additional element, another texture altogether reimposed onto the moving tableau. The rigid, even steps of high heels, the soft hum of a mechanical floor buffer, move in another dimension, haunting the film with the tactile effects of the real. When used as concatenation between cuts in rare instances, sounds startle rather than smooth transitions. The announcement "The court," for example, just before a close-up of the rich fold of red cloth signifying the law (as opposed to the conventionally boring pan shot of a courtroom with heavy furniture and people awaiting the law), provides a Brechtian banner instead of a "naturalistic" transition. Water flowing, bills crackling, a purse popping shut — these everyday sounds are repeated throughout the film both to estrange us from the image as well as to enrich the tableau. Bazin describes this phenomenon while discussing Bresson's "realism": "They are there deliberately as neutrals, as foreign bodies, like a grain of sand that gets into and seizes up a piece of machinery. If the arbitrariness of their choice resembles an abstraction, it is the abstraction of the concrete integral. They are like lines drawn across an image to affirm its transparency, as dust affirms the transparency of a diamond; it is impurity at its purest."[11] Not real, not symbol, Bazin explains, Bresson's sonic punctuations work to highlight the corporeality of things while at the same time confirming them as representation and not real. Or, as Bresson himself put it, they "retouch some real with some real."[12] Bresson's way of using sound as "dust" to affirm the image's transparency and its purity partakes of the "equipment-free aspect" of the image in full measure. In this, Bresson performs what Miriam

Hansen refers to as "technological innervation," which Benjamin had seen as part and parcel of that very aspect. "Benjamin," says Hansen, "sees the cinematic crossing of supreme artificiality with physiological immediacy as a chance — to rehearse technological innervation in the medium of the optical unconscious."[13] This is accomplished, to a significant extent, by measuring out diegetic sounds, increasing them a consistent decibel from the real, rationing them out. Amplified from the diegetic norm, they cross the image with artifice, but at the same time they touch the acoustic nerve with their singular presence. Estranged through magnification and the elimination of other sounds, these object noises at times take on the subjectivity of a voice-over. They frame the tableau, but as they do so, they make it immediate.

Although repetition, a long-standing tenet of modern design, is elemental to Bresson's cinematography in *l'Argent,* neither its general appeal nor its particular efficacy in this film is obvious. Just what are "all those effects you can get from repetition (of an image, of a sound)"?[14] Think of the many odd doors in the film or, specifically, the scene of the floor cleaner traversing a tableau of wooden cell doors in one of the rare delineations of deep space. This shot anticipates Yvon's encounter with Lucien, who is a sort of demon/angel figure Yvon meets in prison and who is in some way responsible for Yvon's incarceration. Yet the shot has a visual warmth that is contrary to the conventional meaning of imprisonment and justice's rationalization of people according to cells, to numbers, or to the law. How is this so?

As a rule, if Bresson shoots something at all, he shoots it twice in *l'Argent.* When the prisoners are delivered for incarceration by a blue bus, it reverses slowly, the inmate's parcels appear, then the three prisoners are led out (objects, as always, come first). Twice, this is recorded on film with the meticulousness and redundancy of a bureaucrat. Doors that are opened, no matter how long they remain so, must be closed; money paid must receive its change. At times, Bresson's repetition is just this side of camp. The color blue is repeated to the point of absurdity: Yvon is a blue-collar worker, his work and prison uniform are both blue, as is the shirt he wears in the final segment of the film. Police uniforms, police cars — there is an accretion of blue such that there is no doubt that the plastic container for the prison mail must be blue, and even the doomed woman's water bucket is, inevitably it seems, the color of the state. Most peripheral people and objects come in sets of threes: three prisoners each time, three policemen, three judges, three kitchen towels hanging on the line to dry. Like a visual ellipsis, three is just enough of something to denote its **111** infinite repetition.

Susan Sontag characterizes Bazin's understanding of Bresson's rational repetitive style as a kind of dramatic prophecy being laid out.[15] By contrast, Sontag sees it as essentially an antidramatic deadpan effect, a complete lack of conventional suspense that produces, in addition to a space for reflection, a sense that everything is "foreordained" (184). She writes, "The key clatters in the lock; another interrogation; again the door clangs shut; fadeout. It is a very dead-pan construction, which puts a sharp break on emotional involvement" (183). Bresson's use of repetition, for Sontag, at one and the same time provides distancing and a sense of prescience.

Bazin's answer to Bresson's puzzling repetition derives from Kierkegaard, who wrote: "Repetition's love is in truth the only happy love. Like recollection's love, it does not have the restlessness of hope, the uneasy adventurousness of discovery, but neither does it have the sadness of recollection — it has the blissful security of the moment."[16] Kierkegaard defines his "ways of knowing, loving" into three categories: hope, recollection, and repetition: "Hope is a new garment, stiff and starched and lustrous, but it has never been tried on, and therefore one does not know how becoming it will be or how it will fit. Recollection is a discarded garment that does not fit, however beautiful it is, for one has outgrown it. Repetition is an indestructible garment that fits closely and tenderly, it neither binds nor sags" (132). For Kierkegaard, repetition is familiar, mature, but most important, repetition, unlike hope and recollection, is of the present. If Bresson's use of repetition can be derived in part from Kierkegaard, he, too, takes a visual, aural, epistemological comfort in the familiarity repetition produces; but prophecy, at this stage, would be the modern critic's (post Freud) intervention.

It is not clear whether Bresson's "compulsion to repeat" derives from a value on things that have stood the test of time or is itself a compulsion to test time. Shifting from philosophy to psychoanalysis, Laplanch and Pontalis show that Freud found repetition a bit more vexing than did Kierkegaard: "At the level of psychopathology, the compulsion to repeat is an ungovernable process originating in the unconscious; as a result of its action the subject deliberately places himself in a distressing situation, thereby repeating an old experience not recalling this prototype; on the contrary he has the strong impression the situation *is fully determined by circumstances of the moment* [emphasis added]."[17] Given that Bresson's peculiar use of repetition produces a distancing effect, the viewer is not so thoroughly convinced that "the situation is fully determined by the circumstances of the moment." In *L'Argent*, the water running after the scene of each murder, for example, harks back instead to the "ungovernable process" of repetition. Yvon, by contrast, gives the impression that he is merely responding to the circumstances of the moment. However shocking his responses may in fact seem in the rational light of day, they do not appear so while watching the film: They seem inevitable. The compulsion to repeat is a compulsion because it is cut off from its origins and becomes an "autonomous factor," which for Freud was not reducible to a conflict between the interplay of the pleasure principle and the reality principle but, in the final analysis, expressed the instinct's conservationism (which resonates well with Kierkegaard's old but snug-fitting clothing). But can we not also see *repetition* as an action or image cut off from its means of production? Is it possible that it is a kind of "reification of experience"? Could "conservationism," then, not be a fetishization of experience?

Lukács's theory of reification, of mechanical repetition, is a relevant model here. The mass production of commodities and identical thingness whose phantom splendor was derived from the fact that it masked the very conditions of its production and denied a relation between people approximates the effect and the means by which Bresson achieves his abstract reality. The camera's image appears free of its machinery, machinery that gives a phantom subjectivity to things and spirits the life out of people.

Not only does Bresson repeat the same shooting style from scene to scene but all his actors must act in the same way throughout the film: "It is necessary for the images to have something in common, to participate in a sort of union. For this reason, I seek to give my characters a relationship and ask my actors to speak in a certain manner and behave in a certain way which, furthermore, is always the same."[18] By repeating gestures, Bresson empties actions of their old, "inherent" meanings and estranges them. This, it seems to me, bespeaks for Bresson an allegiance to the primacy of the present world rather than to the machinations of fate or a spirit that is by default speaking the subject, as Bazin and Sontag both argue.

Bresson leaves the ultimate act of repetition, the reproduction of the image itself, to a thing. Echoing Bazin's and Epstein's sentiments about the impassive lens, he writes of the camera: "What no human eye is capable of catching, no pencil, brush, pen of pinning down, your camera catches without knowing what it is, and pins it down with a machine's scrupulous indifference."[19] The machine is the final autonomous organ of his phantasmagoria. "Scrupulous indifference" or a sense of cut-off-ness is the essence of Bresson's film form.

A series of tableaux often begin with the close-up of an object, itself an integral actor in the sequence of the ensuing shots. For instance, the film begins with a shot of a money machine, thus paving the way for the anonymity, rationality, and capriciousness that will be attributed as characteristics of money, one of the actors in the film. Another necessity of modern life, again a technology that disembodies, the telephone, begins the fateful sequence of the passing of the false note. An object that conceals identity, the red rubber gloves, part thing, part person, oily black from the fuel of the modern economy, return a gas hose to the pump. Next we see an oil gauge, the machine that measures and distributes capitalism's life's blood. Close-ups of these three objects form the establishing shots to initiate Yvon's ambiguous agency. The gloves themselves are a mark of this ambiguity.

Although the lively objects, the gloves, are an extreme example, close-ups of objects are continually used to ground medium shots that follow just as establishing shots are used in more conventionally shot films. This device gives to the object something not unlike an ontological presence, a point of view, a piece of the subjectivity that guides the film. Objects are, on a formal level at least, speaking the text if not its subjects. Bresson's repeated, insistent filmic demand that the spectator yield subjectivity to the "mysterious, silent" object answers Epstein's "wish to understand the lives of objects" in full measure.[20]

We can all but witness objects accrue their fetish power by their incessant repetition. The first shot of Yvon is a shot of his gloved hands. Already, they are more like independent things than part of his body.[21] A close-up of his hand then signals the first violent action in the film, his attack on the café owner. His hands are shot close-up again and again, accruing violent meaning but also becoming things in themselves, embodying these past actions. After he kills the hotel manager, they are foreign matter. When he walks down the hotel stairway after this first murder, the initial shot of the red oily gloves comes back to haunt the scene. As he walks down the stairs we see not his head but a bloody hand attached to a body in a medium to deep distance shot. The rich sounds of the water run from the sink where he washes them, but they exist now as a violent, repeatable fact such that only the bloody water needs to be shown. The missing shot of the hands signals a dark moment of transformation of thing into fetish. A bloody imprint of his hand in close-up on the house door of his penultimate victims, along with the sound of a single drop of water, are enough to signal the final violence that will ensue. When seated at the table awaiting his cognac at the film's end, he stares at his hands; strangers to him now, they have a life of their own.[22]

Money, a very particular object, comes alive in *L'Argent*, acting out and estranging its force as a demonic, unnatural commodity. Money's first appearance in the form of an allowance for one of the boys who will later initiate the counterfeit bill is quite modest. Money denied is seductive; when the mother's black purse is snapped closed it is framed such that it looks like Pandora's box. In the bedroom of the boy's friend, the counterfeit note supersedes the exchange of a watch, and before leaving, the boy looks through an album of nude women as though some mysterious power had been unleashed. When the false note is finally passed, the change — the effortlessly produced false profit (but effacing a world of social relations with devastating consequences) — crackles like lit gunpowder. Money, as hyberbolized capital through counterfeiting, is a "live monster" that is "fruitful and multiplies." Money maintains a role in the film until its end, when Yvon's final victim goes to the bank to get a large amount of money that is barely contained by her purse. Before he delivers his final blow he asks again for the money, although it's difficult to fathom why, so affectless has he become that he appears without desire altogether.

Although Bresson was faithful to Tolstoy's story, this is not the same money that changed hands in 1904 rural Russia. By counterfeiting a banknote, the boys in Tolstoy's story enacted the creation of capital, always a strange and mysterious commodity, but which then still *appeared* strange. After the wood salesman, on whom the note was forced, loses it to the café owner and is thrown in jail for the night as a drunk, he takes up stealing horses and becomes quite successful until he is killed by a character who becomes a murderer like Yvon. This character then is reformed by his last victim's forgiveness and becomes an ascetic pacifist who tells stories that circulate and in turn inspire people to do good works. Upon hearing one of his stories, for example, two prisoners, ordered to perform an execution in a neighboring village, refuse. The anonymous, mysterious power of capital to change people's lives is cut short as waste in the hands of the café keeper and transformed into storytelling. By contrast, in Bresson's story the capital is allowed to live out its devilish life, and Bresson goes on to tell the tale.

115

Another instance of estranged capital, the folklore of the custom of an illegally baptized peso bill in Cauca, Colombia, occurred in a society that lived at the crossroads between capitalist and precapitalist modes of production. Money that was secretly slipped into a child's Catholic baptism destroyed the ritual's effect on the child and came to embody the unnatural and unsettling power of capital. In one story, the baptized *billete,* alive with spirit force, comes to blows with another such *billete* when they meet up in a merchant's cash till.[23] The money takes on a life of its own and precipitates fortune or misfortune, ruining or producing great yields, for instance, from the cash crops for which it had provided the capital. The striking feature of all these examples (Bresson's money, Tolstoy's banknote, and the Cauca valley *billete*) is the way money embodies the anonymity and fatalism of magic. In none of these instances is the passing of the note guided by chance alone; certain people are in a better position to question, others must give change. Men are more disposed to the devil contract and its easy money than are women. The upper-class boys wield their class authority over the merchant woman such that she must accept the questionable bill. Yvon doesn't question the notes, and when he later protests, his class position defeats him. Yet money's anonymous agency does more than link the film together. Money, live and monstrous, makes things happen.

Some objects shimmer as material fetishes. The still life of carrots that burst forth from his living room as Yvon opens his front door, for example, is an object that just "looks as if it wants to be there."[24] Such an image, with its strange placement of an everyday object where it doesn't belong and its vibrant color, has no latent meaning; it is above all pure matter. The materiality of such an image has a likewise material effect. It addresses the viewer as a "corporeal-material being," seizing her, as Kracauer put it, "with skin and hair."[25] As with Benjamin's "innervation," the image grabs the senses, Miriam Hansen, and pulls them into direct contact: "The material elements that present themselves in film directly stimulate the *material layers* of the human being: his nerves, his senses, his entire *physio-logical substance.*[26] Held to their substance, objects so featured in *l'Argent* use film equipment in the way Benjamin and Kracauer had in mind.[27] Bresson's use of objects for their materiality is the visual equivalent of his use of sound. Tinkering this time in the holy land of the living room — the private space for the public sphere that is never so occupied — Bresson "retouches" this domestic tranquility with a bunch of carrots. Such optics crash through the mise-en-scène like peals of timpani where a doorbell normally suffices.

Jewish tradition contains a disinclination to measure men with a foot-rule because the corpse is measured in this way for the coffin. This is what the manipulators of the body enjoy. They measure each other, without realizing it, with the gaze of a coffin maker.[28]

When Yvon returns to the photography store where he was passed the counterfeit note to clear his name, he means to right the injustice done to his character. Dressed in the uniform of submission, Yvon does not speak but is spoken for by the policemen who have escorted him there. The question is asked, the lie delivered, and Lucien, a petit bourgeois dilettante who is here the shop assistant, is called in to confirm the lie that they did not give him the note. With a slight gesture of pique, an apparently spontaneous raising of his eyebrows, Lucien, who will later join Yvon in prison, puts on a real acting job, a virtuoso performance of commedia dell'arte mannerism. Instead of protesting, Yvon just turns away quietly and murmurs, "They are mad," with his back to the camera. He wears his understanding of his social place as plainly as his uniform. When he is fired from his job as a result of this trouble, and freed from his uniform, his gait bearing his social class doesn't change. He carries his leather bags, one over each shoulder, as if he were a burro.

Bresson's training for actors is that of subjugation or the erasure of the subject. In his *Notes on the Cinematographer,* he instructs directors to say to their "models": " 'Don't think what you're saying, don't think what you're doing.' And also: 'Don't think about what you say, don't think about what you do."[29] The subject is always tranquilized (it is the hand that acts out violence), and nothing seems more absurd than the scene in which they **117** administer Valium to Yvon, nothing more right than that his rebellion would be to attempt to tranquilize himself to death, as if merely finishing the injection. Equally numb is Yvon's final victim, well-schooled in accepting her lot. The scene in which we see her perform her daily chores is a dance of perpetual motion choreographed long ago. Each task leads effortlessly to the next without hesitation, no matter how spontaneous it must be. She moves from ironing shirts to cleaning up a broken wine glass as if she were dancing her version of "The Mind Is a Muscle" for Yvonne Rainer's *Trio A.*[30]

Although objects perform many a star turn in this film, Bresson devoted much thought to the training of actors. He did not want drama from his actors, but rather the unthought gestures that characterize much of how we behave in daily life. Real life is hardly dramatic, Bresson writes: "Nine-tenths of our movement obey habit and automatism. It is anti-nature to subordinate them to will and to thought." He trains his "models" to likewise become automatic. Once they have been trained by repetition and calculation they will be "right": "Models who have become automatic (everything weighed, measured, timed, repeated ten, twenty times) and are then dropped in the middle of the events of your film—their relations with the objects and persons around them will be right, because they will not be thought."[31] Bresson drains his models of spontaneity and habit so that they become zombies, filmic reified subjects playing out the last acts of capitalism's midnight show. They are right because they are not thought. To achieve this the Bressonian process bears some resemblance to methods of torture: "Model. Reduce to the minimum the share his consciousness has. Tighten the meshing within which he cannot any longer not be him and where he can now do nothing that is not useful" (48).

In *L'Argent,* the same form of acting serves for all of the characters, except of course when they are "acting," as with Lucien's overt dissimulation. What looks like elegance and reserve on the part of the upper-class characters in the film (the child's mother and father) becomes the merchant's keen eye for business and the accommodation of class structures (the shopkeeper's wife, in particular, as she reluctantly assents to accept the forged note), and finally serves just as easily to render submission and victimization (Yvon and his wife). The same deliberate and inexpressive acting style is, at all times, right.

Bresson's characters are right because they appear to exist effortlessly as social subjects in a highly rationalized world, their class uniforms and social assumptions fitted tightly over their skins. The people in *l'Argent* are not so much characters as walking social facts. Lukács saw the similarity (and virtual interchangeability) of all workers, regardless of what it is they do, by virtue of the fact that they were under someone else's control: "The hierarchic dependence of the worker, the clerk, the technical assistant, the assistant in an academic institute and the civil servant and soldier has a comparable basis: namely that the tools, supplies and financial resources essential both for the business-concern and for economic survival are in the hands, in the one case, of the entrepreneur and, in the other case, of the political master."[32] Lukács goes on to say, quoting Weber, that "the modern capitalist concern is based inwardly above all on calculation." Bresson's calculators (the gas pump meter, the money machine, the cash registers) and his formal calculating methods throughout the film are of a more ambiguous agency than the simple entrepreneur or political master. The objective camera lens, by its very indifference, bears the subjectivity of calculation itself. In its "scrupulous indifference," Bresson's camera shares the calculating gaze of the coffin maker.

Justice, meted out three times in the film, is equally calculated. Weber maintained that the system of capitalism required "a system of justice and administration whose workings can be rationally calculated, at least in principle, according to fixed general laws, just as the probable performance of a machine can be calculated."[33] At the pronouncement of Yvon's three-year sentence, the court disperses and Yvon is led back to prison in handcuffs. A shot of his wife precedes a shot of the exit door over which we hear the severe, even clack of high heels beating out the time of this sequence's final tableau. Bresson uses the familiar sound to estrange and to emphasize the law's calculation. We see it here in all its devilishly smooth, ritualistic rationality.

In addition to the camera and the law, another subject, the body, and particularly the female body, performs a silent role. The walls of the interiors are adorned with images of women, often nude. The frame and photo shop where the counterfeit bill is baptized is discreetly decorated with women's images and a single large "artistic" nude hangs upstairs, where the owners live. Perhaps the most striking set of women's images are those that form collages over the beds of each of the prisoners in their cells. Although Bresson refuses to give life to the live people's bodies— to animate the actors at all—he haunts the film with exotic pictures of women's bodies. This love-hate relationship with the body bears the traces of a phenomenon that Horkheimer and Adorno maintained in 1945 "colors all recent culture." Because of the unnatural division of body and spirit, they wrote, "The body is scorned and rejected as something inferior, and at the same time desired as something forbidden, objectified, and alienated."[34] Bresson resorts to the representation of the body as picture and photo perhaps because unlike the spirit, the body is something that can be got at, but only grasped as an object without spirit. "Culture," they wrote, "defines the body as a thing which can be possessed . . . a distinction is made between the body and the spirit, the concept of power and command, as the object, the dead thing, the 'corpus'" (232). The division between body and spirit pits them against each other. Repeatedly framing the body as photo (think of the young boys evenly turning the black pages of the photo album before they do their mischief), Bresson names the body as corpus, the dead thing.

Yvon's murders, in turn, might be seen as nature's revenge, as characterized by Horkheimer and Adorno: "In man's denigration of his own body, nature takes its revenge for the fact that man has reduced nature to an object for domination, a raw material. The compulsive urge to cruelty and destruction springs from the organic displacement of the relationship between the mind and body" (233). Because "the body cannot be remade into a noble object it remains the corpse." The corpse/body Yvon becomes nature's advocate for the body in the all-out "rancor for reification" that characterizes the entire film. Like a werewolf, he is akin to those destructive characters Horkheimer and Adorno strive to understand, who "repeat, in their blind anger against the living object all that they cannot unmake: the division of life into spirit and its object" (234).

The godless desert that dictates in Bresson's object world is "the new urban-industrial phantasmagoria dream-world, in which neither exchange value nor use value exhausted the meaning of objects."[35] Bresson "rouses" objects, in the form of the material detail, from their "death-sleep."[36] If Bresson has a "spiritual style," it is akin to Benjamin's notion of redemption through "redeemable wish-image." For Benjamin, however, "it was as 'dream images of the collective' — both distorting illusion and redeemable wish-image — that they took on political meaning." The lived experience of all this, "the false consciousness of a collective subjectivity, at once deeply alienated and yet capable of entering into the commodity landscape of utopian symbols with uncritical enthusiasm is what Benjamin called 'dream consciousness.' "[37] Bresson operates on the all too perilous divide between alienation and dream consciousness. His cinematic power to neutralize the image, using medium shots and gentle camera movement, soft-pedals through the phantasmagoric landscape and avoids detonating the land mines of commodity fetishism to explode into the redeemable wish image on the one hand or fall into the murky waters of mere melo-drama on the other.

Bresson's cool negotiation through the phantasmagoria gives his film its tension. Through his somnambulist aesthetic, his insistent repetition usurps the power of the dream state to create a state of profound fatigue. Although the fetish is inexhaustible, the Bressonian subject is always tired, fatigued. The power in *L'Argent,* the feeling of external control, is the power of the fetish.

L'Argent produces, both textually and formally, the modern elements of the phantasmagoria: alienation, repetition, reification, fetishization, the objectification and degradation of the body, and money as a live, un-natural thing. It is a world of fatigued, affectless subjects, shimmering objects, and tactile sounds. What we do in this phantasmagoria, whether or not it is the dream world from which we can retrieve our wish images, is still an open question. Perhaps this accounts for why one thinks, imme-diately upon viewing the film, that Bresson somehow got it "right" — and the numb stammering that realization produces.

In light of Bresson's narcotic poetics, it is somehow right that, when Patti Smith fell off the stage and broke her neck, she had a projector installed in her hospital room and watched movies: "for awhile there was only one film — *Au hasard, Balthazar.* i saw it several times under mild sedation. for a time my mind was a notebook of stills, annotation and the art of this century."[38] As Bresson put it: "Cinematography: a new way of writing, therefore, of feeling."[39]

Sacrifice is heat, in which the intimacy of those who make up the system of common works is rediscovered. — Georges Bataille, *The Accursed Share*

The collapse of conscious cognition into fatigue, distraction, or exhaustion produced fertile terrain for the animation of the object world. Although conditions do not appear to bode well, my interest here is in the emancipation we experience in illuminated images. Such is the nature of the reverie released when "the human motor"[1] turns toward the light, and the light of the cinema in particular. To return to the devastation Tess D'Urberville suffered by the ricks' domination, recall that while her senses were utterly broken apart from the machine's vibrations and the endless mechanical movement in which her body automatically participated, Hardy describes her condition in the following way: "The incessant quivering, in which every fibre of her frame participated, had thrown her into a stupefied reverie in which her arms worked on independently of her consciousness."[2] The "stupefied reverie" into which Tess was thrown by the brutal fusion of her body with the machine results for all of its violence in a fantastical, animated vision, the vision of a yellow river running up-hill: "Against the grey north sky; in front of it the long red elevator like a Jacob's ladder, on which a perpetual stream of threshed straw ascended, a yellow river running up-hill, and spouting out on the top of the rick" (426). This visual animation's appearance is provoked by the numbing effects of the machine on the sensate body as well as the social intimacy lost to rationalized labor. In this it presents a model of film spectatorship: an audience at a sensate and social loss with everything to gain in the cinema.

When Wolfgang Schivelbusch charted the felt effects of changes in lighting over the past two hundred years that culminate in the electric light-bulb, he began with the hearth fire. The breaking of the unity of the hearth fire, at once used for cooking, heating, and light, brought with it the dispersion of people in common spaces and the loss of what he calls the dreamlike quality of watching the flames, or flame in later gas lighting. This, he concludes, is what we look to when we turn from modernity's darkness toward the cinema: "Common to all these media, from the diorama to the cinemascope screen, is a darkened auditorium and a brightly illuminated image. . . . The world of the diorama and the cinema is an illusory dream world that light opens up to the viewer. He can lose himself in it in the same way that he can submerge himself in contemplating the flame of a camp-fire or a candle. In this respect, the film is closer to the fire than to the theatre. . . . The power of artificial light to create its own reality only exists in darkness. In the dark, light is life."[3]

I want to lay claim to this element of cinema's archaic past by taking up Eisenstein's connection between the animated cartoon and fire to suggest some further attributes of fire's reverie, and in so doing, show another side to Tess's otherwise morbid story.

Between 1940 and 1941, Sergei Eisenstein produced the core of a monograph on Walt Disney, whom he had befriended in Hollywood in September 1930. Eisenstein's abiding concern with art practices' "dual unity" differentiates him from Epstein and Benjamin, whose interests were in the way cinema spectatorship circumvented conscious cognition and led to a bodily felt mode of perception. This monograph, however, like his musings on sensual thinking in his earlier 1935 essay, "Film Form: New Problems," dwells mainly in the arena of "attraction," which was, after all, as Gunning indicates, originally Eisenstein's term coined very early on in his career as a dramaturge to connote the sensate spectatorship of the amusement park ride. Eisenstein's fascination with fire, whose moving flames prefigure the amorphous quality of the cartoon, touches on a phenomenon that bears on attracted spectatorship as well as the creative process.

The monograph on Disney is representative of the final trajectory of Eisenstein's thought away from a materialist, cognitive construction of cinema as a rational system of causes and effects whose efficacy resides in the images onscreen alone, toward primordial associations he investigates through his readings in anthropology and folklore. More important for us now, however, is that he attempts here to understand the very attraction of attraction, which has since gained new theoretical currency.[4] Constructively aligned with Benjamin's tactile (rather than contemplative) form of perception, the astonishments produced by the cinema of attraction are understood as a form of modern shock. On the one hand, it is representative of all that smarts when experience loses its final bits of ground to representation, but on the other, astonishment also produces an immediate sensation, a moment of physical joy.[5] In theory, this construction unfurls a profoundly modern nostalgia, repeating the moment of loss while the referent is long gone. Insofar as we turn away from explanation toward attraction's theoretical revelry, we regain the immediacy and the intimacy lost to what Bataille calls labor's "operations," the same loss, albeit in the far more sedate form of "reading," that Tess suffered at the hands of the rick.[6] The attraction of attraction, like the flame's intoxication, lies in its visual heat, heat that sustains thaumaturgical mental activity.

Reusing and rethinking material with which he had been occupied since his trip to Europe, America, and finally Mexico, Eisenstein points to the way the cartoon awakens and momentarily satisfies the human desire to become something else with its metamorphosing drawings. Like the playful nature of his subject, Eisenstein's text consists of fragments and free associations around myriad examples taken from a wide cultural and temporal range of images. Key features of this unfinished monograph are the child, the phenomenon of fire, and animism.

Eisenstein's "dual unity" notwithstanding, this monograph is concerned with the emancipation from logic, linear thought, social and even sexual repressions that is suggested to him by the cartoon form. Disney's figures, neither entirely animal nor certainly not human, are free to move, grow, and transform beyond "once and forever prescribed norms of nomenclature, form and behavior."[7] Animated cartoons are totally irresponsible; there are no actors, no biological or physical laws. "Like the sun, like trees, like birds, like the ducks and mice, deer and pigeons that run across his screen," Disney simply is, Eisenstein puts it, "beyond good and evil" (9).

The anthropologist Paul Radin described the famous Trickster of the Winnebago Indians with striking similarity. "In what must be regarded as its earliest and most archaic form, as found among the North American Indians," Radin wrote, "Trickster wills nothing consciously"; he "knows neither good nor evil"; he "possesses no values, moral or social"; he is "at the mercy of his passions and appetites." Although he is identified with certain animals, "Basically he possesses no well-defined and fixed form." As far as Radin can make out, "he is primarily an inchoate being of undetermined proportions, a figure foreshadowing the shape of man. . . . He possesses intestines wrapped around his body, and an equally long penis, like-wise wrapped around his body with his scrotum on top of it. Yet **124** regarding his specific features we are, significantly enough, told nothing."[8] The inchoate, amorphous quality of the cartoon is what fascinated Eisenstein most of all, and he locates its power in the archaic world of folklore and mythology.

The Trickster cycle could well have been used as material by Tex Avery or Chuck Jones, but probably wouldn't have tempted Disney. Disney's identification with the culture industry in Critical Theory, his association with McCarthyism, but especially today with the recent growth of Disney's entertainment parks, whose study is itself becoming an industry, makes it extremely difficult for us to see Disney's cartoons in particular in a radical, liberatory light. Eisenstein's reference to Disney as the supreme capitalist entertainer who provides the freedoms onscreen that are denied in real life does not even begin the criticisms that could and have been leveled. The wholesome American character of all things Disney with which anyone growing up in the United States over the past forty years has been force-fed makes any critique short of fingers down the throat inadequate. Although Eisenstein does consider Disney's cartoons to be the ultimate in capitalist escapism, his analysis concentrates on the formal appeal of animated metamorphoses. Despite the arguments for and against the redemptive character of the Disney cartoon and its reception in a significant public sphere,[9] what is of importance here, following Eisenstein, is not to worry the question of good and evil but to explore such freedoms from moral and physical constraints that are manifest in the animated cartoon, regardless of content or context. As Miriam Hansen has pointed out, these freedoms were not unnoticed by Benjamin, for example, and she reads their combination of technology and nature as a prototype for Benjamin's concept of innervation. "While mechanically produced," she writes, "the miracles of the animated cartoon seem improvised out of the bodies and objects on the screen, in a freewheeling exchange between animate and inanimate world."[10] The appeal of the hybrid creature—the not quite animal, not quite human mouse with gloves on its four fingers—extends to the animated cartoon in general: "The appeal of the animated creature, and this goes beyond Mickey, owes much to its hybrid status, its blurring of human and animal, two-dimensional and three-dimensional, corporeal and neuro-energetic qualities" (44). Eisenstein is using Disney to talk about the cartoon form itself, and the cartoon form itself to talk about a much more basic attraction. Its appeal is old, as old as the Trickster myths, for instance:[11]

"He who chews me, he will defecate; he will defecate!" "Well," thought the Trickster, "I wonder who it is who is speaking. I know very well that if I chew it, I will not defecate." [But he keeps looking around for the speaker and finally discovers, much to his astonishment, that it is a bulb on a bush.] The bulb it was that was speaking. So he seized it, put it in his mouth, chewed it, and then swallowed it. [Later he begins to break wind.] "Well this, I suppose, is what it meant. . . . In any case, I am a great man even if I do expel a little gas." [He breaks wind again and again until "his rectum began to smart." This continues until he is propelled forward by his own wind's force.] Then, again he broke wind. This time the force of the expulsion sent him far up in the air and he landed on the ground on his stomach. The next time he had to hang on to a log so high he was thrown. However, he raised himself up and, after awhile, landed on the ground, the log on top of him. He was almost killed by the fall. [The force of his wind continues to strengthen such that he pulls up by their roots the increasingly larger and stronger trees he has clung to.][12]

Needless to say, the bulb spoke the truth. The story goes on, after ever more fantastical explosions, to tell of his being buried in his own dung, and then it goes on some more. Just as cartoons are often propelled by the drawn figure, the Trickster stories never stop; they slip from one magical event to the next as the Trickster ambles foolishly along, talking to trees, animals, people, and himself along the way, making mischief, doing truly terrible things, and taking care of his penis, which he carries, at this point in the cycle, in a wooden box.[13]

Eisenstein's fascination with Disney's animation is based on "the fantastical, alogical order" in which it is possible to "achieve a mastery and supremacy in the realm of freedom from the shackles of logic, from shackles in general."[14] Disney, says Eisenstein, "constantly gives us prescriptions from folkloric, mythological, prelogical thought—but always rejecting, pushing aside logic, brushing aside logistics, formal logic, the 'logical case'" (23). The freedom Eisenstein speaks of is the elasticity with which animated forms move and change, the amorphous quality of cartoon animation. The "attraction" of what Eisenstein terms "plasmaticness" is characterized by a "rejection of once and forever allotted form, freedom from ossification, the ability to dynamically assume any form" (21). Plasmaticness refers to "a being of definite form, a being which has attained a definite appearance"—the drawing in the cartoon—which nonetheless "behaves like the primal protoplasm, not yet possessing a 'stable' form, but capable of assuming any form" (21). The figure in the cartoon has a definite, but unstable, form. Why, wonders Eisenstein, who had, after all, desperately sought (and failed, in the eyes of increasingly powerful critics) to create films that would be intelligible and attractive to millions, why, he wonders not disinterestedly, is this attraction so attractive?

Eisenstein rehearses a few arguments. First, he considers the possibility that plasmaticness activates a " 'memory' of his own existence at a similar stage—the origin of the foetus or further back down the evolutionary scale." Though he finds this implausible, he does consider it if only to move on to locate the attraction to be an American one, which fills the desire that is as continually evoked as it is denied in capitalist society, the "ability to become whatever you wish" (21). The desire for omnipotence, to become something else, is of course, easily generalized, and he does just that by extending this desire to eighteenth-century Japan as well as high European society.

Although an urge to expand the reason for the cartoon's appeal even further emerges in the text with more examples, he doesn't claim that the appeal is universal. He concludes his exploration by leaving that question open: "A lost changeability, fluidity, suddenness of formations—that's the 'subtext' brought to the viewer who lacks all this by these seemingly strange traits which permeate folktales, cartoons, the spineless circus performer and the seemingly groundless scattering of extremities in Disney's drawings" (21). The desire for the ability to become "whatever you wish" bears a strong resemblance to the desire Benjamin articulated in his essay on the mimetic faculty. Here Benjamin refers not to the cartoon but to the human faculty for mimicry: "[Man's] gift of seeing resemblances is nothing other than a rudiment of the powerful compulsion in former times to become and behave like something else."[15] And indeed, the breadth of Eisenstein's examples—*Alice in Wonderland* (1872, UK), *Max und Moritz* (1865, Germany), the famous French satirist Grandville (1842)—would suggest that this desire is not specific to American capitalism. When Eisenstein refers plasmaticness to "a lost changeability," he is certainly contemplating something more basic than yet not uncongenial to the conditions of noncapitalistic society.

If one follows Eisenstein's logic, there is a sense in which the cartoon, though drawn, still belongs to the unfettered medium of film, with its direct transfer of reality, as Bazin referred to it. Eisenstein finds cartoon **127** drawing to be similar in form to early cave drawing, which he maintains was automatic and merely deployed the body to trace the contours of animals and objects. The "stroke drawing, a line with only one contour, is the very earliest type of drawing — cave drawings. In my opinion, this is not yet a consciously creative act, but the simple automatism of 'outlining a contour.' It is a roving eye, from which movement the hand has not yet been separated."[16] As a primitive form of copying, animation answers the desire for mimicry, which for Eisenstein was primitive in nature: "Such is the stage [the first stage] where the 'animalization' (the opposite process of the 'personification' of an ape, moving forward) of man, with the effect of the reconstruction of the sensuous system of thought, occurs not through identification (cf. the second stage — Bororo), but through *likening*" (51; emphasis added).

Although he does generalize the components of the attraction of the cartoon, finding its roots in animistic belief and the appeal of fire, Eisenstein remains firm that the desire for such displacement as the cartoon offers is rooted in repression: "It's interesting that the same kind of 'flight' into an animal skin and the humanization of animals is apparently characteristic for many ages, and is especially sharply expressed as a lack of humaneness in systems of social government or philosophy, whether it's the age of American mechanization in the realm of life, welfare and morals, or the age of . . . mathematical abstraction and metaphysics in philosophy" (33). Repression reactivates the "compulsion in former times" and invigorates that "lost changeability" to burst out of one form and into another, returning the archaic mimetic faculty, this time, as cartoons.

At the point in Eisenstein's text where he seems to founder to explain the reason for the attraction of plasmaticness, Naum Kleinman notes that Eisenstein had once put in, but then removed, the following reference to fire: " 'Between plasmation and fire.' But there is yet another element, even more plasmatic, more free in its diversity, more tempestuous in the rate at which it engenders the most unexpected outlines. And of course, it too is rendered its due by Disney's creative imagination. *The Moth and the Flame* is the name of this film" (22). Eisenstein brings in this film and the amorphous phenomenon of fire a few pages later on, but the direction toward fire and the reasons for its association when foundering on the rocks of reason, when trying to explain this compulsion, may well rest with the captivating nature of fire itself. The connection between animism and fire is basic, according to the French philosopher Gaston Bachelard (1884–1963). Put simply, "When one gets to the bottom of animism, one always finds calorism. What I recognize to be living — living in the immediate sense — is what I recognize as being hot."[17]

Though Bachelard's remark refers to animism rather than animation, Eisenstein linked the two in the same way he had earlier linked cinema identification, metaphor, and metonymy to primitive belief:[18] "The very idea, if you will, of the animated cartoon is like a direct embodiment of the method of animism. Whether a momentary supplying of an inanimate object with life and a soul, which we also preserve when we bump into a chair and curse it as though it were a living being, or whether a long-term supplying with life, with which primitive man endows inanimate nature. And thus, what Disney does is connected with one of the deepest-set traits of man's early psyche."[19] As if animated himself at the warm sign of life from the fire's glow, Eisenstein abruptly launches into a theme that he will sustain throughout the work: "The ghostly mask which prophesies to the witch in *Snow White,* appears in . . . fire. And what, if not fire, is capable of most fully conveying the dream of a flowing diversity of forms!? And thus arises *The Moth and the Flame.* Its hero is — fire" (24).

For Eisenstein, fire was an important element to consider as a foundation for the cartoon's attraction because of its movement, the way the shapes change while we watch it. Like music, its images flow continuously; they are eternally changeable, "like the play of its tongues, mobile and endlessly diverse." "Visions in fire seem to be a cradle of metonymies" (33). The animation produced by fire provides an opening through which sensuous thought can emerge: "Persistent suggestion through fire, the appearance of fire, the play of fire, images of fire, is capable in certain cases of provoking 'unconscious' and 'impulsive' conditions — that is, of bringing 'sensuous thought' to the foreground, and forcing 'consciousness' into the background" (32–33).

For sexologists and criminologists, Eisenstein noted, fire released repressed sexuality and aggression. He suggests that the attraction to fire is primitive, which explains why pyromania strikes the essentially immature: "When sensuous thought predominates — that is childhood." He gives the account of a fourteen-year-old girl whose case he discovered in his reading in German sociology: "Her desire to commit arson arose in periods of a sort of unaccountable melancholy and inner unrest. It was then that the desire to see fire would arise, then after she would always be calm." Like a **129** sexual release, "At the sight of a blazing fire, her heart tickles with joy, then relief and serenity" (32).

In "Acinema," François Lyotard goes further than this when he uses a lit match to characterize *jouissance* and that which is truly creative in film. Fire, which expends energy, can burn so as to be of use: "A match once struck is consumed. If you use the match to light the gas that heats the water for the coffee which keeps you alert on your way to work, the consumption is not sterile, for it is a movement belonging to the circuit of capital: merchandise/match–merchandise/labor power–money/wages–merchandise/match."[20] Lyotard overlooks the excess inherent in capital itself; that is to say, the system works far less rationally than he represents it here and it only really flowers when use value and merchandise explode into inutility. The distinction Lyotard wants to make between utility and pleasure is, however, clear enough: "But when a child strikes the match-head to see what happens — just for the fun of it — he enjoys the movement itself, the changing colors, the light flashing at the height of the blaze, the death of the tiny piece of wood, the hiss of the tiny flame. He enjoys these sterile differences leading nowhere, these uncompensated losses; what the physicist calls the dissipation of energy" (351). Lyotard identifies the dissipation of energy, these uncompensated losses, the child burning a match just for the fun of it, with *la jouissance*. By sterility Lyotard means that which has no issue: "Intense enjoyment and sexual pleasure insofar as they give rise to perversion and not solely propagation, are distinguished by this sterility." Furthermore, for Lyotard, such inutility is essential to the creation of a work of art: "It is essential that the entire erotic force invested in the simulacrum [in this case, cinema] be promoted, raised, displayed and burned in vain." Art must not only consume; ideally, it should consume itself: "It is thus that Adorno said the only truly great art is the making of fireworks: pyrotechnics would simulate perfectly the sterile consumption of energies in *jouissance*" (351).

Bachelard's interest in fire stems from his preoccupation with reverie. Like Eisenstein's "extasis," reverie takes one out of oneself. Like *jouissance*, extasis and reverie are preconditions of creativity. What we first learn about fire, however, says Bachelard, "is that we must not touch it."[21] With this interdiction comes "our first general knowledge"; thus the "child's problem of obtaining a personal knowledge of fire is the problem of clever disobedience. . . . Like a little Prometheus he steals some matches" (11). As with Eisenstein and Lyotard, Bachelard associates fire with the child and the childlike fascination with phenomena. Most important, fire is not essentially utilitarian but an object of contemplation, of reverie: "It is a phenomenon both monotonous and brilliant, a really total phenomenon: it speaks and soars, and it sings" (14).

Reverie, thought Bachelard, was the first and the "truly human use of fire." Its other uses, such as for cooking and heating, were secondary. Even its sensation of warmth is secondary to its visual stimulation of the mind: "To be sure, a fire warms us and gives us comfort. But one only becomes fully aware of this comforting sensation after quite a long period of contemplation of the flames; one only receives comfort from the fire when one leans his elbows on his knees and holds his head in his hands" (14). As Eisenstein had also observed, this contemplation is archaic by nature and most easily assumed and observed in children: "This attitude comes from the distant past. The child by the fire assumes it naturally. Not for nothing is it the attitude of the Thinker" (14).

Fire's attraction is unlike the linear involvement of the dream or the distanced perspective of a critic. Bending over toward the hearth "leads to a very special kind of attention which has nothing in common with the attention involved in watching or observing. . . . When near the fire, one must be seated; one must rest without sleeping; one must engage in reverie on a specific object" (14–15). Furthermore, reverie before the fire is less deep, more intellectualized than the experience of dreaming: "In our opinion, this reverie is entirely different from the dream by the very fact that it is always more or less centered upon one object. The dream proceeds on its way in linear fashion, forgetting its original path as it hastens along. The reverie works in a star pattern. It returns to its center to shoot out new beams" (14). Fire provokes intellectual yet nonlinear thought that occupies a space between the dream world and conscious cognition, enslaved neither to the dream's incessant linearity nor to the shackles of logic. While Bachelard goes on to call fire the "metaphor of metaphor" (111), the star pattern he evokes above, whose flames return to the center to shoot out new beams, provides an apt image for Eisenstein's claim noted earlier, that fire is "a cradle of metonymies." Eisenstein saw the cartoon's appeal, its unfettered, metonymic associations that went beyond good and evil, as a repetition of fire's attraction.

As with Eisenstein and Lyotard, Bachelard's fire is externalizing, it is **131** joyful, and it is excessive in its essence. He describes a medley of cookery that his grandmother prepared with eggs, soup, potatoes, and a waffle iron: "Rectangular in form, it would crush down the fire of thorns burning red as the spikes of sword lilies. And soon the *gaufre* or waffle would be pressed against my pinafore, warmer to the fingers than to the lips. Yes, then indeed I was eating fire, eating its gold, its odor and even its crackling while the burning gaufre was crunching under my teeth. And it is always like that, through a kind of extra pleasure — like dessert — that fire shows itself a friend of man. It does not confine itself to cooking; it makes things crisp and crunchy. It puts the golden crust on the griddle cake; it gives material form to man's festivities" (15). Even when it is functional, when used for cooking, fire always delivers an extra pleasure — "it makes things crisp and crunchy."

The possibilities for the meaning of fire, Bachelard pointed out, are limitless: "Fire is both cookery and the apocalypse" (7). In the context of Eisenstein, however, fire is freedom from static form, freedom from logic and cognitive thought; it is anti-authoritarian, and, with its built-in interdiction, its danger excites disobedience, even crime.

There is a further emancipation in fire's reverie, which, like the alienating evolution from the hearth fire to the electric lightbulb, is specific to the conditions of modernity. This is the emancipation from labor's fatigue, labor that so confounds the senses and so destroys intimacy that such a turn toward the animated light becomes not only a form of reverie, extasis, but also intimacy. In Schivelbusch's *Disenchanted Night,* the hearth fire, which is the original site of reverie and intimacy, is displaced by the sobriety and dispersion of electric lighting. Schivelbusch sees the turn toward the light of the cinema as a lonely one for a bereft, modern subject: "The illuminated scene in darkness is like an anchor at sea. This is the root of the power of suggestion exercised by the light-based media since Daguerre's time. The spectator in the dark is alone with himself and the illuminated image, because social connections cease to exist in the dark."[22] Although Schivelbusch may have film theoretical and psychological literature in mind to support the notion that "social connections cease to exist in the dark," this statement rings hollow. For darkness, even as it is evoked by Schivelbusch himself in reference to the campfire, cloisters intimacy. Just as the turning off of a lamp on the film screen conventionally signals that friends have become lovers, darkness shrouds the strangeness of strangers in the cinema and binds them, however weakly and momentarily, with the thrill of stranger intimacy.[23]

Whereas for Schivelbusch, "light is life," for Barthes it was the darkness of the cinema that was "the very substance of reverie." Entering the movie hall from the "twilight reverie which precedes it and leads him from street to street, from poster to poster, finally burying himself in a dim, anonymous, indifferent cube where that festival of affects known as a film will be presented," Barthes pens down the fecundity of the "urban dark."[24] He writes, "Not only is the dark the very substance of reverie . . . it is also the 'color' of a diffused eroticism; by its human condensation, by its absence of worldliness . . . by the relaxation of postures . . . the movie house . . . is a site of availability (even more than cruising), the inoccupation of bodies, which best defines modern eroticism—the big city." Unlike the "legitimate theatre," private screenings, or films on television, the "cocoon" of the theater houses subjects on the loose: "It is in this urban dark that the body's freedom is generated." This roving, anonymous, untendered consciousness ambles from the twilight of the out-of-doors to darkness inside: "In this darkness of the cinema (anonymous, populated, numerous) . . . lies the very fascination of the film (any film)." Such unrelated relations, such loose (social) connections, like those of the big city make their best appearance, for Barthes, in the dark.

I want to further suggest not that we turn, fatigued and alone, from darkness to light, nor merely from alienation to proximity, but that with the purchase of a movie ticket, we turn away from the rational to the excessive. Like the meanings set loose by labor's exhaustion, the light of the cinema partakes of the qualities of freedom that Eisenstein, Lyotard, and Bachelard illustrate with the phenomenon of fire. The scale alone in the cinema is excessive. Magnification, and in particular the close-up, wrote Epstein, "is the soul of the cinema."[25] He describes its effect on him:

I will never find the way to say how I love American close-ups. Point blank. A head suddenly appears on screen and drama, now face to face, seems to address me personally and swells with an extraordinary intensity. I am hypnotized. Now the tragedy is anatomical. The decor of the fifth act is this corner of a cheek torn by a smile. Waiting for the moment when 1,000 meters of intrigue converge in a muscular *dénouement* satisfies me more than the rest of the film. Muscular preambles ripple beneath the skin. Shadows shift, tremble, hesitate. **133** Something is being decided. A breeze of emotion underlines the mouth with clouds. The orography of the face vacillates. Seismic shocks begin. Capillary wrinkles try to split the fault. A wave carries them away. Crescendo. A muscle bridles. The lip is laced with tics like a theater curtain. Everything is movement, imbalance, crisis. Crack. The mouth gives way, like a ripe fruit splitting open. As if slit by a scalpel, a keyboard-like smile cuts laterally into the corner of the lips. (9)

Cinema too can produce the flames' amorphous star pattern of associative thought, just as it re-creates, albeit in darkness's isolation, quiet's secrecy, and in the crowd's public space, the intimacy we associate with gathering round the fire.

Fire's final seduction, of course, is bound to its initial interdiction. Bachelard cites the self-immolation of moths to flames in George Sand's *Dreamer's Story,* itself a slow-motion scene in close-up: "Why have I not the eyes of an ant in order to admire this burning birch log? With what transports of blind joy and of love's frenzy these swarms of little white moths come to hurl themselves into it! For them this is the volcano in all its majesty. This is the spectacle of an immense conflagration. This dazzling light intoxicates and exalts them as the sight of the whole forest on fire would do for me."[26] The "true axis" of this "*magnifying* reverie" for Bachelard is the unity of "death, love, and fire." This description of someone watching minute creatures and reacting on a larger human scale hits upon the final theme that binds fire to attracted spectatorship, which lies in its excessive nature. "The lesson taught by fire is clear," wrote Bachelard: "After having gained all through skill, through love or through violence you must give up all, you must annihilate yourself" (17).

The excessive nature of fire upon which Bachelard insists, and to which Lyotard connects Anemic Cinema, the cinema that is beyond good and evil—this sterile burning—is a release from the repression of usefulness. Bachelard invokes Aztec sacrifice, borrowing Giono's likewise hyperbolic prose. Such is the urge "among the Aztecs, among people whose religious philosophy and religious cruelty have rendered anaemic to the point of total desiccation so that the head has become merely a globe of pure

intelligence" (17–18). "Only these intellectualized people," says Bachelard, "these individuals subjected to the instincts of an intellectual," and
here he cites Giono's *Les Vraies Richesses* again, "can force the door of the
furnace and enter into the mystery of the fire" (18).

Self-annihilation destroys the working body—its utility—altogether.
Labor destroyed intimacy "from the start," according to Bataille, whether
it was slave or wage labor, because it parceled out people so that they
became things, mere parts of a scheme, and so destroyed their life's immediacy while working. He writes: "The introduction of *labor* into the world
replaced intimacy, the depth of desire and its free outbreaks, with rational
progression, where what matters is no longer the truth of the present
moment, but, rather, the subsequent results of *operations*. Once the world
of things was posited, man himself became one of the things of this world,
at least for the time in which he labored. It is this degradation that man has
always tried to escape. In his strange myths, in his cruel rites, man is in
search of a lost intimacy from the first."[27] By binding oneself to labor's
"operations," which involves effacing the present, one becomes a mere
thing, just an element in an operation. The "cruel rites," whose sum and
substance must be expenditure, inutility, excess, perform the intimacy that
is lost through such routine degradations of the soul.

It is labor's useful, material product that makes it so arduous and so
soul-destroying. Even subsistence farming, where the worker is bound
neither to wage nor market, is drudgery in this sense. The following tale
shows the change in attitude toward gardening when the fruits of labor
were reduced to serve a utilitarian rather than an excessive purpose. When
Donald Tuzin revisited the New Guinea village of Ilahita many years after
his fieldwork in the early seventies, he found, among the many dramatic
changes that occurred because the men had destroyed their secret cult, a
shift toward more efficient farming: "One important casualty was the male
prestige complex centered on the production, display, competition, and
exchange of long and short yams. Apart from the loss of periodic excitement and pageantry, the change removed the cultural incentive for the
production of food surpluses."[28] Because the yams had lost their cultural,
ceremonial function, far fewer yams were cultivated. Tuzin reports that
now, instead of the competitive overplanting and its attendant magical
practices, people merely plant yams for food: "People now plant only
according to estimated subsistence needs, having recently decided that

European missionaries were correct all along in insisting that the surpluses were wasteful and their purposes evil. The men now accept that the
competitions fueled by the surpluses were socially disruptive, which is
much less than half true, and that the magic used to grow the yams was
heathenish, which is true only in a name-calling sense" (34). The most
bitter consequence of the yam's reduction from ritual to victual function is
the way people now feel about laboring in the garden: "One interesting
consequence of this change is that garden work was converted from meaningful endeavor into unredeemed drudgery. In the past people at work
would sometimes remark on how hot it was, but never would they com-
plain about the work itself. Today, complaints about gardening are fre-
quent. People resent the labor, even though today's gardens are smaller
and shabbier than before, and the time spent in them is clearly much less"
(34). In this sense, all labor that is slave to utility alone is slave labor.

The same sort of loss occurs as light, in the form of raw flame, is contained and metered out by electrical means. Schivelbusch writes: "The
open flame of gaslight linked it, however distantly, with the old unity of
fire and light, but no reminiscence of this lingered with the incandescent
electric light. According to Bachelard, the incandescent bulb 'will never
allow us to dream the dreams that the light of the living oil-lamp conjured
up. We live in the age of administered light.'"[29] Furthermore, such "administered light" has a "sobering" effect on that which it illuminates.
Although objects appear more clearly, the lightbulb "flattens objects" such
that they lose their "poetic element," says Schivelbusch. He draws the
following illustration from an art historian who, during the air raids of
World War II, was forced to use candlelight: "This is something that is lost
in electric light: objects (seemingly) appear much more clearly, but in
reality it *flattens* them. Electric light imparts too much brightness and thus
things lose body, outline, substance — in short, their essence. In candlelight objects cast much more significant shadows, shadows that have the
power actually to create forms. Candles give as much light as things need
in order to be what they are — optimally, so to speak — and allows them to
retain their poetic element" (178).[30] With the loss of the candle flame's
shadows, which move such "that they have the power actually to create
forms," things lose their substance. Rational, electric light reduces things
from their "poetic element" to what I would call their functional element.

For Bataille, an overcast day had the same effect on things as did the electric lightbulb. The absence of the sun's brilliance brings things more clearly into view, or, as above, "objects (seemingly) appear more clearly." One does not turn toward the sun nor is one besotted by its impressive illumination, so that one sees things in all their dull utility. And just as the poetic brilliance of things gives way to their functional element in such undistracting light, so too, wrote Bataille, "slavery brings into the world the absence of light that is the separate positing of each thing, reduced to the *use* that it has."[31] A barn, for example, is just a barn that houses animals; its redness does not shine, it has lost the sun's excessive halo of inutility. Slavery casts this dull pall over all who so toil, as they are reduced to mere use. To circumvent this reduction to use, Bataille wrote, "Light, or brilliance, manifests the intimacy of life, that which life deeply is, which is perceived by the subject as being true to itself and as the transparency of the universe" (56).

The ritual of Aztec sacrifice in flames represents consumption, rather than production, par excellence. Inasmuch as it exceeds utility, it regenerates the intimacy lost to labor. Bachelard's and Lyotard's interdictions against fire's utility, the attraction of Eisenstein's plasmaticness, and indeed the renewed attraction of the theory of attraction, stand against the concept of utility. Bataille writes, "The victim of the sacrifice cannot be consumed the same way as a motor uses fuel. What the ritual has the virtue of rediscovering is the intimate participation of the sacrificer and the victim, to which a servile use had put an end" (56).

The turn toward the light of the cinema is not the dark, lonely one that Schivelbusch described, but rather a return to fire's excess, in which "the world of *intimacy* is as antithetical to the *real* world as immoderation is to moderation, madness to reason, drunkenness to lucidity" (57). And here we can add . . . as cinema is to real life.

CHAPTER 10

Pyrotechnical Reproduction

When a Cuna Indian is very sick, the curer takes illustrated magazines, trade catalogues, and newspapers, and places them around the sick person's hut. Then they burn the images, releasing their souls or *purbas*. The souls of the burnt images then go about setting up a store or emporium full of fascinating items. When the evil spirits come to invade the sick person, they are so taken by the show of wares that they do not enter the sick person's body. Instead of killing the sick person, the evil spirits, in effect, go shopping.[1]

Think of the animation of objects and their power to distract that was unleashed by the Cuna's burning of photographs as a cinematic event. The images, merely culled from old catalogues and magazines, themselves are utterly arbitrary; they move from the reified object beyond commodity fetishism with fire's speed. Not only are the photos hollowed out and interchangeable, as in the case of reified images; not only do they serve as ciphers, as in the case when fetish meaning rushes in apace with our rapidly discarded things; but the spiritual incarnation of these photos has the power to seduce attention, to attract and to distract, and in so doing creates its own world that competes so successfully with reality as to shelter the real body from harm.

For the film theorists and films with which I deal, the most critical feature of cinema is, as Benjamin put it, "not what the neon sign says, but the fiery pool reflected in the asphalt below."[2] Not the image itself, but its smoky second nature. This spectacular analogy of Cuna ritual to film presents us with a model for the structure of the relationship of the film image to reality. The Cuna *purba* is an exact copy, a spiritual double of a thing or person. What is more, everything — plants, animals, man-made things — all have invisible spiritual copies of their physical bodies.[3] The word that the first Cuna informant used to describe the uses of what is now called *purpa*[4] and translated from Cuna into English as "spirit" was actually "image": "Anywhere we want to go for image we can go. If I want to go far up in the blue sea I can go there for image and I can go under there too."[5] By using the spirit double it is possible to "go" anywhere. Recalling Epstein's description of film viewing, which repeatedly bears the traces of an encounter with a magical world, film's relationship to reality is the very source of its pleasure and its horror: "I see this unreal thing and I see it exactly."[6] The *purba* in Cuna curing is the animation of reality's other, or "this unreal thing," as Epstein says, such that the spectacle of animation has power over the *purba*'s other, that is to say, reality.

The curative potential of film images — how they might meet the political and cultural task to hand of transforming a society in peril, in part at least because of the very technology and mode of production that characterize cinema — was central to both Walter Benjamin's and Siegfried Kracauer's interest in the medium. The ability to both represent reality's thinglike nature and to move those images, to see them close up, in detail, from many different angles, to not only move the spectator through new configurations of space but to expand, change time as well, offered a way of seeing that met the demands of representation in the modern world. A world that was fragmented and drained of living meaning, a world in which history, in particular, was erased by empty progress.

Understanding photography's properties was a necessary step for both Kracauer and Benjamin as they assessed the stakes when these still images were shattered onto the film screen. The American artist and writer Hollis Frampton (1936–1984) marked his transformation from photographer to filmmaker in the film *nostalgia* (1971) by burning photos he had taken in the prior eight years along with one found photograph. In that act of burning Frampton performs the arrest and release of time and the optical unconscious Benjamin had theorized. The film also addresses Kracauer's issue of history's absorption by unlanguaged static images, as well as the shattering of the surface haunting the exits of every picture palace.[7] The animation of the object from an old static image into its lively spiritual double and power of distraction to avert bodily harm, which is unleashed by the Cuna's burning of photographs, becomes a protofilmic event. In Frampton's film, the deathlike or residue-laden nature imputed to the photograph by Benjamin and Kracauer, respectively, are reordered to bring souls and things back to life from utter arbitrariness. Frampton's aim, achieved by releasing the spirits from his photographs by burning them while animating them with language, is to unlock temporality in this new medium so as to hold off the desultory effects of melancholia. Let us not forget, at the same time, that setting things on fire also partakes of the rites of an adolescent prank, which Frampton, as the film shows, was certainly not above. The aim of this chapter, however, is to demonstrate the manner by which the fetish character of the film image can be ignited and reanimated as a dialectical image and thus truly become a modern magical form.

139

nostalgia, a series of photos identical in size, narrated not by their own story but by the story of the photo yet to come, moves only when the fire burns, the smoke twists and turns, and the burnt carbon image quivers. Language, spoken by a narrator, which emerges only at those moments of burning, refers explicitly to times now gone, to memories. But the language, which is a description of an image, refers to the future diegetic time, to the next image we will see. By then, however, the time of this image will have passed. The film's story moves from the beginning to the end of Frampton's history as a photographer, from "the first photograph I ever made with the direct intention of making art" to the narration that precedes the film's final image. Then, after blowing up a "tiny detail" of a photograph over and over again, he was faced with an image that "fills me with such fear, such utter dread and loathing, that I think I shall never dare to make another photograph again." He pauses, and, turning the film over to the spectator, he says, "Look at it. Do you see what I see?" The final image is a complete exposure of black that fills the entire screen.

This abysmal plenum, which haunts every partial exposure, is the unspeakable residue stored in the thousands of dots that make a photograph. It is to the possibility of reanimating unintelligible, archaic nature that lays hidden, dormant in the photograph that Benjamin and Kracauer turn as they theorize the redemptive power of film. Frampton's film produces such a reanimation because of his rigorous engagement with this new form, fueled perhaps particularly in *nostalgia* by his passion for temporality, which, as formerly pursued in photography, had run up against that form's intrinsic limits.

Such an engagement, along with Frampton's written work on photography and history, provides favorable ground on which to illuminate the terms Benjamin and Kracauer set in their discussions of photography and film for history's redemption. Whereas, for Kracauer, the photograph was indeed capable of representing the reified world, it was through the spectacle of reification par excellence, the "mass ornament" that we must lead our attention. To do otherwise was a "flight from its reality."[8] And when looking at the mass ornament we should not be concerned with baser forms of meaning such as narrative, but with its shimmering surface of mechanical movement, disembodied limbs, repetition (70). Here we recall that in turning toward the mass ornament Kracauer is counting on its "double-edged nature"; that the apparent unity of the mass ornament is a false unity in the sense that it is made up of arbitrary fragments on the one hand, but a true unity because this fragmentation accurately reflects the state of the modern-day world on the other. It thus awaits its undoing. In turning toward Frampton's film and away from popular spectacle, we look, I suggest, in a more fruitful direction. In so doing, we turn toward film practice that by virtue of its formal structural interrogation emphasizes the filmic and, ironically enough, can really be said to be a cinema that goes through the mass ornament. Kracauer's emphasis on the disintegrating, shattering spectacle of film serves well as an announcement of Frampton's film.

Looking at Frampton's *nostalgia* in terms of Benjamin's dialectical image provides an opportunity for their cross-illumination. Benjamin's suggestions in the "Work of Art" essay about an optical unconscious stimulated by film's fluidity of movement and the shock value of montage,[9] though fundamental to Benjamin's theory and eminently present in *nostalgia,* become especially relevant when these properties work in the service of the dialectical image. If one takes the optical unconscious to be that which reawakens the language-mind that once signified in the constellations of archaic meaning when word and thing were one, it is important to sort out the mechanisms by which these archaic meanings can be reactivated. Now they are available to us only in new constellations that can be set forth through shock and awakening, through our ingenious facility to form nonsensuous correspondences, and through the tactile effects of modern media that circumvent contemplative perception. In this way, one can see film — perhaps not Benjamin's viewing of films but surely his idea of what they were — as fundamental to Benjamin. He describes the *Passagenwerk,* a work that was meant to create dialectical images from modernity's residue, as a "dialectical fairy scene (*dialektische Feen*)."[10] The form of the work, evoking both the dream-sleep and the devices of montage, is so similar to the speculations he made about film that the book could be characterized as cinematographic, with its attention to the tableau of shop windows and his exploration of the interstices of distraction.

As a documentary of Frampton's movement from photography to film, **141** *nostalgia* articulates, in a form that is minimal, tightly ordered, overly structured, and at the same time always subject to the arbitrariness that is controlled only by nature, many of the filmic redemptive qualities Benjamin and Kracauer felt lay in store. Frame after frame, the disjunction between sound and image, the chaos of the burning, thwarts our ability to create a continuous narration. *nostalgia* runs on the tension between the past and the present, between wild images and sure language. Its project, illuminated by Allen Weiss, is to work through a slice of Frampton's personal history and thus perform melancholia.[11] Weiss sees nostalgia and melancholia as the same emotional condition, the latter of which can be rearticulated from the more general, social term for psychoanalytic discussion. Melancholia is the work of cathexis and anticathexis from the many objects and things that stand in for the lost object. For Freud, one of melancholia's crucial problems was that you no longer know why you miss the person, or even who it is you pine for. In song form, it is easy to understand:

My old flame,
Oh what became of my old flame,
Even though I can't quite
Recall his name,
I just know I'll never be the same,
Till I find out what became,
What became of my old flame.[12]

Billie Holiday's singing of this Sam Laslow and Arthur Johnston song suggests not only the meaning of melancholia but the nature of its effect. It is not a strong passion. It abides. It flickers.

The object of melancholia, like the moment of the photograph, is lost. In a similarly ephemeral fashion, the power of history for a "society which strenuously attempts to appear ahistorical"[13] is also inchoate. The way the photograph effaced history and context was a significant property of photography for Kracauer. This presses to the surface today as kitsch, with nostalgia lying somewhere between the private and the public and organized around both speakable and unspeakable history. Although *nostalgia* is only about some small piece of one artist's manufactured history, the way Frampton uses film to address the problem of history is instructive. It suggests that film can rework the irrecuperable past in new constellations of meaning with a new temporality, however transitory, that is experienced in the present, and in so doing, it can bring time itself to life. The abiding modern disease was the waning of experience, the loss of felt time and the ascent of representation, or mediated experience. In rescuing the experience of temporality, Frampton uses the cinema as a form of magical healing.

To Benjamin and Kracauer, history placed an abiding strain on representation, even and perhaps especially in those cases where history and context appear entirely absent, as in the static old photograph. Photographs absorbed and contained time. For Kracauer, writes Heide Schlüpmann, "truth occurs — if at all — only in the realm of nature and only with the advent of a new temporality which is no longer the temporality of historical linearity."[14] When Kracauer says nature, Schlüpmann explains, he means that it occurs only in an earthly realm, in contradistinction to Kant's Christian metaphysics, in which truth was considered to be beyond an earthly realm. Placing truth within nature brings it back to earth, but it remains independent of human subjectivity. Film, neither beyond the earthly realm (for Kracauer) nor dominated by human subjectivity, could provide a venue for such an understanding of truth.[15]

Temporality was the key feature of the photographic medium that informed Kracauer's film aesthetics, according to Miriam Hansen: "The arbitrary photograph" could, to his mind, catch the alienated, historical reality that masquerades as objective reality and "render it strange."[16] Frampton refers to the moving camera's ability to catch otherwise hidden moments in his remarks on Ray Birdwhistell's filming of a schizophrenic child: "Birdwhistell filmed the mother in the banal and repetitive act of diapering the third child, a baby girl a few months old. Careful, frame-by-frame analysis of the cinema strip revealed that, during one moment in the process, the mother appeared to give the child simultaneous and contradictory signals, putting her in a confusing double-bind." Temporality in the sense of the movement of time that film can slow down, stop, catch, and examine is no less crucial for Frampton than it was for Kracauer. Frampton remarks on this examination, "If there is a monster in hiding here, it has cunningly concealed itself within time." The camera is a mechanism that can release the monsters time has trapped. "If it is dragons we seek," wrote Frampton, "or if it is angels, then we might reconsider our desperate searches through space, and hunt them with our cameras, where they seem to live: in the reaches of temporality."[17] For both Kracauer and Frampton, the camera beats a path to temporality, which is not a sublime but an earthly category, yet it escapes human subjectivity; it is the realm of dragons and angels. Temporality is a magical realm, to be got at by magical means.

With that ability to capture time, to seek out angels and dragons, the photographer perhaps could make a particular "incision" in time that could recover and release something from that instant. Temporality, so far predominantly a bestial domain, is nonetheless time we live and, more problematically, try to represent. The impossibility of satisfying that desire, of fixing a moment in time, maintaining its vitality, while living in yet another moment, becomes the subject of Frampton's *nostalgia*. He thus lays out the stakes for his new form (cinema), while ritualistically destroying its predecessor (photography) in his artistic career.

Benjamin presents an image that attests to the perilous nature of temporality with Klee's *Angelus Novus*. The angel, facing toward the past, is being blown toward the future while history's wreckage piles skyward in front of him:

A Klee painting named "Angelus Novus" shows an angel looking as though he is about to move away from something he is fixedly contemplating. His eyes are staring, his mouth is open, his wings are spread. This is how one pictures the angel of history. His face is turned toward the past. Where we perceive a chain of events, he sees one single catastrophe which keeps piling wreckage upon wreckage and hurls it in front of his feet. The angel would like to stay, awaken the dead, and make whole what has been smashed. But a storm is blowing from Paradise; it has got caught in his wings with such violence that the angel can no longer close them. This storm irresistibly propels him into the future to which his back is turned, while the pile of debris before him grows skyward. This storm is what we call progress.[18]

My interest here is not so much in the carbon that sits silently in front of your eyes — the "wreckage" that piles up beneath the feet of the angel of history — but in temporality. Temporality is the smoke, the text, the "torsion"[19] of the burning, which, though often thought destructive, is also, after all, the release of energy. Release and destruction combine as the excess of ritual sacrifice as the flames and smoke twist and turn over the distorted photograph. "Burning a photograph," Philippe Dubois suggests, "is only an extension of the photographic process: the photograph is a sensitive surface (like the soul) burned by the light that strikes it, and gnawed from within by the very things that allow it to exist: light and time."[20] Both a compelling object of contemplation and an elemental subject that can change and destroy, the significance of fire is limitless. Bachelard's observation that "Fire is both cookery and the apocalypse" is particularly relevant for a film that burns photographs on a hot plate.[21] Just as relevant is Benjamin's assertion that when delving into the secrets of modernity — its technology, for instance — the archaic is never that far off.[22]

Though all of these associations might serve *nostalgia,* Frampton's connection of fire to time is its central importance to the film. The following anecdote exemplifies Frampton's concern with their relationship. Writing about the problem of representing temporality in his essay "Incisions in History/Segments of Eternity," Frampton is captivated by the story of a race car driver whose car, going 620 miles per hour, went out of control and "sheared off a number of handy telephone poles, topped a small rise, turned upside down, flew through the air, and landed in a salt pond" in the period of "some 8.7 seconds." The driver, Breedlove, was unhurt. Breedlove made a tape to record his thoughts during those seconds. The tape lasts an hour and thirty-five minutes. Still, Frampton says, Breedlove was condensing, curtailing, making an even longer story short, at a ratio of some "655 to one."[23]

Frampton compares Breedlove's temporal expansion to Proust, Joyce, and Beckett. But Breedlove's most amazing remark, for Frampton, is what he uttered when he emerged from the wreckage: "For my next act, I'll set myself on fire" (99). The hour-and-thirty-five-minute monologue is, in some important way, that act of burning. Perhaps burning is the condensation of the experience into carbon and its release in smoking words, never quite adequate to the task. Or it is equally possible that Frampton sees Breedlove's words as an alternative to burning. Though I can never adequately explicate what fascinated Frampton about Breedlove's line, the connection between setting something on fire (in this case, Breedlove's own body) and the problem of representing the enormity of what a second contains — temporality — is central to an understanding of *nostalgia.*

The choice between burning, on the one hand, and baroque but always inadequate language, on the other, is a model for the representation of past time that is useful to keep in mind as we turn now to a description of the film itself.

In Greek the word means "the wounds of returning." Nostalgia is not an emotion that is entertained; it is sustained. When Ulysses comes home, nostalgia is the lumps he takes, not the tremulous pleasures he derives from being home again. — Hollis Frampton, in *Hollis Frampton: Recollections and Recreations,* by Bruce Jenkins and Susan Crane

Men are by nature tilers and inclined to every calling, save that of abiding at home. — Pascal, *Pensées*

A photograph appears on the screen in silence for about ten seconds (although the time varies, it is usually just enough time to see it and begin to make sense of it). The photograph is on a hot plate. A half-interested male voice begins to account for the photo in the first person, giving its place in time and space. The photograph remains static during this descriptive portion of the narration. As the narration begins to elaborate in the form of anecdote, description, or formal analysis, the image begins to burn. Shoots of flame and puffs of smoke narrate the narration. For example, when he refers to the gums and varnishes of a minor rival, the flames shoot up a little from the burning photo of a storefront, which in turn looks like a cubist painting, with all of its reflections and paraphernalia. The narration is a little confusing because the things he describes in the photos aren't there. You feel you've missed something. You'll look closer next time. The anecdote winds to a close, the burning ends, and the carbon flutters weakly over the hot coil in silence. This silence, accompanied by the spent image, lasts quite a while, almost as long as the storytelling itself. With the appearance of the next photograph it becomes clear that the task of setting the photograph to the sense of the words is less difficult than it seemed—it is impossible. The text refers, not to the image before you during the story, but to the next image. The image that burns in front of your eyes is never that which is enacted in language, never what you hear, and perhaps not even what you experience.

The moments of burning, burning the image whose story you have already heard but never had fixed to the image, and burning the words that can only partially be retrieved by its image to follow, make the viewer acutely aware of temporality. The language, so calm, so sure of itself, so soothing with its pleasant little narratives, is in no way anxious about this.

In her book *Black Sun,* Julia Kristeva characterizes melancholic speech that can be understood as the psychoanalytic variant of nostalgic speech. It is "repetitive" and "monotonous": "A repetitive rhythm, a monotonous melody emerge and dominate the broken logical sequences changing them into recurring, obsessive litanies. Finally, when that frugal musicality becomes exhausted in its turn, or simply does not succeed in becoming established on account of the pressure of silence, the melancholy person appears to stop understanding as well as uttering, sinking into the blankness of asymbolia or the excess of an unorderable cognitive chaos."[24]

Frampton's — or rather Michael Snow's, for it is he who reads Frampton's words — narration remains in the tenor of a monotonous melody, but toward the end of the film his interpretation of images suggests the descent "into the blankness of asymbolia" Kristeva describes. There is, perhaps, a mild sorrow about time no longer spent with some friends, but it remains separate from the viewer's busy task of watching the unrelated photo burn. The narration provides the time the photograph was taken, records some anecdote around it, marks references to other photographs, other exposures taken from the chosen one you see, or even other prints of the same photograph. Often, he analyzes the photo or at least assesses its merit. The dull, declarative sentences, the repetitive forms bore you, while the threat of "cognitive chaos" builds toward fatigue.

In the fifth frame (fourth story) the narration moves from portraits to other artistic forms. He mentions imitating action painting, produces a carving in clay that he casts in plaster, ponders the distinction between craft and art. Looking at the photo of Frank Stella (who we still haven't seen), he is reminded, "unaccountably, of a photograph of another artist squirting water out of his mouth, which is undoubtedly art. Blowing smoke rings seems more of a craft. Ordinarily, only opera singers make art with their mouths," calling attention to his own monologue. The photo of the artist James Rosenquist, which appears about halfway through the film, is the happiest memory, the photograph that "pleases me as much as anything I did." None of the normal dissatisfaction with either the photo or the event mark this story. If only in double negative, the memory abides: "James Rosenquist and I live far apart now, and we seldom meet. But I cannot recall one moment spent in his company that I didn't completely enjoy." The photograph is almost ecstatic in the spiraling movement of spattered light, as close to motion as any photo can be. Like a still from von Sternberg's *Der Blaue Engel,* it is stuffed full of things; at least three sources of light stretch the photograph's dimension far back into the room but also push its subject toward that space in front of the frame. The sour notes (the job was a "washout" and "we seldom meet") foreground the temporality of such ecstasy.

The next three photos aren't portraits but refer to ideas. Frampton was taken with the photographs of Lartique: "I wanted to make photographs as mysterious as his, without, however, attempting to comprehend his wit." Though it is the only photo in the film that has words in it — "I like my new name," printed on a dusty window — its meaning is mysterious. Mystery is overturned in the next story, which burns this "difficult" negative, with an iconographic study of two toilets. Interpretation surrenders to time and nature in a frame from a very slow stop-action series, a photo of moldy Franco-American spaghetti he selected out of a series that records the decay of the spaghetti over a period of two months.

The next to last image in the film is a found photograph from a newspaper. He works through this photograph in three ways, first as a photo of a person without a living referent, like the ahistoric, old photograph in the hands of strangers in Kracauer's study of photography: "A stubby, middle-aged man wearing a baseball cap looks back in matter-of-fact dismay or disgruntlement at the camera. It has caught him in the midst of a display of spheres, each about the size of a grapefruit, and of some non-descript color. He holds four of them in his cupped hands. The rest seem half-submerged in water, or else lying in something like mud. A vague, mottled mass behind the crouching man suggests foliage."[25] In the iconographic study of the two toilets, nature was ignored for referents in quite different time and space. In the photo of spaghetti, the passing of time and the growth of mold was recorded as an abstract image and refers mainly to itself. But this photo has no context, no reference at all, Frampton claims. It is a photograph without a history. For Kracauer, the ahistorical photograph creates a spatial continuum that is devoid of meaning, and effacing history, records only the remnants of nature. This facility to record empirical nature is not "nature in a positive sense, i.e. the immediacy of physis, but rather nature as a negativity of history. When photography records history it simultaneously annihilates every historical context."[26] Nature, the vague, mottled mass, emerges from the anonymous photograph much as Kracauer described it: "As long as the object is still present outside the photograph, the latter will be read as a sign of a reality. Only when even the memory of this reality has disappeared does the mimetic aspect of photography come to the fore; it becomes an archive of the residues of nature which are devoid of meaning, unintelligible, and, indeed, have never been perceived."[27] Mud, foliage, the residue of nature in this otherwise referentless photo proffer not plenitude but the possibility of a void — melancholia on a grand, natural scale: "I am as puzzled and mildly distressed by the sight of this photograph as its protagonist seems to be with the spheres. They seem absolutely alien, and yet not very forbidding, after all."[28] While on the one hand Frampton seems to suggest that a context, an anecdote like the others, would resolve the alienation the photograph provokes when he offers a plausible scenario — a fruit grower is assessing the damage to his grapefruit orchard by a hurricane — this arbitrary reasoning to make sense of the photo isn't completely satisfactory. Freed from historical reality, the photograph shifts through time and changes its significance once again: "Were photography of greater antiquity, then this image might date from the time of, let us say, Pascal; and I suppose he would have understood it quite differently." This third interpretation takes us back, back to "natural" referents, back to the ravages of entropy, back to fire.

Pascal, to my mind the philosopher of melancholia, might have seen the image as a model of a man perplexed by infinity: "But if imagination halts there [in the stars], let imagination pass beyond; it will fail to form a conception long before Nature fails to supply material. The whole visible world is but an imperceptible speck in the ample bosom of Nature. No notion comes near it. Though we may extend our thought beyond imaginable space, yet compared with reality we bring to birth mere atoms. Nature is an infinite sphere whereof the centre is everywhere, the circumference nowhere. In short, imagination is brought to silence at the thought, and that is the most perceptible sign of the all-power of God."[29] Pascal shows that finitude is impossible to reach either through pursuing

Nature's vast heavens or its most tiny progeny, which puts man, both a small speck within infinity and a body that contains still another infinite universe, in a state of eternal homesickness, to which one can only be **149** resigned, finally, through God: "We sail over a vast expanse, ever uncertain, ever adrift, carried to and fro. To whatever point we think to fix and fasten ourselves it shifts and leaves us; and if we pursue it escapes our grasp, slips away, fleeing in eternal flight. Nothing stays for us. That is our condition, natural, yet most contrary to our inclination; we have a burning desire to find a sure resting place and a final fixed basis whereon to build a tower rising to the Infinite; but our whole foundation cracks, and the earth yawns to the abyss. Let us then cease to look for security and stability" (25). Pascal was preoccupied early on not only with disproving the secure notion that Nature abhors a vacuum but more important, with challenging the reigning ideas that follow that notion—the need itself to see Nature a plenum. The image that begins his declaration of the faith required, that accepts the possibility of a void in Nature, that accepts man's eternal homesickness, is that of Fire.[30]

The final image of the film is a black photograph.[31] This is the enlargement of a twice-reflected speck, the "tiny detail" Frampton saw when developing a photograph that he developed over and over again. This is the image that, the narrator says, "fills me with such fear and such dread that I think I shall never dare to make another photograph again." This is an enlargement of one of the millions of dots Kracauer must ignore to see the diva, the waves, and the hotel beginning his essay on photography. Here, Kracauer imagines using a magnifying glass and sees "the millions of little dots that constitute the diva" on the cover of an illustrated magazine.[32] In Kracauer's terms, the black speck would represent history's residue, which so defies representation within the limits of photography. In the story of the film, Frampton approaches the taking and reproduction of the final image cautiously and obsessively. This stubborn speck is the unseen, uncontrollable time and space that, when exposed, even magnified, persists as black residue.

If fire is the signature of faith and redemption in a world haunted by infinity, by epistemic melancholia, and if the temporality of film portends our modern rescue, this black speck, the literal representation of the unfilled, unfillable vacuum of what persistently resists capture, is surely the imprint of modernity's hell. So the viewer sits, perched precariously between the temporality of fire's burning and its narrative score, and the continual reminder of silence and burnt carbon.

The anonymous photo's text, whose explication ranges from a news item to a philosophy, is but an extreme example from *nostalgia* that will neither fix meaning nor deny it. In this film, however, this is more significant than generic avant-garde insouciance. The context of the photos, and thus history itself, is both shifting within and essential to the film's form. This shifting is part and parcel of the stories Frampton tells, the lumps he takes as he returns home. Think how trite, indeed how wrong, a film on nostalgia would be that, for example, told those tales while the "correct" image burned. That would suggest, simply, that the experience of the narrator was there once and now is gone. This is not unlike what happens in the final image of *Citizen Kane,* where the mystery word peels and burns and history and meaning go up through the chimney in diegetic smoke, leaving viewers with the sense that they grasp something that is otherwise irretrievable. That mnemonic bonfire, its referents already fixed into the film, produces pathos. Only a heavy organ pedal is left to settle the score, leaving merely the notes' resonance to register the far trickier issue of what remains.

Frampton's method, by contrast, casts doubt on what was there, unfixes the image from its story, and places the story, which is, after all, a narrative form in the present, in constant peril of being subsumed by the burning image (that is, the past). In this, the film not only enacts nostalgia and melancholia but shock as well. The state of constant peril in which the spectator's ability to contemplate is mercilessly, repeatedly placed, produces such anxiety that a "breach in the shield against stimuli"[33] renders him or her vulnerable to the film's tactile ballistics. Another viewer describes the film's effect on him: "The end result [of the entire film] is the ruin of representation and a fascinating experiment in time. The psychic effect produced by the continuous viewing of the photograph's auto-consumption is intense, as if we felt physically that this carbonization of memory-images were actually taking place. We are left with the shriveled fragments of a life that in the end is little more than ashes. Something irreparable has happened before our very eyes."[34]

Constantly shifting between moments of intangibility and destruction, silence and the frenzy of language, the film's simple, albeit confounding, structure is unstable, nerve-wracking, exhausting. Like the central nervous system (which Frampton refers to as a constant in his autobiography, as opposed to his body, which has been replaced more than once), the film is "first system, then nervous." The nervous system itself, Taussig tells us, is no more stable: "A common impulse in epistemic panic is to run for biological cover, to escape from the whirlygigging of the NS: first nervous, then a system, — nerve center and hierarchy of control, escalating to the top-most echelon, the very nerve center, we might say, as high as the soul is deep, of the individual self."[35] Nonetheless, in citing the nervous system as a constant, Frampton is repeating a biological verity: "The tissue is irreplaceable. Its cells are unregenerative." And of course most of the other cells of the body (but by no means all) are regenerative. More exactly, if less poetically, Frampton would be left with quite a few specialized organs and his nervous system.[36] But his attraction to the nervous system is obvious. As Taussig maintains, "Even while it inspires confidence in the physical centerfold of our worldly existence — at least that such a center-fold truly exists — and as such bespeaks *control, hierarchy* and *intelligence* — it is also (and this is the damnedest thing) somewhat unsettling to be centered on something so fragile, so determinedly other, so nervous."[37] The nervous system is a constant reminder of the ephemeral nature of temporality. The film's fatiguing tension, however, cannot be accounted for without the virtual battle it enacts between words and images. Language creates this nervous tension. Strife between words and images seems to be a premier feature of melancholia, of homesickness.

An extended, more visually luscious, but hardly more restful version of this same tension can be seen in James Benning's *North on Evers* (1984), which, like *nostalgia*, could be looked at as a curing trip. In this film, Benning records a trip that he made on a motorcycle, filming the people and places that are his past, riding from his present home in California to his past homes in New York and Wisconsin and back again. Instead of a speaking sound track, he crafted a strip of handwritten text over the film-strip. This he calls "the road" for a road movie that otherwise has no road. Benning's refusal to put in the road, I think, is very similar to Frampton's not burning the correct images to the text. There is also atemporal mismatch with the words of the text, which describe things we have not yet seen, but the road itself would have been wrong regardless, for nostalgia is not a simple journey backward. It's the pall of the past on the present.

Like Bachelard's "little Prometheus," Frampton is also breaking a taboo with his fires. "Bomb the Museum!" he once said. "I will part gladly with the work of five years, into the bargain."[38] The burnt images represent photographic work from six, not five years of Frampton's career; however, his sacrifice of his own work pales by comparison to the destruction he metes out. Like dadaists and surrealists before him, Frampton disapproved of the elevation of art. "Carl André, old friend," he said, "I here accuse you of believing that art, first and foremost, should be elevating. I suggest instead that we elevate ourselves."[39] His treatment of these fellows in the film, not only André but Stella, the nameless painter upstairs in his building, and even Rosenquist, amounts to a dadaist assault. He burns their paints and varnishes, steals their girlfriends, and takes ridiculous pictures of them. Frampton's venture into sculpture, for example, *A Cast of Thousands,* whose unveiling before a neighboring couple resulted in an outrageous kiss from the attractive girl and the displeasure of her boyfriend, amounts to a silly joke.

Frampton makes sport of or otherwise defaces all the plastic arts, yet he leaves written forms unscathed. He aligned himself with Duchamp and, more specifically, his attention to language: "The rumor anyway that my mother's name was Rrose Sélavy is substantially correct, and I thank she has something to teach us all about the intimacy of the ties between language and perception."[40] Most odious to Frampton about abstract expressionism, specifically, was the elevation of art over language: "The terms of the indictment [by the painters of the '50s and '60s] were clear: language was suspect as the defender of illusion, and both must be purged together, in the interest of a rematerialization of a tradition besieged by the superior illusions of photography. Only the poetics of the title escaped inquisition, for a time."[41] That the monologue in *nostalgia* always coincides precisely with the image's destruction acts as a kind of retaliation for the primacy of the image brought to a head with abstract expressionism: words burning images. This linguistic arson goes a long way to redress the primacy of the image and tries to reinstate language, not only language as expression and language that might reduce mythic artistic authority but also language as a tactile force, albeit a monotonous force, into artistic practice.

The return of language to art practice in itself does not bring with it the clear calm of reason. Indeed, as discussed in chapter 2, cinema was thought to solve problems of expression by forgoing language altogether.

By putting in words that compete with the image, Frampton is pushing the limits of filmic expression, not merely to do so but because the subject requires it.

Frampton frequently articulates the tension between customary dirty language and the apparently pure images that early theorists had hoped film would sort out. In addition, words and images share a common problem: time. Neither photography nor writing can represent the present. Although one could argue that the tension between language and image and between present and past are the abiding concerns of all writing, the particular way this tension operates as the motor force in both Frampton's and Benjamin's writing on history illuminates the inadequacy of thinking about history as a continuum as well as the sheer futility of simply writing it out sequentially.

Among the many similarities between the problems Benjamin and Frampton encounter regarding language in general, they both make the same sort of remark about their subject's — that is, history's — specific demands. Frampton inserts a comment that simply registers the difficulty of the task: "At times, [history] seems impervious to language."[42] Frampton complains that while he sits and writes about history he cannot, at the same time, convey the window out of which he looks nor the desires he compresses. "Instead," he says, "I am enmeshed in these words. But I can't find the words to tell you what it is like to be writing them" (97).

Like Frampton, Benjamin often refers to the process of writing and making history at the same time. In "'[N]' Theoretics of Knowledge, Theory of Progress," he tries to incorporate the moment of writing into the text: "Say something about the method of composition itself: how everything that comes to mind has at all costs to be incorporated into the work one is doing at the time. Be it that its intensity is thereby disclosed, or that from the first, the ideas bear the work within them as telos. So it is with the present [text], which should characterize and maintain the intervals of reflection, the distances between the most intensively extroverted, essential parts of the work."[43] Benjamin's continual insistence that the form of the work be the nerve center of meaning makes it crucial that the process of writing about history be written into the next. Both Frampton and Benjamin pause frequently to alert the reader to the author's task. Often this takes the form of a preoccupation with windows, the desire prompted by the language-free world of images that is only to be complicated by the knowledge that those images are always, in an urgent way, laden with language. Both texts are driven by the tension between the primacy of the inchoate image on the one hand, and the power of language to fix meaning on the other. The window, for example, that Frampton wants to write into his scholar's study "and escape through it into the sunshine of an abrupt summary" suggests the abiding seduction of the image. But the written window, which displaces that other window through which Frampton looked to find images, is inadequate and injurious to the complexities of meanings he thinks and sees. Benjamin looks out a real window that he keeps free from the fetters of language: "the glassed-in spot in front of my seat at the State Library; a space never violated, terrain vierge for the souls of figures I conjured up" (2).

In the midst of their seduction by lucid language, they both voice the necessity to refrain from violating the image. Frampton voices his "irrational suspicion" of language in reference to Diane Arbus's photographs: "Freaks, nudists, transvestites, masked imbeciles, twins and triplets, inhabit an encyclopedia of ambiguities buried *so far beneath language* that we feel a familiar vague terror at the very suggestion of being asked to speak of them . . . an irrational suspicion that, should we ever find and utter a name for what these images mean to us we would so profane them that they might vanish like Eurydice, or fall to dust."[44] In *nostalgia*, the profaned image, the burnt photograph spent by language that quivers in front of us, registers this fall precipitated by language. That this is the same language that Frampton now chooses to write but that also served as a weapon against the authority of the image accounts for the most devastating sense of "torsion" in the film as well as the periodic allusions to fire, smoke, and violence in his text. This torsion of language on images and images on words is completely caught up in that other torsion I spoke of earlier, that of the past turning on the present while the present turns on the past. Both Benjamin and Frampton mean to harness this past/present/language/image torsion's power.

Benjamin and Frampton, both concerned with pulling images out of "historic time," articulate that action as awakening. Returning to Proust, Benjamin writes, "Just as Proust begins his life story with waking, so must ever presentation of history begin with waking; in fact, it should deal with nothing else."[45] In turn, thinking of Joyce, Frampton writes, "Even James Joyce, the most ardent of newsreel devotees, said that history was a nightmare from which he was trying to awake."[46] Their shared aversion to continuous, historical time sets them looking for a way to shock moments, images, ideas, monads out of that time and hold them in an instant. For **155** Frampton, "lasting amusement" and "sustenance" are achieved in the awakening to an "alternate and authentic temporality of ecstasy." He goes on: "It is obvious that historic time, though quite well suited to the needs of matter, is a terrain too sparse to afford the mind any lasting amusement or sustenance. So we must clear out, stand aside, and enter, if we can, the alternate and authentic temporality of ecstasy. I assume that everybody knows what that is" (96). In the spirit of Frampton's melancholia, temporality's foil, it is tempting to reply, I wish I did. For Benjamin, no stranger to melancholia, waking was no less revolutionary and equally lofty. He begins section "N" of the *Passagenwerk* with a line from one of Marx's letters: "The reformation of consciousness lies *solely* in our waking the world . . . from its dream about itself."[47] In *nostalgia,* Frampton wrests the image out of its place in a historical continuum, out of the "infinite cinema" to then "arrest consciousness and suspend its objects of contemplation, outside the ravages of entropy."

Waking and burning, shocking and blasting — clearly history's demands on representation are violent and urgent ones to Frampton and Benjamin. And all this for a representation that is only transitory: "The dialectical image is like lightning. The past must be held like an image flashing in the moment of recognition. A rescue thus — and only thus — achieved, can only be effected on that which, in the next moment, is already irretrievably lost" (21). This passage from Benjamin suggests, in one highly condensed burst, the important affinity for fiery history that Frampton shares. But, unlike "the prophet's gaze, which catches fire from the summits of the past" (21), the fire here comes from old photos. The film is both a systematic rationing out of these images, to be understood in the context of a text now hardly completely recoverable but nonetheless assimilable through memory and curiosity in a rough manner to the next image, and a nervous play of mnemonics. The ungovernable way in which a burn coincides with a text enacts the erasure of one meaning and the reenchantment by another.

Benjamin puts a portion of a letter from Adorno, busy trying to rearticulate the concept of a dialectical image in no-nonsense prose, into the *Passagenwerk.* Adorno's recapitulation separates the concept into stages in a way that would never have tempted Benjamin, but these stages are useful not only to explicate the concept but to see how, with their temporary clarity, Frampton's use of the photographs in *nostalgia* can approach the status of dialectical images and thus illuminate a new sort of life, or afterlife, of objects.

Benjamin's quotation from Adorno begins with an account of the object's descent from use value to exchange and reification: "As things lose their use value, they are hollowed out in their alienation and, as ciphers, draw meanings in." Moving quickly from their short-lived, hollowed-out object status, Adorno then characterizes their fetishization, or their second nature: "Subjectivity takes control of them, by loading them with intentions of wish and anxiety" (6). Frampton uses one photo to stand in for another by inserting a photo whose meaning has already been spent in front of us while we listen to the story of another photo. Quite literally, "things stand in for other things." Frampton then takes control of them with his text and loads them with "wish and anxiety" (7). For example, while the text expresses regret about using lettering inappropriate to a photographed poster for an exhibit by Michael Snow, the text reads, "I wish I could apologize to him for that."[48] This is but a very literal example of the wish and anxiety that recur in the text as well through the disturbing smoky form the image takes on during its narration. Adorno further characterizes fetishization: "Because the dead things stand in as images of subjective intentions, these latter present themselves as originary and eternal." At this point it is clear that Frampton, like Benjamin, short-circuits the image's fetishization. Though Frampton loads his text with "wish and anxiety," he does not merely fetishize the image, for he doesn't attach this new meaning—the text—to the image you see. Instead, he burns that image.

It is at this point, the point of burning, the point of fetishization or refixing the image, that Adorno's definition of the dialectical image can begin. Benjamin was trying to theorize (and practice in writing) a way we could harness the power of the fetish: "Dialectical images are constellations of alienated things and thorough-going meaning, pausing a moment in the balance of death and meaning."[49] His definition articulates an apt description of Frampton's burning, then quivering, images. The alienated things (the photographs) are momentarily caught in the balance between death (burnt carbon) and meaning (its story, which lays waiting in the next sequence along with its replacement). In this liminal stage, the burning image is balanced in a "constellation of new meaning."

This new and transitory meaning is governed by the all but arbitrary fit of the irrelevant text to the photo, and also the very direct materiality of flames and smoke. The meaning produced here relies on the temporality of this complex conjunction or, in other words, on the properties of cinema itself. The film is hyperfilmic in these instances, relying on the tension between movement and time as well as language's narration. Even cinema's reproducibility has a particularly double-edged significance in this film's case. For the question remains whether the photos are really ever burned, on the one hand, and if the film can ever really be reseen, on the other. Frampton removes the very possibility of the distance contemplation requires, with his fiery assault and disjunction of narration to image. He so confounds contemplation as to make the desire for cognition, not normally associated with tactility, itself a palpable one. There is no moment when a photo can be considered with its story, yet by using these stories he repeatedly invokes the pleasure of such relaxing contemplation only to deny it over and over again until the film's final frame. For the fatigued viewer, temporality is everything, with each and every frame.

The quick and barely containable act of burning is crucial to temporality—that is, the containment of a piece of language-laden, image-filled time. Frampton's concern with temporality in this complex sense, like Kracauer's faith in a "new temporality," is similar to the dialectical tension Benjamin wants to create between the past and the present with the dialectical image: "It isn't that the past casts its light on the present or the present casts its light on the past: rather, an image is that in which the past and the now flash into a constellation. In other words: image is dialectic at a standstill. For while the relation of the present to the past is a purely temporal, continuous one, that of the past to the now is dialectical—isn't development but image[,] capable of leaping out. —Only dialectical images are genuine (i.e., not archaic) images; and the place one encounters them is language."[50]

Adorno's distinct yet, in practice, simultaneous phases, illustrates how the power of the fetish could be harnessed to form dialectical images. This seemed to Benjamin the most powerful way to renegotiate meaning in his industrial age. He thus amended Adorno's passage when he placed it in the *Passagenwerk* with the remark, "In the context of these reflections, one must keep in mind that, in the nineteenth century, the number of 'hollowed out' things increases at a pace previously unknown, because technical progress is continually putting more utensils out of circulation" (12).

Frampton's concern, however, is not to refunction commodity fetishism. It is both more general and more specific. Frampton's images are fetishes of the past. Like the commodity fetish, their meanings now bear a different yet powerful relationship to their original and long gone context while appearing to have none at all. Whereas the dialectical torsion of the film enacts the same kind of temporality that Benjamin theorizes and Kracauer demands, Frampton in his written work pits ecstatic, authentic temporality against the ravages of "entropy" (not against mythic authority) as artistic representation's abiding concern, "as if to repudiate, in the spasmodic single gesture of a revulsion only half-sensed, the wavering concerns of painting, purifying and reclaiming for itself those perfected illusions, spatial and tactile, which alone could arrest consciousness, and suspend its objects of contemplation, outside the ravages of entropy."[51] Entropy is a far less historical or political diffusion of meaning than the alienation-charged mystification that concerned Benjamin. But for filmmaking and aesthetics, the way Frampton works language and images away from entropy toward temporality, and from photography toward film, *nostalgia* could hardly be more so charged. Through his new medium, Frampton refunctions the "utensils" of artistic practice.

Amid the throes of technology's rapid acceleration, the task of refunctioning images and exposing disintegration was, for Benjamin, an urgent one: "at once a consequence and condition of technology. . . . 'The world of memory breaks up more quickly, the mythic in its surfaces more quickly and crudely, a completely different world of memory must be set up even faster to oppose it. That is how the accelerated pace of technology looks in the light of today's prehistory.'"[52] Frampton hits on the utopian possibilities of cinema while discarding photography in favor of cinema. In our present electronic age, which Frampton marks with the advent of radar, it is inconceivable that one could rework discarded utensils apace with technology. (Although it is possible to see Frampton's voracious mastery of ever newer technologies' specific powers in that way.) Instead, Frampton hones away at the crucial properties of cinema — movement, language, reproducibility — and compounds its two modes of perception: contemplative distance and tactile immediacy. By so producing that which most evades consciousness — both ecstatic temporality and its horrid inverse — Frampton restores cinema's magical power to curse and to cure.

Conclusion

A generation that had gone to school on a horse-drawn streetcar now stood under the open sky in a countryside in which nothing remained unchanged but the clouds, and beneath the clouds, in a field of force of destructive torrents and explosions, was the tiny, fragile human body. — Walter Benjamin, "The Storyteller"

This scene describes the predicament of the modern person after the Great War, but it also sums up the situation in which Benjamin found himself as he wrote these lines, four years before his death in 1940, after his arduous scramble over the Pyrenees to Port Bou. The other film theorists discussed here, who survived World War II, can also be pictured in this scene, as they too witnessed modernity's vast transformations of their landscape. Insofar as they share a sense that experience and contemplative thought were losing ground to representation and the fragmentation of perception, their writings bear the marks of the storyteller's grasp. Since then, representation has so outpaced and even consumed experience that the only defining difference left between them is that experience risks the life of the "fragile human body." Representation, no matter how "tactile," does not. Many of the things that used to fall within the realm of daily living are now a packaged tour instead of an exploration. Perhaps the paucity of bodily felt and contingent experience accounts for why films "touch." If this is so, it is also the reason why cinema needs to touch those parts of us that are in the most danger of atrophy.

It is easy to understand the depths of that generation's despair as they shivered under the open sky; we understand the grounds of theoretical skepticism all too well. Although the enthusiasms of these early-twentieth-century theorists are not so easily assimilated to an understanding of cinema as a recourse from this despair, it is nonetheless useful, and even gratifying, to try to understand the heights of their hopes. Their hopes rested, to a large degree, on what cinema could regain of our primitive, archaic past.

Caught between the modern future and the archaic past, these theorists produced texts that are by turns melancholic, exuberant, tentative, and willful. As singular as their voices sound, themes cohere: extending a theory of language to rescue what modernity would obscure; the sense that the primitive, like a monad that remains unchanged, is able to break open and render if not fathomable at least substantive a new time like an "anchor at sea"; and an increasing respect for the things and images that were in the process of reorganizing daily life as well as shaping modern poetics.

The concept of the primitive and the concept of modernity are big, solid, and ubiquitous. Modernity has its dates, its rich historical trimmings, its causes and effects. The primitive has real practices, beliefs, and places to live. Yet they float through time, they're always somewhere else, they threaten from afar, and they are always, always on the wane. There is always someone more primitive downstream, and the turbine of modernity upstream hums the constant threat that it will soon destroy our tenuous footing and wash away all that we have, all that we love. Small wonder then that modernity borrows so heavily from a kindred spirit, that which is solid but eternally awaits rescue.

In a book that deals with modern primitivist constructions, *Prehistories of the Future,* the editors characterize the enigmatic relationship in the following, similarly infinite way: "For a hundred years, the West has used the non-Western world to contemplate the prehistories of its future, and the contradictory results have shaped a multitude of social discourses worldwide. There seems to be no end to that dynamic, and no reason to suppose that the present has been freed from working out its complicity in it."[1] If there is indeed no end to that dynamic, nostalgia defines the modern condition and talk of "social construction" begins to sound more like a barker's snake oil or a miracle vaccine than the enormous care necessary to any real treatment.

The river in front of my window runs into the Hudson, which then empties into the Atlantic Ocean at New York City. Next to the river runs a canal, built by Irish navvies in the 1820s to carry coal from Pennsylvania to the city. From the Delaware to the Hudson Rivers donkeys dragged long narrow boats back and forth along this canal connecting them, and soon industries from textiles to cement cropped up alongside these water beds, using the river for power, cooling, drainage, and sustenance and the canal for transport. For the river's flow is too unstable, too much a victim of nature to serve such industrial transport. The canal, too calm, too lifeless **161** to sustain health and industry, depended on the river's water to regulate its depth. Together, for some seventy-five years, these two waterways provided resources to electrify the city, build its roads and bridges, warm its citizens, and employ those who lived along the way. Indeed, local lore takes much pride in the fact that our cement was transported along the canal to build the Brooklyn Bridge. And Roebling himself came up this way to rebuild the canal's aqueducts, which at points traverse the tempestuous river. The canal was a construction with high costs in money and poorly paid arduous labor. The traces that remain, finely cut granite and limestone fitted together like the stones of Macchu Pichu, inspire, as do all such monuments that store effaced labor within, a similar kind of awe. The river still has toxins as a result of its heavy industrial use.

Rather than thinking of a river that flows in one direction somewhere else along which "the primitive" and "modernity" can be placed, no matter which is privileged, I prefer to think of these terms as a system, like the canal and the river. Although the canal was constructed with money to serve a material need, and the materials it carried changed dramatically over this period because of industrial shifts, it nonetheless used the water from the river *and* the stone from its bed. The canal prospered for almost a century because of the continual replenishment from river to canal and canal to river. This system, with its sordid exploitation and its dazzling engineering, relied on unquestionably real things as well as on monumental construction in order to function. The system is now in shambles. The canal has been filled in at places in favor of manicured lawns. The locks tumble into disarray under large pylons built for high-tension wires that zoom along the river's edge, for the power company had the foresight to purloin the corridor in which the system had so prospered. Now 69,000 and soon 120,000 volts run along the tow path between the canal and the river where donkeys dragged the canal boats carrying coal. Progress follows a well-worn path. And inasmuch as modernity and the primitive both represent socially real and carefully served-up concepts that work in tandem, they too form a path that will not easily become overgrown. Like the Brooklyn Bridge, their monuments are too useful and too beguiling to escape continuous traffic and admiration.

There is no denying that cinema offers a safer passage than real life. But it also can travel farther over spatial and temporal distances. The canal is a more serviceable alternative to the river, but it depends on the river's material, its water and its stone, to deliver the goods in safety. The ruins that remain now, with tree roots pushing the finely honed rocks apart, confuse and tease at such an easy distinction not only between what is real and what is made up but also what sort of value each has for us. It is these ruins' intertwining of the archaic and the modern that now fascinates. For the nature *before* second nature, the nature from which these monuments were once so ingeniously fashioned, inevitably keeps pace with such dazzling feats of progress. Benjamin inserted the following extract into his "Theory of Progress": "The thoroughly transformed landscape of the 19th century remains visible to this day, at least in traces. It was shaped by the railroad. . . . Wherever mountain and tunnel, ravine and viaduct, torrent and funicular, river and iron bridge . . . are intimately related, we find the focal points of this historical landscape. . . . Curiously, they testify that nature did not sink into namelessness or imagelessness under the triumph of technological civilization, and that the construction of a bridge or a tunnel did not become the exclusive feature of the landscape; rather, the river or mountain immediately rallied to their side, not as victim to victor, but as a friendly power. . . . The iron train entering the walled portals of the mountains . . . seems . . . to be returning to its homeland, where the raw materials lie out of which it was made."[2] Like a locomotive zooming out of the mountain's tunnel bringing the iron ore with it, prehistory breaks open on the modern world. Traversing the line between raw material and material film, pro-filmic and filmic, reality and make-believe, nature and second nature, light and shadow move on a square, white piece of cloth. Like the locomotive, crafted in iron, that soars from the old to the new, the camera, crafted as much by archaic beliefs and desires as by glass lenses, joins the primitive to the modern.

Cinema rescues all that experience allows, save risking the body. In so doing, it provides a magical double with which directors can practice their craft, manipulating the spirit world so as to affect the real counterpart. In Frampton's combustion of photographs to produce temporality and Bresson's renewal of our sensitivity to violence that is nearby, both of these films, to my mind, touch endangered parts — not of the human body, but parts of our consciousness and poetic capabilities with regard to representation. I have attempted to show how this is done by analyzing the deployment of our fetishes, our mode of production and perception — in short, a cosmology of modern magic.

Most of us can recall, somewhere in the pockets of childhood memory, **163** the time when someone, not without a small amount of glee, exposed magic as a sham. The confirmation that magic really works, incessantly tested by children, is inevitably denied one disenchanting day. Mine was when Miss K. informed me that Mary Poppins was all a movie trick; she couldn't really fly. My daughter's was when she looked out at Sydney Harbour for the fairies I had assured her would glide across the water and all she saw were ferryboats. Could not the question of credulity of the spectator, of the degree to which seeing is believing, take part in the same enchanted desire to determine the efficacy of magic so worried by children? Unlike most cultures, our culture operates with a remarkably inelastic spirit world and is the only one in which people don't devote a fair amount of time and money to some magical form of ritual healing, divination, or spirit possession. The camera is our one magical tool flush with animistic power to possess, enchant, travel through time and space, and bewitch. In light of this, our theoretical speculations about the cinema are akin to the child looking furtively behind the curtain or checking out Santa's beard, whether to debunk the magician — or to confirm that there is such a thing as magic. The question of the degree to which cinema affects real life, like the issue of whether or not magic really works, is moot. The point remains that we, now, do not work without it.

Notes

Introduction

1 *Photogenie* refers to those properties of film that are specific to the form, the capabilities that differentiate it from other forms such as slow, fast, and reverse motion, pans and close-ups; the term was introduced into French film theory by Louis Delluc and further explored by French avant-garde filmmakers Germain Dulac and Jean Epstein.

2 There is obviously a lot more to be said about this film about newsreel fakery and cinematic authenticity, directed by Harold Rossen and shot, in part, in Dutch Guiana. However, none of the actors are Djukas, none of the dances are indigenous to them, nor is their language or ritual gear authentic. The canoes, paddles, and huts are authentic. Sally and Richard Price, anthropologists who have worked in this area for twenty years, pointed out these infidelities to me and also remarked that this film shows only Djuka men, whereas, they assure me, in real life there are women Djukas as well. Chapter 3 discusses the deployment of primitives' reactions to modern technology in the cinema.

3 Jean Epstein, in *"Bonjour cinéma* and Other Writings," trans. Tom Milne, *Afterimage* no. 10 (1981), referred to "the Bell and Howell" as a "metal brain" (14).

4 Given the properly refined analytical tools and more modest theoretical ambition than has been customary, films and their workings can be explained, Bordwell and Carroll assert, through logical analysis based on empirical data and sound reasoning. David Bordwell and Noël Carroll, eds., *Post Theory: Reconstructing Film Studies* (Madison: University of Wisconsin Press, 1996).

5 For a different set of dissatisfactions to cognitive theory, see Richard Allen, *Projecting Illusion* (Cambridge: Cambridge University Press, 1995).

6 Tom Gunning, "An Aesthetic of Astonishment: Early Film and the (In)credulous Spectator," *Art & Text* 34 (spring 1989): 31.

7 Ibid., 43.

8 Christian Metz, *The Imaginary Signifier,* trans. Celia Britton et al. (Bloomington: Indiana University Press, 1982), 73. The quotes that follow are drawn from 72–73.

9 Marcel Mauss, *A General Theory of Magic,* trans. Robert Brain (New York: Norton, 1975), 19.

10 "On the contrary, conditions at a film-show induce the spectator to feel as if he were in total isolation . . . the spectator's condition is close to solitary, intimate contemplation — he observes, as it were, somebody's dream" (Boris Eikhenbaum, "Problems of Cine-Stylistics," in *The Poetics of Cinema,* trans. Richard Sherwood, ed. Richard Taylor [Essex: RTP Publications, 1982], 10).

11 Guliana Bruno delineates this feature of spectatorship in the context of early Neapolitan cinema in "Streetwalking around Plato's Cave," *October* 60 (spring

1992). Clearly pushing aside a psycholanalytic understanding of a powerless spectator, she argues for its exteriority by analogy to the modern "panoramic gaze" as well as its central position in the public sphere. "Founded on the physical/emotional experience of both intimacy and collectivity," she writes, "film spectatorship dwells on the borders of interior/exterior. It offers 'an imaginary private sphere from the vantage point of public space'" (124).

12 I employ the term *inner speech* as defined by Paul Willemen, who dubs inner speech the "frontier creature," "where the subjective and the social are articulated" ("Cinematic Discourse: The Problem of Inner Speech," in *Looks and Frictions* [Bloomington: Indiana University Press, 1994], 52).

13 This description is a generalization from visiting *curanderos* in Venezuela, Colombia, Equador, and Peru over a ten-year period beginning in 1983.

14 Maya Deren, "Notes on Ritual and Ordeal," *Film Culture* 39 (winter 1965): 10.

15 Maya Deren, "An Anagram of Ideas on Art, Form and Film," *Film Culture* 39 (winter 1965): 20.

16 Ibid., 18–20, 26–29, 37–41 respectively.

17 Annette Michelson, "On Reading Deren's Notebook," *October* 14 (fall 1980): 49.

18 Stan Brakhage, "Metaphors on Vision," in *The Avant Garde Film,* ed. P. Adams Sitney (New York: New York University Press, 1978), 124.

19 Walter Benjamin, *One Way Street,* trans. Edmund Jephcott and Kingsley Shorter (London: New Left Books, 1979), 114.

20 Vachel Lindsay, *The Art of the Moving Picture* (New York: Macmillan, 1922), 32.

21 Georg Simmel, *The Sociology of Georg Simmel,* ed. and trans. Kurt H. Wolff (London: The Free Press of Glencoe, 1964), 409–24.

22 Walter Benjamin, *Illuminations,* trans. Harry Zohn (New York: Schocken, 1969), 84.

23 E. E. Evans-Pritchard, *Theories of Primitive Religion* (Oxford: Clarendon Press, 1965); see, for example, 26–28. The book is a critique of theories of primitive religion as understood not just by early anthropologists but by the "great mythmakers" of the last century: Darwin, Marx-Engels, Freud, Frazer, and perhaps Comte.

24 Raúl Ruiz compares filmmakers to shamans in "For a Shamanic Cinema," chapter 5 of his book, *Poetics of Cinema,* trans. Brian Holmes (Paris: Éditions Dis Voir, 1995). Like magic or witchcraft, the films that he considers shamanic are "crafted," and he calls on one of the Spanish terms for sorcery, *hechizo,* a preterit form of *hacer,* "to make," to enable a definition. See especially 74–78.

Chapter 1   The Moderns

1 Wolfgang Schivelbusch, *The Railway Journey: The Industrialization of Time and Space in the Nineteenth Century* (Berkeley: University of California Press, 1986); Lynne Kirby, *Parallel Tracks* (Durham, NC: Duke University Press, 1997).

2 Wolfgang Schivelbusch, *Disenchanted Night,* trans. Angela Davies (Berkeley: University of California Press, 1988).

3 Anson Rabinbach, *The Human Motor: Energy, Fatigue, and the Origins of Modernity* (Berkeley: University of California Press, 1992).

4 Thomas Hardy, *Far from the Madding Crowd* (1874; London: Penguin Books, 1985).

5 Thomas Hardy, *Tess of the D'Urbervilles* (1891; New York: Harper & Brothers, 1935), 414.

6 For an account of the ascent of the image, see Anton Kaes, "Literary Intellectuals and the Cinema," trans. David Levin, *New German Critique* 40 (winter 1987): 23–28.

7 For a study of the billboard advertisement, see Marcus Verhagen, "The Poster in *Fin-de-Siecle* Paris," in *Cinema and the Invention of Modern Life,* ed. Leo Charney and Vanessa Schwartz (Berkeley: University of California Press, 1995).

8 Karl Marx, "The Fetishism of Commodities and the Secret Thereof," in *Capital,* trans. Samuel Moore and Edward Aveling (New York: International Publishers, 1967), 76.

9 Noël Burch, "Primitivism and the Avant-Gardes," in *Narrative, Apparatus, Ideology,* ed. Philip Rosen (New York: Columbia University Press, 1986), 483–506.

10 Roger Shattuck, *The Banquet Years: The Origins of the Avant Garde in France — 1885 to World War I* (New York: Vintage Books, 1968), 80–81.

11 Ibid., 170–71.

12 Burch, "Primitivism," 487.

13 See, for example, John Goldwater's 1938 pioneering and still authoritative study of the subject in *Primitivism in Modern Art* (Cambridge, MA: Belknap Press, 1986); and William Rubin's two-volume book of essays that accompanied a large exhibition on the topic, *"Primitivism" in 20th Century Art* (New York: Museum of Modern Art, 1984).

14 Goldwater, *Primitivism in Modern Art,* xxiv.

15 Ibid., xxv.

16 For a sustained attack on the use of the primitive in the term "modern primitive" in art critical circles, see Maya Deren, *An Anagram of Ideas on Art, Form and Film,* (Yonkers, NY: The Alicat Book Shop Press, 1946), 14–17. A similar attack is leveled, with the specific example of comparing the cultural meaning of Warlpiri acrylics in their traditional verses with their market value, by the late Eric Michaels, "Bad Aboriginal Art," *Art and Text* 28 (1988): 59–73.

17 Michael Taussig, *Shamanism, Colonialism and the Wild Man* (Chicago: University of Chicago Press, 1985).

18 Richard Huelsenbeck, *Memoirs of a Dada Drummer,* trans. Joachim Neugroschel (Berkeley: University of California Press, 1991), 61–62. "This is probably one of the many manifestations in our time of the primitivistic tendency. I am reminded of the rediscovery of Negro art, the drawings in the caves at Altamira and Lascaux, the rediscovery of children's art, folk art, and so on. All of this is in line with an aesthetic and moral renewal."

19 See, for example, Marianna Torgovnick, *Gone Primitive* (Chicago: University of Chicago Press, 1990). For a critique and corrective to Torgovnick, see Marjorie Perloff, "Tolerance and Taboo: Modernist Primitivisms and Postmodernist Pi-

eties," in *Prehistories of the Future,* ed. Elazar Barkan and Ronald Bush (Stanford: Stanford University Press, 1995), 339–54.

20 Hal Foster, "The 'Primitive' Unconscious of Modern Art," *October* 34 (fall 1985): 45–70; James Clifford, "On Ethnographic Surrealism," *Comparative Studies in Society and History* 23, no. 4 (October 1981): 539–64.

21 Annette Michelson, "On Reading Deren's Notebook," *October* 14 (fall 1980): 49.

22 Clifford, "On Ethnographic Surrealism," 119.

23 Ibid., 120.

24 These examples are mine, not Clifford's. I refer first to Richard Huelsenbeck's dada sound poems using African drumming in Berlin 1915 in Huelsenbeck, *Memoirs*; second, to Georges Bataille's many uses of primitive customs such as Aztec sacrifice and Kwakiutl potlatch to reinterpret the general economy in terms of expenditure and consumption instead of scarcity and production in *The Accursed Share,* trans. Robert Hurley (New York: Zone Books, 1988).

25 Instances of primitives looking at the camera are often faked or forced by the cameraman to lend authenticity to the film, to show that the primitives were real primitives. Vincent Monnikendam's film *Mother Dao the Turtlelike* (1995, Netherlands) stunningly reveals this in the Dutch footage of Javanese victims of colonization he reassembled to construct the film.

26 Judith Mayne has productively worried the "primitive" as regards both Burch's and Gunning's contributions to the modern refraction of the term to investigate the ways in which — and she pointedly activates the term with scare quotes — the connotations of the term primitive infect and enliven issues that emerge in a consideration of women as filmed primitives, spectator primitives, and filmmakers such as Maya Deren, Trinh T. Minh-ha, and Laleen Jayamanne who deal in primitivism. In this, she is in a minority of scholars who have questioned the innocence of the term, questioned the easy yet fundamental way "primitive cinema" is commonly deployed interchangeably with "early cinema." See *The Woman at the Keyhole* (Bloomington: Indiana University Press, 1990), especially introduction, chaps. 5 and 6, afterword.

27 Elazar Barkan and Ronald Bush, eds., *Prehistories of the Future: The Primitivist Project and the Culture of Modernism* (Stanford: Stanford University Press, 1995), 2.

28 Sergei Eisenstein, *Film Form,* trans. Jay Leyda (New York: Harcourt Brace Jovanovich, 1977), 143–45.

29 Sergei Eisenstein, *Immoral Memories,* trans. Herbert Marshall et al. (Boston: Houghton Mifflin, 1983), 200–203.

30 Naum Kleinman, introduction to *Eisenstein on Disney,* ed. Naum Kleinman, trans. Alan Upchurch (London: Methuen, 1988), 2.

31 Eisenstein, *Film Form,* 28–44.

32 *The Old and the New* (1929), *Que Viva Mexico!* (1930–31), *Bezhin Meadow* (1935–37).

33 Eisenstein, *Film Form,* 122–49; Sergei Eisenstein, *Nonindifferent Nature,* trans. Herbert Marshall et al. (Cambridge: Cambridge University Press, 1987).

34 Vachel Lindsay, *The Art of the Moving Picture* (New York: Macmillan, 1922), 171.

35 Béla Balázs, *Theory of the Film*, trans. Edith Bone (New York: Arno Press and New York Times, 1972), 50, 48.

36 See, for example, E. E. Evans-Pritchard, *Theories of Primitive Religion* (Oxford: Clarendon Press, 1965), in which he critiques this notion as "rubbish" (106).

37 Walter Benjamin, *Illuminations*, trans. Harry Zohn (New York: Schocken, 1969), 236.

38 Georg Lukács, *History and Class Consciousness*, trans. Rodney Livingstone (Cambridge: MIT Press, 1971), 86.

39 I employ this term to describe the body of theory that emerged around the Frankfurt School, but I use the term to include Kracauer, Benjamin, and Lukács, who were not among its members.

40 Gertrud Koch, "Mimesis und Bilderverbot in Adornos Asthetik," *Babylon*, no. 6 (1989): 36–45.

41 Walter Benjamin, "Work of Art," in *Illuminations*, 233.

42 Walter Benjamin, "On Language as Such and the Language of Man," in *One Way Street and Other Writings*, trans. Edmund Jephcott and Kingsley Shorter (London: New Left Books, 1979), 114: "Things are denied the pure formal principle of language — sound. They can only communicate to one another through a more or less material community. This community is immediate and infinite, like every linguistic communication; it is magical. The incomparable feature of human language is that its magical community with things is immaterial and purely mental, and the symbol of this is sound."

43 Jean Epstein, "*Bonjour cinéma* and Other Writings," trans. Tom Milne, *Afterimage*, no. 10 (1981): 22.

44 Benjamin, *Illuminations*, 234.

45 Epstein, "*Bonjour cinéma*," 17.

46 Gertrud Koch conjures this image in a powerful probe of Kracauer's deflection of Holocaust atrocities: " 'Not yet accepted anywhere:' Exile, Memory and Image in Kracauer's Conception of History," *New German Critique*, no. 54 (1991): 97–98.

47 Siegfried Kracauer, *Theory of Film: The Redemption of Physical Reality* (London: Oxford University Press, 1960), 305.

48 See, for example, Koch, " 'Not Yet Accepted Anywhere' "; and Miriam Hansen, *Babel and Baylon: Spectatorship in American Silent Film* (Cambridge, MA: Harvard University Press, 1991), 112. In a refined analysis of the relationship of *Theory of Film* to Kracauer's earlier work, Hansen suggests that there is more likeness than has heretofore been acknowledged, and that his concern with materiality by no means vanished, but went unnoticed. See "With Skin and Hair," *Critical Inquiry* 19 (spring 1993): 437–69.

49 André Bazin, *What Is Cinema?*, trans. Hugh Gray (Berkeley: University of California Press, 1967), 9–10.

50 Walter Benjamin, " 'N' [Theoretics of Knowledge; Theory of Progress]," *The Philosophical Forum* 15, nos. 1–2 (fall–winter 1983–84): 6.

51 On melancholia in Benjamin, see Fredric Jameson, *Marxism and Form* (Princeton: Princeton University Press, 1971), 60–83.

169

Chapter 2   Savage Theory / Savage Practice

1 A remark that Bohr made to Heisenberg, which Frampton cites as an analogy to the circles of confusion ingrained in the very medium of photography. Cited in Hollis Frampton, *Circles of Confusion* (Rochester, NY: Visual Studies Workshop Press, 1983), 10.
2 Cited in Sergei Eisenstein, *Film Form*, trans. Jay Leyda (New York: Harcourt Brace Jovanovich, 1977), 84. Eisenstein uses this segment from Joyce's *Ulysses* to begin the essay "A Course in Treatment" (1932), in which he introduces the "inner monologue" in relation to his script for *An American Tragedy*.
3 Eisenstein, *Film Form*, 143–45.
4 Horkheimer and Adorno, *Dialectic of Enlightenment*, trans. John Cumming (New York: Continuum, 1989), 60.
5 Horkheimer and Adorno, *Dialectic*, 60.
6 Walter Benjamin, "On Language as Such and the Language of Man," in *One Way Street*, trans. Edmond Jephcott and Kingsley Shorter (London: New Left Books, 1979), 119.
7 Walter Benjamin, *Selected Writings*, Marcus Bullock and Michael W. Jennings (Cambridge, MA: Belknap Press, 1996), 1:88.
8 Béla Balázs, *Theory of the Film*, trans. Edith Bone (New York: Arno Press and New York Times, 1972), 41–42.
9 Jean Epstein, *"Bonjour cinéma* and Other Writings," trans. Tom Milne, *Afterimage*, no. 10 (1981): 34.
10 Eisenstein, *Film Form*, 130.
11 This was given as a speech at the All-Union Creative Conference of Workers in Soviet Cinematography, Moscow, January 1935.
12 Paul Willemen, *Looks and Frictions* (Bloomington: Indiana University Press, 1994), 27–28. This is also stated emphatically at the beginning of Benjamin's essay, "On Language as Such," 114.
13 Willemen, *Looks*, 27–55.
14 Boris Eikhenbaum, *The Poetics of Cinema*, ed. Richard Taylor, trans. Richard Sherwood (Essex: RTP Publications, 1982), 12.
15 Willemen, *Looks*, 46.
16 Willemen is citing Freud, *The Interpretation of Dreams* (Harmondsworth: Penguin Books, 1976), 468.
17 Sergei Eisenstein, *Immoral Memories*, trans. Herbert Marshall et al. (Boston: Houghton Mifflin, 1983), 201. These memoirs were written in 1946 while Eisenstein convalesced in hospital after suffering a heart attack. This section is not included in the new, preferred translation, *Beyond the Stars*, ed. Richard Taylor, trans. William Powell (Calcutta: Seagull, 1995).
18 Eisenstein translates *tierra caliente* more poetically than the customary "hot country."
19 These are by no means the only origins. In tracing the roots of "intellectual montage," Yuri Tsivian has argued that "the very idea of a character's inner monologue based on a network of puns comes from Symbolist prose," as the making of

October predates his reading of Joyce in 1928. Yet Eisenstein seems to conflate Bely and Joyce as "impulses towards the revision of the narrative technique of the film medium." A primary characteristic of this influence, "from a bowl of soup to the British vessels sunk by England [Eisenstein referring to Joyce]," is one of clever and imaginative, rather than meandering and sensuous associations. See "Eisenstein and Russian Symbolist Culture: An Unknown Script of *October*," in *Eisenstein Rediscovered*, ed. Ian Christie and Richard Taylor (London: Routledge, 1993), 141–42.

171

20 Eisenstein, *Film Form*, 130.
21 Inga Karetnikova, *Mexico According to Eisenstein* (Albuquerque: University of New Mexico Press, 1991). See also Annette Michelson, "On Reading Deren's Notebook," *October* 14 (fall 1980): 47–54; and Sergei Eisenstein, "Letters from Mexico," trans. Tanaquil Taubes, *October* 14 (fall 1980): 55–64.
22 Sigmund Freud, *The Complete Psychological Words of Sigmund Freud*, ed. and trans. James Strachey (London: Hogarth Press, 1975), 14:169.
23 Eisenstein, *Film Form*, 126.
24 Sir James George Frazer, *The Golden Bough* (London: Macmillan, 1976), part 1, vol. 1: 54.
25 Roman Jakobson, *Language in Literature*, ed. Krystyna Pomorska and Stephen Rudy (Cambridge, MA: Belknap Press, 1987), 113. The essay "Two Aspects of Language and Two Types of Aphasic Disturbances" in which he discusses this connection was written in 1956.
26 Both of these examples are in Eisenstein, *Film Form*, 143.
27 Lucien Lévy-Bruhl, *How Natives Think*, trans. Lillian A. Clare (Salem, MA: Ayer Publishers, 1984), 77, 48.
28 Balázs, *Theory of the Film*, 50.
29 Lévy-Bruhl, *How Natives Think*, 46.
30 Eisenstein, *Film Form*, 137–38.
31 Wilhelm Wundt, *Elements of Folk Psychology* (London: Macmillan, 1928), 69.
32 Eisenstein, *Film Form*, 144.
33 Freud, *Complete Works*, 14:171.
34 Eisenstein, *Film Form*, 144.
35 Mikhail Yampolsky, "The Essential Bone Structure: Mimesis in Eisenstein," in *Eisenstein Rediscovered*, ed. Ian Christie and Richard Taylor (London: Routledge, 1993), 180.
36 Benjamin, *Selected Writings*, 61; the citations that follow in this paragraph are all from 51.
37 See, "On Semblance," in ibid., 224.
38 Benjamin, "On the Mimetic Faculty," in *One Way Street*, 160.
39 Sergei Eisenstein, *Eisenstein on Disney*, ed. Naum Kleinman, trans. Alan Upchurch (New York: Methuen, 1988), 21.
40 Benjamin, "On the Mimetic Faculty," 160–61.
41 Karl Marx, *Economic and Philosophic Manuscripts of 1844*, trans. Martin Milligan (New York: International Publishers, 1964), 139.
42 Benjamin, in *One Way Street*.

43 Benjamin, "On the Mimetic Faculty," 161.
44 Sergei Eisenstein, *Film Sense*, trans. Jay Leyda (New York: Harcourt Brace Jovanovich, 1975), 14–15.
45 Benjamin, "On the Mimetic Faculty," 162.
46 Ibid. "And just as the film does not present furniture and façades in completed forms for critical inspection, *their insistent, jerky nearness* alone being sensational."
47 Walter Benjamin, *Illuminations*, trans. Harry Zohn (New York: Schocken, 1969), 236.
48 In "Mimesis und Bilderverbot in Adornos Asthetik," *Babylon* 6 (1989), Koch describes the infant who cannot physically reach an object and so grasps it with his or her eyes. Similarly, Rosalind Krauss uses the figure of John Ruskin as a child who, when denied toys, made seeing his form of play. See *The Optical Unconscious* (Cambridge, MA: MIT Press, 1993).
49 Benjamin, *Illuminations*, 236.
50 Miriam Hansen, "Of Mice and Ducks," *South Atlantic Quarterly* 92, no. 1 (winter 1993), especially 37–48; Hansen's introduction to the new edition of Siegfried Kracauer, *Theory of Film* (Princeton: Princeton University Press, 1997), xii; Hansen, "America, Paris, the Alps," in *Cinema and the Invention of Modern Life*, ed. Leo Charnay and Vanessa Schwartz (Berkeley: University of California Press, 1995), 381–84.
51 Hansen, "Of Mice and Ducks," 38. Here she is citing the first version of the "Work of Art" essay from *Gesammelte Schriften*, 1:445.
52 Annette Michelson, introduction to *Kino-Eye*, by Dziga Vertov, ed. Annette Michelson, trans. Kevin O'Brien (Berkeley: University of California Press, 1984), xxxix.
53 AKA *The Donbass Symphony (Symfoniya Donbassa);* director, Dziga Vertov. Ukrainfilm 1930.
54 Benjamin, "On the Mimetic Faculty," 236.
55 Leon Trotsky, *The History of the Russian Revolution*, trans. Max Eastman (London: Sphere Books, 1967), 1:376. "Leo Tolstoy looked deeper into the soul of the muzhik than anyone else." Trotsky goes on to compare the clever resistance by the muzhiks in the early days of the revolution to Tolstoy's idea of nonviolence.
56 Leon Trotsky, *My Life*, trans. Max Eastman (New York: Pathfinder Press, 1971), 88.
57 Sergei Eisenstein, *The Film Factory*, ed. Richard Taylor and Ian Christie, trans. Richard Taylor (Cambridge, MA: Harvard University Press, 1988), 257. Eisenstein refers to a contemporary slogan.
58 AKA *The General Line (Staroe i novoe).*
59 A. V. Chayanov, *The Theory of Peasant Economy*, ed. Daniel Thorner et al., trans. Christel Lane and R. E. F. Smith (Homewood, IL: Irwin, 1966), 174–75.
60 In contrast to the clear incentives called for by the likes of Chayanov, the ideology of the film as well as its portrayal of collective organization is obscure, as David Bordwell suggests in his analysis of the film, *The Cinema of Eisenstein* (Cambridge, MA.: Harvard University Press, 1993), 106–7.
61 *The Old and the New* coincides with the extension of the "state farms' drive to new

regions to create veritable cereal factories, which were to deliver the marketable surplus that was harder and harder to obtain as the peasant, lacking incentive, retreated into his shell" (Chayanov, *The Theory of Peasant Economy,* lx).

62 Sergei Eisenstein, "The Milk Separator and the Holy Grail," in *Nonindifferent Nature,* trans. Herbert Marshall et al. (Cambridge: Cambridge University Press, 1987), 39.

63 David Bordwell describes much the same shift in this sequence, but emphasizes instead the eroticism of such liquid excess. See *The Cinema of Eisenstein,* 107–8.

64 This subtle camera movement was pointed out by Annette Michelson. Look for it; it happens twice.

65 This is Annette Michelson's term.

66 Benjamin, *Illuminations,* 240.

67 Eisenstein, *Film Form,* 131.

68 Eisenstein, *Nonindifferent Nature,* 53.

Chapter 3 First Contact

1 See Tom Gunning, "An Aesthetic of Astonishment: Early Film and the (In)credulous Spectator," *Art & Text* 34 (spring 1989): 31–45.

2 This is Tom Gunning's term in "Cinema of Attraction," *Wide Angle* 8, nos. 3–4 (1986): 63–70. Gunning likened early film spectatorship to the attraction of a fairground spectacle.

3 I am indebted to Tom Gunning for this observation, confirmed by Lynne Kirby, *Parallel Tracks* (Durham, NC: Duke University Press, 1997) 20, though their dates differ.

4 Béla Balázs, *Theory of the Film,* trans. Edith Bone (New York: Arno Press and New York Times, 1972), 49–51.

5 Vachel Lindsay, *The Art of the Moving Picture* (New York: Macmillan, 1922), 8.

6 Gunning, "Cinema of Attraction," 63–70. Gunning's article argues that early cinema spectatorship was based on the attraction to the spectacle, equally present in Méliès and Lumière, rather than an "absorption" into the narrative.

7 Lindsay, *The Art,* 10.

8 Siegfried Kracauer, *The Mass Ornament,* ed. and trans. Thomas Y. Levin (Cambridge, MA: Harvard University Press, 1995), 75–88.

9 Lindsay, *The Art,* 13.

10 Karl Marx, *Capital,* trans. Samuel Moore and Edward Aveling (New York: International Publishers, 1967), 1:76.

11 Lindsay, *The Art,* 32–33.

12 Sergei Eisenstein, *Film Form,* trans. Jay Leyda (New York: Harcourt Brace Jovanovich, 1977), 144.

13 Lindsay, *The Art,* 184.

14 Rev. John Casper Lavater, *Essays on Physiognomy for the Promotion of Knowledge and Love of Mankind,* trans. Rev. C. Moore (London, 1797), 1:19. Moore appears to have translated his name as well.

15 For a historical account of this appeal, see Antonia Lant, "The Curse of the Pharoah, or How Cinema Contracted Egyptomania," *October* 59 (winter 1992): 86–112.

16 Lindsay, *The Art*, 236.

Chapter 4 Close Contact

1 Béla Balázs, *Theory of the Film*, trans. Edith Bone (New York: Arno Press and New York Times, 1972), 41.

2 Gertrud Koch, "The Physiognomy of Things," *New German Critique*, no. 40 (winter 1987): 172.

3 Tom Gunning, "Cinema of Attraction: Early Film Its Spectator and the Avant-Garde," *Wide Angle* 8, nos. 3–4 (1986): 66.

4 Balázs, *Theory of the Film*, 24.

5 Miriam Hansen, "Benjamin, Cinema and Experience: The Blue Flower in the Land of Technology," *New German Critique*, no. 40 (winter 1987): 179–224.

6 Balázs, cited in Gertrud Koch, "The Physiognomy of Things," *New German Critique*, no. 40 (1987): 173.

7 Peter Sloterdijk, *Critique of Cynical Reason*, trans. Michael Eldred (Minneapolis: University of Minnesota Press, 1987), 139.

8 Bálazs, *Theory of the Film*, 58.

9 Koch, "Physiognomy," 168–69.

10 The late Epicurean Titus Lucretius wrote the poem variously translated as *On the Nature of Things* and *The Nature of the Universe* sometime between 100 and 55 BC.

11 Balázs, *Theory of the Film*, 65.

12 Siegfried Kracauer, *From Caligari to Hitler* (Princeton: Princeton University Press, 1974), 128.

13 Balázs, *Theory of the Film*, 64–65. I cannot positively identify to which film Balázs refers in this passage.

Chapter 5 The Secret Life of the Object

1 Jean Epstein, "On Certain Characteristics of *Photogenie,*" in *"Bonjour cinéma* and Other Writings,*" trans. Tom Milne, *Afterimage* no. 10 (1981): 20–23, delivered as a lecture in the fall of 1923, 22.

2 Sergei Eisenstein, *Film Form*, trans. Jay Leyda (New York: Harcourt Brace Jovanovich, 1977).

3 Roman Jakobson saw the meaning of the analogy between metaphor and metonymy on the one hand, and homeopathic and sympathetic magic on the other using distinctions formulated by Frazer in the *Golden Bough*. See "Two Aspects of Language and Two Types of Aphasic Disturbances," in *Language in Literature*, ed. Krystyna Pomorska and Stephen Rudy (Cambridge, MA: Belknap Press, 1987), 113.

4 Eisenstein, *Film Form,* 132.
5 Eisenstein does not distinguish between these two kinds of magic in his written work. However, this differs from his film practice. As Annette Michelson once verbally pointed out, in Eisenstein's cinematic representations of people, the upper classes are always metaphoric (homeopathic magic) and the peasant is always metonymic (sympathetic magic).
6 Georg Lukács, *History and Class Consciousness,* trans. Rodney Livingstone (Cambridge, MA: MIT Press, 1971), 86. The term appears in his chapter "Reification and the Consciousness of the Proletariat," where he writes, "Only then [when the commodity becomes a universal category] does the commodity become crucial for the subjection of men's consciousness to the forms in which this reification finds expression and for their attempt to comprehend the process or to rebel against its disastrous effects and liberate themselves from the servitude to the 'second nature' so created."
7 Karl Marx, *Capital,* trans. Samuel Moore and Edward Aveling (New York: International Publishers, 1967), 1:77.
8 Walter Benjamin, *Illuminations,* trans. Harry Zohn (New York: Schocken, 1969), 233.
9 Jean Baudrillard, *Simulations,* trans. Paul Foss et al. (New York: Semiotext(e), 1983).
10 Miriam Hansen, "Benjamin, Cinema and Experience," *New German Critique,* no. 40 (winter 1987): 204.
11 Fredric Jameson, "Reification and Utopia in Mass Culture," *Social Text,* no. 1 (winter 1979): 135.
12 Carel Rowe, "Illuminating Lucifer," in *The Avant Garde Film,* ed. P. Adams Sitney (New York: New York University Press, 1978), 116.
13 Jameson, "Reification," 137–38.
14 Walter Benjamin, *Charles Baudelaire: A Lyric Poet in the Era of High Capitalism,* trans. Harry Zohn (London: New Left Books, 1973), 56.
15 Walter Benjamin, *Das Passagen-Werk,* 2 vols., ed. Rolf Tiedemann (Frankfurt am Main, 1982); Konvolut H degree, 1, as cited by Susan Buck-Morss, "Benjamin's *Passagen-Werk:* Redeeming Mass Culture for the Revolution," *New German Critique,* no. 29 (spring–summer 1983): 214.
16 Susan Buck-Morss, "Walter Benjamin—Revolutionary Writer (1)," *New Left Review,* no. 128 (July–August 1982): 71.
17 Benjamin, "Work of Art," cited in Andreas Huyssen, "Introduction to Adorno," *New German Critique,* no. 6 (1975): 9.
18 I refer here to Northrop Frye's *The Great Code,* in which he reads Western literature against the biblical narrative (New York: Harcourt Brace Jovanovich, 1982).
19 Susan Buck-Morss, "Walter Benjamin—Revolutionary Writer (1)," says that for Benjamin, "The desire for pleasure, understood in its most material and sensual form, was a force of resistance against both capitalism and fascism, because their very existence required that this desire not be fulfilled" (64).
20 Robert Bresson, *Notes on the Cinematographer,* trans. Jonathan Griffin (London: Quartet Books, 1986), 101.

21 Naomi Schor, *Reading in Detail: The Aesthetics of the Feminine* (New York: Methuen, 1987), 61.

22 William Pietz, "The Problem of the Fetish, 1," *RES* 9 (spring 1985): 14–16.

23 Thomas Elsaesser, "Tales of Sound and Fury: Observations on the Family Melodrama," in *Home Is Where the Heart Is*, ed. Christine Gledhill (London: BFI, 1987), 43.

Chapter 6   The Metal Brain

1 Jean Epstein, "Cine-Mystique," trans. Stuart Liebman, *Millennium Film Journal*, nos. 10–11 (1984): 192–93.

2 Tom Gunning, "Phantom Images and Modern Manifestations," in *Fugitive Images*, ed. Patrice Petro (Bloomington: Indiana University Press, 1995), 45.

3 In a sequel, *Topper Returns* (1941, produced by Hal Roach, directed by Ray del Ruth), a far less outrageous assault on reality has the only truly magical moment witnessed by the chauffeur, played by Eddie Anderson, when Joan Blondell, an invisible ghost, walks with Cosmo Topper and he sees the footprints she makes in the snow. The rest of the supernatural movements of objects are seen only by Topper, who knows the ghost, and scant sightings that are shrugged off as eyes playing tricks.

4 The figure of the drunk as the observer of the fantastical has a healthy heritage. In Méliès's *The Inn Where No Man Rests* (1897), the poor, tired drunk is all but done in by his animated room. In Capra's *It's a Wonderful Life* (1946), it is the drunk who first sees the angel, Clarence. The spirit-seeing drunk himself becomes the subject of Henry Koster's 1950 *Harvey*. Elwood P. Dowd's (a full-time drinker) belief in the existence of his invisible friend, Harvey (a "pooka," which is a mischievous figure from Irish folklore), is contested and by turns sustained in increments until the film's end, when the pooka's existence is finally confirmed as the camera shows a change purse moved back into the aunt's purse by the invisible pooka. And in Lubitsch's *Ninotchka* (1939), the patriotic comrade played by Greta Garbo is drunk and sleepy when the photograph of Lenin she keeps on her nightstand changes his somber expression into a smile.

5 John Walker, ed., *Halliwell's Film Guide* (New York: Harper Collins, 1994), 1222.

6 Jean-Louis Comolli, "Machines of the Visible," in *Narrative, Apparatus Ideology*, ed. Paul Rosen et al. (New York: Columbia University Press, 1986), 753.

7 André Bazin, *What Is Cinema?*, trans. Hugh Gray (Berkeley: University of California Press, 1967), 110.

8 Philip Rosen, "History of Image, Image of History: Subject and Ontology in Bazin," *Wide Angle* 9, no. 4 (1987): 15.

9 Bazin, *What Is Cinema?*, 1:47.

10 Rosen, "History of Image," 15.

11 Bazin, *What Is Cinema?*, 1:48.

12 Siegfried Kracauer, *The Mass Ornament*, ed. and trans. Thomas Y. Levin (Cambridge, MA: Harvard University Press, 1995).

13 This discussion deals with the ornament in the mass ornament, rather than the "mass." For a discussion of the mass, see Miriam Hansen, "America, Paris, the Alps," in *Cinema and the Invention of Modern Life,* ed. Leo Charney and Vanessa Schwartz (Berkeley: University of California Press, 1995), and Gertrud Koch, *Kracauer zur Einführung* (Hamburg: Junius, 1996), 39–52.

14 Kracauer, *The Mass Ornament,* 79.

15 Tom Levin's footnote, in ibid., 356. The "Tiller Girls" are but the most famous example of a very popular form of entertainment. For a detailed history of such entertainment as well as an account of its mimicry of the Taylorist mode of production, see Günter Berghaus, *"Girlkultur,* Feminism, Americanism, and Popular Entertainment in Weimar Germany," *Journal of Design History* 1, nos. 3–4 (1988): 193–219.

16 Quoted in Ronald Haymen, *Brecht* (New York: Oxford University Press, 1983), 111–12.

17 Kracauer, *The Mass Ornament,* 79.

18 Karl Marx and Friedrich Engels, *The Communist Manifesto,* trans. Samuel Moore (New York: Washington Square Press, 1970), 63: "All that is solid melts into air, all that is holy is profaned, and man is at last compelled to face his real conditions of life, and his mutual relations with sober eye."

19 Kracauer, *The Mass Ornament,* 327.

20 Miriam Hansen notes Kracauer's reactions to Lukács's essay in "America, Paris, the Alps," 362–402, an essay that distinguishes Kracauer for his intimate association with the popular and the everyday and for constructing models for us at times more relevant than others of his ilk (Benjamin, in particular), because his thought is so concretely rooted in twentieth-century contemporary, rather than nineteenth-century literary material.

21 Georg Lukács, *History and Class Consciousness,* trans. Rodney Livingstone (Cambridge, MA: MIT Press, 1971), 90.

22 This essay had a profound influence on Benjamin too, when he read it in 1923. His argument about consciousness appears in *Charles Baudelaire,* trans. Harry Zohn (London: New Left Books, 1973), 58.

23 Ibid., 58.

24 Hansen, "America, Paris, the Alps," 370.

25 Kracauer, *The Mass Ornament,* 76.

26 Two key texts on the ideology of the apparatus are Jean Baudry, "Ideological Effects of the Basic Cinematographic Apparatus," in *Apparatus,* ed. Theresa Hak Kyung Cha (New York: Tanam Press, 1980), and Jean-Louis Comolli, "Machines of the Visible," *Film Theory and Criticism,* 3d ed., ed. Gerald Mast and Marshall Cohen (New York: Oxford University Press, 1985), 741–60.

27 Bazin, "Ontology of the Photographic Image," in *What Is Cinema?,* 12.

28 Philip Rosen, in "History of Image, Image of History: Subject and Ontology in Bazin," discusses Bazin's (or our) "obsession with realism" and emphasizes that the indexical nature of the image gives it both credibility and a sense of "pastness." "The Mummy Complex" is at once a defense against time, a preservative, and by virtue of the fact that the film image must come after, places the subject in a

fraught dialectical relationship to history. Prefiguring Deleuze's discussion of Italian neorealism, he writes, "The contradiction between the time-filled and the timeless requires its own understanding, in a peculiar balancing act" (29).

29 Aristotle, *Poetics,* in *Critical Theory Since Plato,* ed. Hazard Adams (New York: Harcourt Brace Jovanovich, 1971), 50.

30 Bazin, *What Is Cinema?,* 14.

31 Aristotle, *Poetics,* 50.

32 Bazin, *What Is Cinema?,* 11.

33 Maya Deren, "An Anagram of Ideas on Art, Form and Film," *Film Culture* 39 (winter 1965): 30.

34 Walter Benjamin, *Illuminations,* trans. Harry Zohn (New York: Schocken, 1969), 236.

35 Jean Epstein, *"Bonjour cinéma* and Other Writings," trans. Tom Milne, *Afterimage,* no. 10 (1981): 19.

36 Epstein, "Ciné Mystique," 192.

37 Epstein, *"Bonjour,"* 22.

Chapter 7 The Tired Lens

1 See, for example, Jonathan Crary, *Techniques of the Observer* (Cambridge, MA: MIT Press, 1992); Rosalind Krauss, *The Optical Unconscious* (Cambridge, MA: MIT Press, 1993); and Martin Jay, *Downcast Eyes* (Berkeley: University of California Press, 1993).

2 David Bordwell, for example, implies that the notion that "modernity altered human perception" is based on such scanty evidence as Benjamin's meager citation of fifth-century art for this broad assumption in the "Work of Art" essay. See David Bordwell and Noël Carroll, eds., *Post-Theory* (Madison: University of Wisconsin Press, 1996), 21.

3 This looseness is remarked upon and critiqued by Miriam Hansen in "America, Paris, the Alps," in *Cinema and the Invention of Modern Life,* ed. Leo Charney and Vanessa Schwartz (Berkeley: University of California Press, 1995), 363–66.

4 Jean Epstein, "Cine-Mystique," trans. Stuart Liebman, *Millennium Film Journal,* nos. 10–11 (1984): 192–93.

5 Stuart Liebman, "Jean Epstein's Early Film Theory, 1920–22" (Ph.D. diss., New York University, 1980), 111.

6 Liebman's source is Jean Epstein, "Le Phénomène littéraire," *L'Esprit Nouveau* 8 (n.d.): 860.

7 Liebman, "Jean Epstein's Early Film Theory," 111.

8 Walter Benjamin, *Illuminations,* trans. Harry Zohn (New York: Schocken, 1969), 91.

9 Siegfried Kracauer, "Boredom," in *The Mass Ornament,* ed. and trans. Thomas Y. Levin (Cambridge, MA: Harvard University Press, 1995), 334.

10 See Anson Rabinbach, *The Human Motor: Energy, Fatigue and the Origins of Modernity* (Berkeley: University of California Press, 1992). This book draws on an immense number of materials that range from physiology to Flaubert.

11 Jean Epstein, "Magnification and Other Writings," trans. Stuart Liebman, *October* 3 (spring 1977): 13.
12 Georg Lukács, *History and Class Consciousness,* trans. Rodney Livingstone (Cambridge, MA: MIT Press, 1971), 89: "In consequence of the rationalisation of the work-process the human qualities and idiosyncrasies of the worker appear increasingly as *mere sources of error."*
13 Marcel Proust, *Remembrance of Things Past,* trans. C. K. Scott Moncrieff (London: Chatto & Windus, 1964), vol. 1, part 1, 57.
14 Walter Benjamin, "Proust," in *Illuminations,* trans. Harry Zohn (New York: Schocken Books, 1969), 202.
15 Roger Shattuck, *Proust's Binoculars* (New York: Vintage, 1967), 150, calls these moments Proust's "moments bienheureux"; Samuel Beckett simply refers to them as Proust's "Fetiches."
16 Miriam Hansen, "Benjamin, Cinema and Experience," *New German Critique,* no. 40 (winter 1987): 179–224; Krauss, *The Optical Unconscious;* Kracauer, *The Mass Ornament,* 291–306.
17 Heide Schlüpmann, "Phenomenology of Film: On Siegfried Kracauer's Writings of the 1920's," trans. Tom Levin, *New German Critique,* no. 40 (winter 1987): 97–114; Sabine Hake, "Girls and Crisis: The Other Side of Diversion," ibid., 147–66.
18 Liebman, "Jean Epstein's Early Film Theory," 66–67.
19 Walter Benjamin, *One Way Street and Other Writings,* trans. Edmond Jephcott and Kingsley Shorter (London: New Left Books, 1979), 89–90.
20 The cryptic sense of melodrama in Benjamin's phrase "people whom nothing moves are taught to cry again" was cleverly captured by Thomas Elsaesser's essay on Douglas Sirk with the subtitle, "How to Make Stones Weep." See Thomas Elsaesser, "Tales of Sound and Fury," in *Home Is Where the Heart Is,* ed. Christine Gledhill (London: BFI, 1987), 43.
21 Benjamin, *One Way Street,* 90.
22 Kracauer, *The Mass Ornament,* 378, n. 6.
23 Epstein, "Magnification," 10. Ankylosis is a fusion in the spinal bones that prevents one from bending one's back.
24 Jean Epstein, *Le Livre d'Or du Cinema,* 1947–48, trans. Robert Lamberton, Anthology Film Archive Notes, unpaginated.
25 Although he is not citing this film, Ken Jacobs has made an entire film out of this shot (my favorite moment in cinema so far) in one film of his *Nervous System* series entitled *The Sea.*
26 Epstein, "Magnification," 11.
27 Jean Epstein, *"Bonjour cinéma* and Other Writings," trans. Tom Milne, *Afterimage,* no. 10 (1981): 36.
28 Eric Michaels, "A Primer of Restrictions of Picture-Taking in Traditional Areas of Aboriginal Australia," *Visual Anthropology* 4 (1991): 259. The evidence for this early on, he admits, is by no means conclusive. I would venture that such reported reactions could just as easily be a product of the modern belief in the magical quality the camera projected, by such anthropologists as Baldwin Spencer, who brought the camera to the field for the first time in 1901.
29 Epstein, "Magnification," 10.

30 Epstein, *"Bonjour,"* 3. This is refuted by Italian futurist experiments with music such as that of Luigi Russolo, who recorded the noises of modern machines and weapons and made new instruments for use in technological recording; by contemporary music; and by Jimi Hendrix's "Machine Gun," the likes of which Orna Panfil mobilized to outline an "auditory unconscious" in a talk of that title at Columbia University's Anthropology department, November 1996.

Chapter 8   Bresson's Phantasmagoria

1 Raúl Ruiz, *Poetics of Cinema,* trans. Brian Holmes (Paris: Éditions Dis Voir, 1995), 78.
2 Steve Shaviro, *The Cinematic Body* (Minneapolis: University of Minnesota Press, 1993), 246.
3 For a number of reasons, we can hardly think of the chosen site for passing the note as coincidental. Jonathan Crary writes, for example, "Both [photography and money] are magical forms that establish a new set of abstract relations between individuals and things and impose those relations as the real." *Techniques of the Observer* (Cambridge, MA: MIT Press, 1990), 13.
4 Karl Marx, *Capital: A Critique of Political Economy,* trans. Samuel Moore and Edward Aveling (New York: International Publishers, 1967), 1:77.
5 Walter Benjamin, quoted in Susan Buck-Morss, "Benjamin's Passagenwerk: Redeeming Mass Culture for the Revolution," *New German Critique,* no. 29 (spring–summer, 1983): 213.
6 Marx, *Capital,* 1:189.
7 Roland Barthes, "Brecht, Diderot, Eisenstein," in *Image, Music, Text,* trans. Stephen Heath (New York: Hill and Wang, 1977), 69–78.
8 The shaman's *pinta*—his painting or image—which may be as meandering as a story or as brief as a metaphor, bears this quality of decoupage: set out with clearly defined edges, set out clearly to ponder, to laugh at, to see, but not, with its clearly defined edges, to lose yourself in. See Taussig, *Shamanism: Colonialism and The Wild Man* (Chicago: University of Chicago Press, 1985), 328–30.
9 Barthes, "Brecht, Diderot, Eisenstein," 70.
10 There are further ways in which Bresson's scenes follow Barthes's meaning. The tableau of Bresson is also a fetish-object in Barthes's sense. The acting at significant moments has the quality of Brecht's social gest, which Barthes includes as a characteristic of the tableau by selecting out "pregnant moments" that depict gestures wherein a whole social situation can be read. See ibid., 71 and 73–74.
11 André Bazin, "The Stylistics of Robert Bresson," in *What Is Cinema?,* trans. Hugh Gray (Berkeley: University of California Press, 1967), 131.
12 Robert Bresson, *Notes on the Cinematographer,* trans. Jonathan Griffin (London: Quartet Books, 1986), 44.
13 Miriam Hansen, "Of Mice and Ducks," *South Atlantic Quarterly* 92, no. 1 (winter 1993): 43.
14 Ibid., 47.

15 Susan Sontag, "Spiritual Style in the Films of Robert Bresson," in *Against Interpretation* (New York: Farrar, Straus & Giroux, 1986), 183.

16 Søren Kierkegaard, *Repetition*, trans. Edna Hong and Howard Hong (Princeton: Princeton University Press, 1983), 131.

17 J. Laplanch and J.-B. Pontalis, "The Compulsion to Repeat," in *The Language of Psycho-Analysis*, trans. Donald Nicholson (New York: Norton, 1973), 78–80.

18 Bresson, quoted in Roy Armes, "Robert Bresson," *French Cinema Since '46*, vol. 1 of *The Great Tradition* (New York: Barnes, 1970), 143.

19 Bresson, *Notes*, 26.

20 Jean Epstein, "*Bonjour cinéma* and Other Writings," trans. Tom Milne, *Afterimage*, no. 10 (1981): 22.

21 Lesley Stern sketches out the significance of two similarly lively objects that become increasingly independent of the body: the red shoes of the 1948 Powell and Pressburger film of that title and Jake La Motta's boxing gloves in Scorcese's *Raging Bull* (1980). They are "clearly supercharged objects; almost magical in their effects." She finds, finally, that "it is not simply as functional, denotative objects that they exist, but as totemic." *The Scorsese Connection* (London: BFI, 1995), 20–21.

22 Christian Metz uses the example of the balloon in Fritz Lang's *M* to suggest that the recurrence of a thing doesn't necessarily symbolize the same thing at all times but that it is the "diversity of the changing configuration in which the (*recurrent*, rather than constant) image of the balloon is 'caught up' as much as . . . their persistence," which constitutes the "problem of *repetition*, which is always a mixture of the invariable and the variable." See *The Imaginary Signifier*, trans. Celia Britton et al. (Bloomington: Indiana University Press, 1982), 191.

23 Michael Taussig, *The Devil and Commodity Fetishism in South America* (Chapel Hill: University of North Carolina Press, 1980), 12–38.

24 Bresson, *Notes*, 101.

25 Miriam Hansen, paraphrasing Kracauer, in "With Skin and Hair," *Critical Inquiry* 19 (spring 1993): 458.

26 Ibid., 460; quoting Kracauer, 458.

27 Miriam Hansen summarizes Kracauer's argument: "The material dimension is that which film has the ability, and therefore obligation, to grasp; film comes into its own when it grasps the material dimension" (ibid., 452).

28 Max Horkheimer and Theodor Adorno, *Dialectic of Enlightenment*, trans. John Cumming (New York: Continuum, 1989), 235.

29 Bresson, *Notes*, 15.

30 Yvonne Rainer's film *Trio A* (1968) films her dance "The Mind Is a Muscle," in which her project is to remove the virtuoso dancer, the dramatic, enunciating self, and substitute instead pure corporeality.

31 Bresson, *Notes*, 22.

32 Georg Lukács, *History and Class Consciousness*, trans. Rodney Livingstone (Cambridge, MA: MIT Press, 1971), 95, quoting Marx's *Capital* 3:809.

33 Lukács, *History*, 95.

34 Horkheimer and Adorno, *Dialectic of Enlightenment*, 232.

35 Buck-Morss, "Benjamin's Passagenwerk," 214–15.
36 Marx, *Capital*, 1:178.
37 Buck-Morss, "Benjamin's Passagenwerk," 215.
38 Patti Smith, *Babel* (New York: Putnam, 1974), 128.
39 Bresson, *Notes*, 28.

Chapter 9   Reverie

1 Anson Rabinbach, *The Human Motor: Energy, Fatigue and the Origins of Modernity* (Berkeley: University of California Press, 1992).
2 Thomas Hardy, *Tess of the D'Urbervilles* (New York: Harper & Brothers, 1935), 425.
3 Wolfgang Schivelbusch, *Disenchanted Night*, trans. Angela Davies (Berkeley: University of California Press, 1988), 220–21.
4 Since Gunning restored the term and pitted it against absorptive, narrative-bound forms of cinema, the cinema of attraction has been discussed in relation to numerous genres, stylistics, and filmmakers. They range, for example, from the kind of spectatorship aimed at in the films of Alexander Kluge by Miriam Hansen, in "Reinventing the Nickelodeon: Notes on Kluge and Early Cinema," *October* 46 (fall 1988): 178–98, to the dynamism of action films by Simon During remarks upon in "Public Culture on a Global Scale: A Challenge for Cultural Studies?" *Critical Inquiry* 23, no. 4 (summer 1997): 808–33. The additions to Gunning's discussion of attraction's remnants found in avant-garde cinema and the musical sections of the musical, spanning ten years and several genres, are so ubiquitous that they suggest the concept itself is an attraction. Here I would obviously insert the animated cartoon, and maybe even postulate something called pyrotechnical cinema.
5 Tom Gunning, "Cinema of Astonishment: Early Film and the (In)credulous Spectator," *Art & Text* 34 (spring 1989): 30–32.
6 Georges Bataille, *The Accursed Share*, trans. Robert Hurley (New York: Zone Books, 1988), 1;57.
7 Sergei Eisenstein, *Eisenstein on Disney*, ed. Naum Kleinman, trans. Alan Upchurch (New York: Methuen, 1988), 10.
8 Paul Radin, *The Trickster* (New York: Bell, 1956), ix–x.
9 See, for example, Susan Willis, ed., *The World According to Disney*, special issue of *South Atlantic Quarterly* 92, no. 1 (winter 1993).
10 Miriam Hansen, "Of Mice and Ducks," *South Atlantic Quarterly* 92, no. 1 (winter 1993): 42.
11 These belong to "the oldest expressions of mankind," according to Radin: "The Trickster myth is found among the simplest aboriginal tribe and among the complex. We encounter it among the ancient Greeks, the Chinese, the Japanese and in the Semitic world" (*The Trickster*, ix).
12 Ibid., 25–26.

13 Ibid., 26–27.

14 Eisenstein, *Disney*, 22.

15 Walter Benjamin, *One Way Street*, trans. Edmund Jephcott and Kingsley Shorter (London: New Left Books, 1979), 160.

16 Eisenstein, *Disney*, 43.

17 Gaston Bachelard, *The Psychoanalysis of Fire*, trans. Alan C. M. Ross (1938; Boston: Beacon Press, 1968), 111.

18 Sergei Eisenstein, *Film Form*, trans. Jay Leyda (New York: Harcourt Brace Jovanovich, 1977), 136–44; *Nonindifferent Nature*, trans. Herbert Marshall et al. (Cambridge: Cambridge University Press, 1987); as well as *Disney*, 49–52.

19 Eisenstein, *Disney*, 44.

20 François Lyotard, "Acinema," in *Narrative, Apparatus, Ideology*, ed. Philip Rosen (New York: Columbia University Press, 1986), 351.

21 Bachelard, *Psychoanalysis of Fire*, 11.

22 Schivelbusch, *Disenchanted Night*, 220.

23 I take the phrase "stranger intimacy" from Mick Taussig, who once used it in conversation to describe the unique pleasure of talking to the airline ticket vendor on the telephone.

24 Roland Barthes, "Leaving the Movie Theater," in *The Rustle of Language*, trans. Richard Howard (Oxford: Basil Blackwell, 1986), 346; all quotes that follow in this paragraph are from this page.

25 Jean Epstein, "Magnification and Other Writings," trans. Stuart Liebman, *October* 3 (spring 1977): 9.

26 Bachelard, *Psychoanalysis of Fire*, 17.

27 Bataille, *The Accursed Share*, 1:56.

28 Donald Tuzin, *The Cassowary's Revenge: The Life and Death of Masculinity in a New Guinea Society* (Chicago: University of Chicago Press, 1997), 34.

29 Schivelbusch, *Disenchanted Night*, 178. Here he also cites Bachelard, *La Flamme d'une chandelle* (Paris, 1961), 90.

30 Citing Wilhelm Hausenstein, *Licht unter dem Horizont, Tagebücher von 1942 bis 1946* (Munich, 1967), 273.

31 Bataille, *The Accursed Share*, 1:57.

Chapter 10 Pyrotechnical Reproduction

1 Erland Nordenskiöld, *An Historical and Ethnological Survey of the Cuna Indians*, ed. Henry Wassen (Goteborg: Goteborgs Museum Etnografiska Avelningen, 1938); this ethnography recounts this event on pages 353, 366, and 398.

2 Walter Benjamin, *One Way Street*, trans. Edmund Jephcott and Kingsley Shorter (London: New Left Books, 1979), 90.

3 Michael Taussig, *Mimesis and Alterity* (New York: Routledge, 1994), 101.

4 In recent ethnographies this is now agreed upon as the correct spelling of the word.

5 Taussig, *Mimesis*, 101.

6 Jean Epstein, "Cine-Mystique," trans. Stuart Liebman, *Millennium Film Journal,* nos. 10–11 (1983): 193.

7 Siegfried Kracauer, "Photography"; "Cult of Distraction"; both in *The Mass Ornament,* ed. and trans. Thomas Y. Levin (Cambridge, MA: Harvard University Press, 1995).

8 Siegfried Kracauer, "The Mass Ornament," trans. Barbara Correll and Jack Zipes, *New German Critique,* no. 5 (1975): 76.

9 Walter Benjamin, *Illuminations,* trans. Harry Zohn (New York: Schocken, 1969), 238: "The spectator's process of association in view of these images is indeed interrupted by their constant, sudden change. This constitutes the *shock effect* of the film by heightened presence of mind. By means of its technical structure, the film has taken the physical shock effect out of the wrappers in which Dadaism had, as it were, kept it inside the moral shock effect."

10 Quoted in Susan Buck-Morss, *The Dialectics of Seeing* (Boston: MIT Press, 1989), 271.

11 Allen S. Weiss, "*nostalgia,* Melancholy and Aesthetic Irony," in "Subject Construction and Spectatorial Identification: A Revision of Contemporary Film Theory" (Ph.D. diss., New York University, 1989), 120–24.

12 Sam Laslow and Arthur Johnston, "My Old Flame."

13 Heide Schlüpmann, "Kracauer's Phenomenology of Film," *New German Critique,* no. 40 (winter 1987): 104.

14 Ibid., 113.

15 Here I am paraphrasing Schlüpmann's explication, "Kracauer's Phenomenology," 113.

16 Miriam Hansen, "With Skin and Hair," *Critical Inquiry* 19 (spring 1995): 453.

17 Hollis Frampton, *Circles of Confusion* (Rochester, NY: Visual Studies Workshop Press, 1983), 103.

18 Benjamin, *Illuminations,* 257.

19 Annette Michelson's term for the effect in her foreword to *Circles of Confusion,* 21.

20 Philippe Dubois, "Photography *Mise-en-Film,*" trans. Lynne Kirby, in *Fugitive Images,* ed. Patrice Petro (Bloomington: Indiana University Press, 1995), 169.

21 Gaston Bachelard, *The Psychoanalysis of Fire,* trans. Alan C. M. Ross (Boston: Beacon Press, 1964), 7.

22 Gary Smith, ed., *Benjamin* (Chicago: University of Chicago Press, 1989), 49.

23 Frampton, *Circles,* 98.

24 Julia Kristeva, *Black Sun: Depression and Melancholia,* trans. Leon S. Roudiez (New York: Columbia University Press, 1989), 33.

25 Bruce Jenkins and Susan Craine, *Hollis Frampton: Recollection and Recreations* (Cambridge, MA: MIT Press, 1984), 68.

26 Quoted in Schlüpmann, "Kracauer's Phenomenology," 103.

27 Quoted in ibid., 105.

28 Frampton, quoted in Jenkins and Crane, *Recollections,* 68.

29 Blaise Pascal, *Pensées,* trans. H. F. Stewart (London: Routledge Kegan Paul, 1950), 116.

30 Blaise Pascal, *The Great Shorter Works of Pascal,* trans. Emeile Cailliet and John C.

Bankenagel (Philadelphia: Westminster Press, 1948), 117: "On Monday night 23rd of November, 1654, Pascal had a mystical experience, a conversion. It lasted about two hours, and he wrote twenty seven lines." The Memorial begins "FIRE/God of Abraham, God of Isaac, God of Jacob, not of the philosophers and scholars./Certitude. Certitude. Feeling. Joy. Peace." He kept this memorial in a spirit not unlike Kierkegaard's repetition, sewn into his snug-fitting, daily-worn coat, and had it resewn into each coat until the time of his death.

31 There is a lot of debate about this image. Frampton initially had his trademark HF as the final image but inserted black leader so HF wouldn't be read as the final image. The point, Tom Gunning thinks, is that he wants no image as the final image to interrupt the cycle. I take liberties with Frampton's reported intention, however, and read it as a completely exposed, frameless filmstrip, for that is what you see, which I take to mean also no image, but in the sense that it can't be photographed. Frampton defined film as anything you can put in the projector's sprockets. In this instance, this appears to have been a severe limitation of the form, which indeed was not unnoticed by Frampton: "Our white triangle is not 'nothing at all.' In fact it is, in the end, all we have. That is one of the limits of the art of film." The black leader can, in this context, justifiably signify the opposite of "all we have" (*Circles*, 194).

32 Siegfried Kracauer, "Die Photographie," in *Das Ornament der Masse* (Frankfurt am Main: Suhrkamp Verlag, 1977), 21. "If one were to look through a magnifying glass one could make out the grain, the millions of little dots that constitute the diva, the waves, and the hotel. The picture, however, refers not to the dot matrix but to the living diva on the Lido. Time: the present" (*The Mass Ornament*, 47).

33 Sigmund Freud, "Beyond the Pleasure Principle," in *The Standard Edition of the Complete Psychological Works of Sigmund Freud,* ed. and trans. James Strachey (London: Hogarth Press, 1960–74), 18:31.

34 Dubois, "Photography *Mise-en-Film,*" 168.

35 Michael Taussig, "The Nervous System: Homesickness and Dada," *Stanford Humanities Review* 1, no. 1 (spring 1989): 46–47.

36 In general, the rule is that the more specialized the organ or cell, the less regenerative they are.

37 Taussig, "Nervous System," 46–47.

38 Carl André and Hollis Frampton, *12 dialogues, 1962–1963* (Halifax: Press of the Nova Scotia College of Art and Design, 1981), 90.

39 Ibid., 87.

40 Jenkins and Crane, *Recollections,* 12, citing Frampton in a 1972 interview.

41 Frampton, *Circles,* 83.

42 Ibid., 97.

43 Walter Benjamin, "'N' [Theoretics of Knowledge; Theory of Progress]," *The Philosophical Forum* 15, nos. 1–2 (fall–winter 1983–84): 2.

44 Frampton, *Circles,* 105; emphasis added.

45 Benjamin, "'N,'" 10.

46 Frampton, *Circles,* 96.

47 Benjamin, "'N,'" 1, quoting Marx in a letter to Ruge Kreuzenach, September 1843.
48 According to Allen Weiss, the story goes that when reading those words, Snow turned to Frampton and asked, "Why, then, don't you?" To which Frampton replied, "I wish I could."
49 Benjamin, "'N,'" 11.
50 Ibid., 7.
51 Frampton, *Circles*, 96–97.
52 Benjamin, "'N,'" 22.

Conclusion

1 Elazar Barkan and Ronald Bush, eds., *Prehistories of the Future: The Primitivist Project and the Culture of Modernism* (Stanford: Stanford University Press, 1995), 19.
2 Dolf Sternberger, *Panorama oder Ansichten vom 19. Jahrhundert* (Hamburg, 1938), 34–35, written sometime between 1938 and 1940, cited in Walter Benjamin, "'N' [Theoretics of Knowledge, Theory of Progress]," *The Philosophical Forum* 15, nos. 1–2 (fall–winter 1982–84): 27.

Works Cited

Allen, Richard. *Projecting Illusion*. Cambridge: Cambridge University Press, 1995.
André, Carl, and Hollis Frampton. *12 dialogues, 1962–1963*. Halifax: Press of the Nova Scotia College of Art and Design, 1981.
Aristotle. *Poetics*. In *Critical Theory Since Plato*, ed. Hazard Adams. New York: Harcourt Brace Jovanovich, 1971.
Armes, Roy. *The Great Tradition*. New York: Barnes, 1970.
Bachelard, Gaston. *The Psychoanalysis of Fire*. Trans. Alan C. M. Ross. Boston: Beacon Press, 1964.
Balázs, Béla. *Der sichtbare Mensch*. Vienna: Deutsch Ostereichende Verlag, 1924.
———. *Theory of the Film*. Trans. Edith Bone. New York: Arno Press and New York Times, 1972.
Barkan, Elazar, and Ronald Bush, eds. *Prehistories of the Future: The Primitivist Project and the Culture of Modernism*. Stanford: Stanford University Press, 1995.
Barthes, Roland. *Image Music Text*. Trans. Stephen Heath. New York: Hill and Wang, 1977.
———. *The Rustle of Language*. Trans. Richard Howard. Oxford: Basil Blackwell, 1986.
Bataille, Georges. *The Accursed Share*. 3 vols. Trans. Robert Hurley. New York: Zone Books, 1988.
Baudrillard, Jean. *Simulations*. Trans. Paul Foss et al. New York: Semiotext(e), 1983.
Baudry, Jean. "Ideological Effects of the Basic Cinematographic Apparatus." In *Apparatus*, ed. Theresa Hak Kyung Cha. New York: Tanam Press, 1980.
Bazin, André. *What Is Cinema?* Trans. Hugh Gray. Berkeley: University of California Press, 1967.
Benjamin, Walter. *Charles Baudelaire: A Lyric Poet in the Era of High Capitalism*. Trans. Harry Zohn. London: New Left Books, 1973.
———. *Illuminations*. Trans. Harry Zohn. New York: Schocken, 1969.
———. "'N' [Theoretics of Knowledge; Theory of Progress]." *The Philosophical Forum* 15, nos. 1–2 (fall–winter 1983–84): 1–39.
———. *One Way Street and Other Writings*. Trans. Edmund Jephcott and Kingsley Shorter. London: New Left Books, 1979.
———. *Reflections*. Trans. Edmund Jephcott. New York: Harcourt Brace Jovanovich, 1978.
———. *Selected Writings*. Vol. 1, *1913–1926*. Ed. Marcus Bullock and Michael W. Jennings. Cambridge, MA: Belknap Press, 1996.
Berghaus, Günter. "*Girlkultur*, Feminism, Americanism, and Popular Entertainment in Weimar Germany." *Journal of Design History* 1, nos. 3–4 (1988): 193–219.
Bordwell, David. *The Cinema of Eisenstein*. Cambridge, MA: Harvard University Press, 1993.

———. "Eisenstein's Epistemological Shift." *Screen* 15, no. 4. (winter 1974–75): 32–46.

188   Bordwell, David, and Noël Carroll, eds. *Post-Theory: Reconstructing Film Studies.* Madison: University of Wisconsin Press, 1996.

Brakhage, Stan. "Metaphors on Vision." In *The Avant Garde Film,* ed. P. Adams Sitney. New York: New York University Press, 1978.

Bresson, Robert. *Notes on the Cinematographer.* Trans. Jonathan Griffin. London: Quartet Books, 1986.

Brewster, Ben, ed. "David Bordwell's 'Eisenstein's Epistemological Shift.'" *Screen* 15, no. 4 (winter 1974–75): 27–32.

Bruno, Giuliana. "Streetwalking around Plato's Cave." *October* 60 (spring 1992): 110–29.

Buck-Morss, Susan. "Benjamin's Passagenwerk: Redeeming Mass Culture for the Revolution." *New German Critique,* no. 29 (spring–summer 1983): 211–40.

———. *The Dialectics of Seeing.* Boston: MIT Press, 1989.

———. "Walter Benjamin — Revolutionary Writer (1)." *New Left Review,* no. 128 (July–August 1981): 50–75.

Burch, Noël. "Primitivism and the Avant-Gardes." In *Narrative, Apparatus, Ideology,* ed. Philip Rosen. New York: Columbia University Press, 1986.

Carroll, Noël. *Theorizing the Moving Image.* Cambridge: Cambridge University Press, 1996.

Charney, Leo, and Vanessa R. Schwartz. *Cinema and the Invention of Modern Life.* Berkeley: University of California Press, 1995.

Chayanov, A. V. *The Theory of Peasant Economy.* Ed. Daniel Thorner et al. Trans. Christel Lane and R. E. F. Smith. Madison: University of Wisconsin Press, 1986.

———. *The Theory of Peasant Economy.* Ed. Daniel Thorner et al. Trans. Christel Lane and R. E. F. Smith. Homewood, IL: Irwin, 1966.

Clifford, James. "On Ethnographic Surrealism." *Comparative Studies in Society and History* 23, no. 4 (October 1981): 539–64.

Comolli, Jean-Louis. "Machines of the Visible." In *Narrative, Apparatus, Ideology,* ed. Paul Rosen et al. New York: Columbia University Press, 1986.

———. "Machines of the Visible." In *Film Theory and Criticism.* Ed. Gerald Mast and Marshall Cohen. New York: Oxford University Press, 1985.

Crary, Jonathan. *Techniques of the Observer.* Cambridge, MA: MIT Press, 1992.

Deren, Maya. *An Anagram of Ideas on Art, Form and Film.* Yonkers, NY: The Alicat Book Shop Press, 1946.

———. "Notes on Ritual and Ordeal." *Film Culture* 39 (winter 1965): 10.

DuBois, Philippe. "Photography *Mise-en-Film.*" Trans. Lynne Kirby. In *Fugitive Images,* ed. Patrice Petro. Bloomington: Indiana University Press, 1995.

During, Simon. "Popular Culture on a Global Scale: A Challenge for Cultural Studies?" *Critical Inquiry* 23, no. 4 (summer 1997): 808–33.

Eikhenbaum, Boris. *The Poetics of Cinema.* Ed. Richard Taylor. Trans. Richard Sherwood. Essex: RTP Publications, 1982.

Eisenstein, Sergei. *Beyond the Stars.* Ed. Richard Taylor. Trans. William Powell. Calcutta: Seagull Books, 1995.

———. *Eisenstein on Disney.* Ed. Naum Kleinman. Trans. Alan Upchurch. New York: Methuen, 1988.

———. *The Film Factory.* Ed. Richard Taylor and Ian Christie. Trans. Richard Taylor. Cambridge, MA: Harvard University Press, 1988.

———. *Film Form.* Trans. Jay Leyda. New York: Harcourt Brace Jovanovich, 1977.

———. *Film Sense.* Trans. Jay Leyda. New York: Harcourt Brace Jovanovich, 1975.

———. *Immoral Memories.* Trans. Herbert Marshall et al. Boston: Houghton Mifflin, 1983.

———. "Letters from Mexico." Trans. Tanaquil Taubes. *October* 14 (fall 1980): 55–64.

———. *Nonindifferent Nature.* Trans. Herbert Marshall et al. Cambridge: Cambridge University Press, 1987.

Elsaesser, Thomas. "Tales of Sound and Fury: Observations on the Family Melodrama." In *Home Is Where the Heart Is,* ed. Christine Gledhill. London: BFI, 1987.

Epstein, Jean. "Anthology Film Archive Notes." Unpublished, nd.

———. "*Bonjour cinéma* and Other Writings." Trans. Tom Milne. *Afterimage,* no. 10 (1981): 2–39.

———. "Cine-Mystique." Trans. Stuart Liebman. *Millennium Film Journal,* nos. 10–11 (1984): 191–93.

———. "Magnification and Other Writings." Trans. Stuart Liebman. *October* 3 (spring 1977): 9–31.

Evans-Pritchard, E. E. *Theories of Primitive Religion.* Oxford: Clarendon Press, 1965.

Foster, Hal. "The 'Primitive' Unconscious of Modern Art." *October* 34 (fall 1985): 45–70.

Frampton, Hollis. *Circles of Confusion.* Rochester, NY: Visual Studies Workshop Press, 1983.

Frazer, Sir James George. *The Golden Bough.* London: Macmillan, 1976.

Freud, Sigmund. *The Standard Edition of the Complete Psychological Works of Sigmund Freud.* Ed. and trans. James Strachey. London: Hogarth Press and the Institute of Psycho-Analysis, 1960–74.

Frye, Northrop. *The Great Code.* New York: Harcourt Brace Jovanovich, 1982.

Goldwater, John. *Primitivism in Modern Art.* Cambridge, MA: Belknap Press, 1986.

Gunning, Tom. "An Aesthetic of Astonishment: Early Film and the (In)credulous Spectator." *Art & Text* 34 (spring 1989): 31–45.

———. "Cinema of Attraction: Early Film, Its Spectator and the Avant-Garde." *Wide Angle* 8, nos. 3–4 (1986): 63–70.

———. "Phantom Images and Modern Manifestations." In *Fugitive Images,* ed. Patrice Petro. Bloomington: Indiana University Press, 1995.

Hake, Sabine. "Girls and Crisis: The Other Side of Diversion," *New German Critique,* no. 40 (winter 1987): 147–64.

Hansen, Miriam. "America, Paris, the Alps." In *Cinema and the Invention of Modern Life,* ed. Leo Charney and Vanessa Schwartz. Berkeley: University of California Press, 1995.

———. *Babel and Babylon: Spectatorship in American Silent Film.* Cambridge, MA: Harvard University Press, 1991.

———. "Benjamin, Cinema and Experience: The Blue Flower in the Land of Technology." *New German Critique,* no. 40 (winter 1987): 179–224.

———. "Of Mice and Ducks." *South Atlantic Quarterly* 92, no. 1 (winter 1993): 27–61.

———. "Reinventing the Nickelodeon: Notes on Kluge and Early Cinema." *October* 46 (fall 1988): 178–98.

———. "With Skin and Hair." *Critical Inquiry* 19 (spring 1993): 437–69.

Hardy, Thomas. *Far from the Madding Crowd.* London: Penguin Books, 1985.

———. *Tess of the D'Urbervilles.* New York: Harper & Brothers, 1935.

Haymen, Ronald. *Brecht.* New York: Oxford University Press, 1983.

Horkheimer, Max, and Theodor Adorno. *Dialectic of Enlightenment.* Trans. John Cumming. New York: Continuum, 1987.

Huelsenbeck, Richard. *Memoirs of a Dada Drummer.* Trans. Joachim Neugroschel. Berkeley: University of California Press, 1991.

Huyssen, Andreas. "Introduction to Adorno." *New German Critique,* no. 6 (1975): 3–11.

Jakobson, Roman. *Language in Literature.* Ed. Krystyna Pomorska and Stephen Rudy. Cambridge, MA: Belknap Press, 1987.

Jameson, Fredric. *Marxism and Form.* Princeton: Princeton University Press, 1971.

———. "Reification and Utopia in Mass Culture." *Social Text,* no. 1 (winter 1979): 130–56.

Jay, Martin. *Downcast Eyes.* Berkeley: University of California Press, 1993.

Jenkins, Bruce, and Susan Crane. *Hollis Frampton: Recollections and Recreations.* Cambridge, MA: MIT Press, 1984.

Kaes, Anton. "Literary Intellectuals and the Cinema." Trans. David Levin. *New German Critique,* no. 40 (winter 1987): 7–33.

Karetnikova, Inga. *Mexico According to Eisenstein.* Albuquerque: University of New Mexico Press, 1991.

Kierkegaard, Søren. *Repetition.* Trans. Edna Hong and Howard Hong. Princeton: Princeton University Press, 1983.

Kirby, Lynne. *Parallel Tracks.* Durham, NC: Duke University Press, 1997.

Koch, Gertrud. *Kracauer zur Einführung.* Hamburg: Junius, 1996.

——— "Mimesis und Bilderverbot in Adornos Asthetik." *Babylon,* no. 6 (1989): 36–45.

———. " 'Not yet accepted anywhere': Exile, Memory and Image in Kracauer's Conception of History." *New German Critique,* no. 54 (1991): 95–109.

———. "The Physiognomy of Things." *New German Critique,* no. 40 (1987): 167–77.

Kracauer, Siegfried. *From Caligan to Hitler.* Princeton: Princeton University Press, 1974.

———. *The Mass Ornament.* Ed. and trans. Thomas Y. Levin. Cambridge, MA: Harvard University Press, 1995.

———. "The Mass Ornament." Trans. Barbara Correll and Jack Zipes. *New German Critique,* no. 5 (1975): 67–76.

———. *Das Ornament der Masse.* Frankfurt am Main: Suhrkamp Verlag, 1977.

———. *Theory of Film: The Redemption of Physical Reality.* London: Oxford University Press, 1960.

————. *Theory of Film: The Redemption of Physical Reality.* Princeton: Princeton University Press, 1997.

Krauss, Rosalind. *The Optical Unconscious.* Cambridge, MA: MIT Press, 1993.

Kristeva, Julia. *Black Sun: Depression and Melancholia.* Trans. Leon S. Roudiez. New York: Columbia University Press, 1989.

Lant, Antonia. "The Curse of the Pharoah, or How Cinema Contracted Egyptomania." *October* 59 (winter 1992): 86–112.

Laplanch, J., and J.-B. Pontalis. *The Language of Psycho-Analysis.* Trans. Donald Nicholson. New York: Norton, 1973.

Lavater, Rev. John Casper. *Essays on Physiognomy for the Promotion of Knowledge and Love of Mankind.* Trans. Rev. C. Moore. London, 1797.

Levin, Tom. "From Dialectical to Normative Specificity: Reading Lukács on Film." *New German Critique,* no. 40 (winter 1987): 35–61.

Lévy-Bruhl, Lucien. *How Natives Think.* Trans. Lillian A. Clare. Salem, MA: Ayer Publishers, 1984.

Liebman, Stuart. "Jean Epstein's Early Film Theory, 1920–22." Ph.D. diss., New York University, 1980.

Lindsay, Vachel. *The Art of the Moving Picture.* New York: Macmillan, 1916.

Lucretius, Titus. *The Nature of the Universe.* Trans. R. E. Latham. Hammondsworth: Penguin Books, 1958.

Lukács, Georg. *History and Class Consciousness.* Trans. Rodney Livingstone. Cambridge, MA: MIT Press, 1971.

Lyotard, François. *Narrative, Apparatus, Ideology.* Ed. Philip Rosen. New York: Columbia University Press, 1986.

Marx, Karl. *Capital: A Critique of Political Economy.* Trans. Samuel Moore and Edward Aveling. New York: International Publishers, 1967.

————. *Economic and Philosophic Manuscripts of 1844.* Trans. Martin Milligan. New York: International Publishers, 1964.

Marx, Karl, and Friedrich Engels. *The Communist Manifesto.* Trans. Samuel Moore. New York: Washington Square Press, 1970.

Mauss, Marcel. *A General Theory of Magic.* Trans. Robert Brain. New York: Norton, 1975.

Mayne, Judith. *The Woman at the Keyhole.* Bloomington: Indiana University Press, 1990.

Metz, Christian. *The Imaginary Signifier.* Trans. Celia Britton, Annwyl Williams, Ben Brewster, and Alfred Guzzetti. Bloomington: Indiana University Press, 1982.

Michaels, Eric. "Bad Aboriginal Art." *Art & Text* 28 (1988): 59–73.

————. "A Primer of Restrictions of Picture-Taking in Traditional Areas of Aboriginal Australia." *Visual Anthropology* 4 (1991): 259–75.

Michelson, Annette. "On Reading Deren's Notebook." *October* 14 (fall 1980): 47–54.

Nordenskiöld, Erland. *An Historical and Ethnological Survey of the Cuna Indians.* Ed. Henry Wassen. Goteborg: Goteborgs Museum Etnografiska Avelningen, 1938.

Pascal, Blaise. *The Great Shorter Works of Pascal.* Trans. Emeile Cailliet and John C. Bankenagel. Philadelphia: Westminster Press, 1948.

————. *Pensées.* Trans. H. F. Stewart. London: Routledge Kegan Paul, 1950.

Perloff, Marjorie. "Tolerance and Taboo: Modernist Primitivisms and Postmodernist Pieties." In *Prehistories of the Future*, ed. Elazar Barkan and Ronald Bush. Stanford: Stanford University Press, 1995.

Petro, Patrice, ed. *Fugitive Images*. Bloomington: Indiana University Press, 1995.

Pietz, William. "The Problem of the Fetish, 1." *RES* 9 (spring 1985): 5–17.

Proust, Marcel. *Remembrance of Things Past*. Trans. C. K. Scott Moncrieff. London: Chatto & Windus, 1964.

Rabinbach, Anson. *The Human Motor: Energy, Fatigue and the Origins of Modernity*. Berkeley: University of California Press, 1992.

Radin, Paul. *The Trickster*. New York: Bell, 1956.

Rosen, Philip. "History of Image, Image of History: Subject and Ontology in Bazin." *Wide Angle* 9, no. 4 (1987): 7–34.

Rowe, Carel. "Illuminating Lucifer." In *The Avant Garde Film*, ed. P. Adams Sitney. New York: New York University Press, 1978.

Rubin, William. *"Primitivism" in 20th Century Art*. New York: Museum of Modern Art, 1984.

Ruiz, Raúl. *Poetics of Cinema*. Trans. Brian Holmes. Paris: Éditions Dis Voir, 1995.

Schivelbusch, Wolfgang. *Disenchanted Night*. Trans. Angela Davies. Berkeley: University of California Press, 1988.

———. *The Railway Journey: The Industrialization of Time and Space in the Nineteenth Century*. Berkeley: University of California Press, 1986.

Schlüpmann, Heide. "Kracauer's Phenomenology of Film: On Siegfried Kracauer's Writings of the 1920s." Trans. Tom Levin. *New German Critique*, no. 40 (winter 1987): 97–114.

Schor, Naomi. *Reading in Detail: The Aesthetics of the Feminine*. New York: Methuen, 1987.

Shattuck, Roger. *The Banquet Years: The Origins of the Avant Garde in France — 1885 to World War I*. New York: Vintage, 1968.

———. *Proust's Binoculars*. New York: Vintage, 1967.

Shaviro, Steve. *The Cinematic Body*. Minneapolis: University of Minnesota Press, 1993.

Simmel, Georg. *The Sociology of Georg Simmel*. Ed. and trans. Kurt H. Wolff. London: The Free Press of Glencoe, 1964.

Sitney, P. Adams, ed. *The Avant Garde Film*. New York: New York University Press, 1978.

———. *Visionary Film*. New York: Oxford University Press, 1974.

Sloterdijk, Peter. *Critique of Cynical Reason*. Trans. Michael Eldred. Foreword by Andreas Huyssen. Minneapolis: University of Minnesota Press, 1987.

Smith, Gary. *Benjamin*. Chicago: University of Chicago Press, 1989.

Smith, Patti. *Babel*. New York: Putnam, 1974.

Sontag, Susan. *Against Interpretation*. New York: Farrar, Straus & Giroux, 1986.

Stern, Lesley. *The Scorsese Connection*. London: BFI, 1995.

Taussig, Michael. *The Devil and Commodity Fetishism in South America*. Chapel Hill: University of North Carolina Press, 1980.

———. *Mimesis and Alterity*. New York: Routledge, 1994.

———. "The Nervous System: Homesickness and Dada." *Stanford Humanities Review* 1, no. 1 (spring 1989): 44–81.

———. *Shamanism, Colonialism and the Wild Man*. Chicago: University of Chicago Press, 1985.

Taylor, Richard, ed. *The Poetics of Cinema*. Essex: RTP Publications, 1982.

Taylor, Richard, and Ian Christie, eds. *The Film Factory*. Cambridge, MA: Harvard University Press, 1988.

———. *Eisenstein Rediscovered*. London: Routledge, 1993.

Torgovnick, Marianna. *Gone Primitive*. Chicago: University of Chicago Press, 1990.

Trotsky, Leon. *The History of the Russian Revolution*. 3 vols. Trans. Max Eastman. London: Sphere Books, 1967.

———. *My Life*. Trans. Max Eastman. New York: Pathfinder Press, 1971.

Tsivian, Yuri. "Eisenstein and Russian Symbolist Culture: An Unknown Script of *October*." In *Eisenstein Rediscovered*, ed. Richard Taylor and Ian Christie. London: Routledge, 1993.

Tuzin, Donald, *The Cassowary's Revenge: The Life and Death of Masculinity in a New Guinea Society*. Chicago: University of Chicago Press, 1997.

Tytler, Graeme. *Physiognomy in the European Novel: Faces and Fortunes*. Princeton: Princeton University Press, 1982.

Verhagen, Marcus. "The Poster in Fin-de-Siecle Paris." In *Cinema and the Invention of Modern Life*, ed. Leo Charney and Vanessa Schwartz. Berkeley: University of California Press, 1995.

Vertov, Dziga. *Kino-Eye*. Ed. Annette Michelson. Trans. Kevin O'Brien. Berkeley: University of California Press, 1984.

Walker, John, ed. *Halliwell's Film Guide*. New York: Harper Collins, 1994.

Weiss, Allen. "Subject Construction and Spectatorial Identification: A Revision of Contemporary Film Theory." Ph.D. diss., New York University, 1989.

Willemen, Paul. *Looks and Frictions*. Bloomington: Indiana University Press, 1994.

Willis, Susan, ed. *The World According to Disney*. Special issue of *South Atlantic Quarterly* 92, no. 1 (winter 1993).

Wundt, Wilhelm. *Elements of Folk Psychology*. London: Macmillan, 1928.

Yampolsky, Mikhail. "The Essential Bone Structure: Mimesis in Eisenstein." *Eisenstein Rediscovered*. Ed. Richard Taylor and Ian Christie. London: Routledge, 1993.

193

Index

Rachel O. Moore is an independent scholar
who lives in New York City.

Library of Congress Cataloging-in-Publication Data

Moore, Rachel O.
Savage theory : cinema as modern magic / Rachel O.
Moore.
p.   cm.
Includes bibliographical references and index.
ISBN 0-8223-2354-0 (alk. paper). —
ISBN 0-8223-2388-5 (pbk. : alk. paper)
1. Motion pictures — Psychological aspects.   2. Motion
picture audiences — Psychology.   3. Magical thinking.
I. Title.
PN1995.M569 2000
791.43'01'9 — dc21   99-14159